Eric and Matt have thought about why most ka poorly designed processes. They have developed a way to align all parts of an organization to eliminate waste of all sorts in production processes *before* the start of production. I'm delighted with their important contribution to Lean thinking that goes far beyond 3P and other methods of process development.

—**James P. Womack,** PhD, Co-founder of the global Lean movement; Co-Author, *Lean Thinking* and *The Machine That Changed the World;* Founder, Lean Enterprise Institute

Making things is important. Making things well with high quality, on time and low cost with improvements everyday leads to success and prosperity. *The Power of Process* both outlines the end goals and provides a realistic story of the path for getting to extraordinary goals. The book is well worth an investment of time and energy.

—**Don Runkle,** Senior Multi-Industry Executive; Former CTO & Board Member, Delphi Automotive Systems; Former Engineering VP, General Motors

With *The Power of Process,* Matt Zayko and Eric Ethington give us something unique in the world of books about continuous improvement, management, and work design, which typically focus on either the product or the people creating it: this book shares a practical approach for engaging people in developing great processes. Anyone involved in designing or managing work should keep this book handy for quick reference on their physical or digital desktop.

—**John Shook,** Chairman, Lean Global Network

The timing for this book could not be better. Many organizations are so very frustrated with their lack of CI progress. This framework is certain to help them to close the gap and adds context to demystifying Lean transformation. And I love the presentation of learning through doing using case studies to cement the approach.

—**Crystal Davis,** Founder & CEO, The Lean Coach Inc.; Experienced Operations and Engineering Leader at Fortune 50 Companies

Finally, a book that lays out how to apply Lean concepts to the process development phase through launch. The authors have done an excellent job of showing the benefits of engaging a cross functional team early on in the process so that touzen (rework) does not take place after launch. I only wish this book would have been in print earlier in my career.

—**Mary O'Neill,** Senior Vice President Lean Manufacturing, Gates Industrial Corp

The Power of Process is a remarkable guide and a must-read primer for anyone considering embarking on their own process design transformation. Through this self-reflective story, we are challenged by the reality in which we live today and inspired to drastically change our future – NOW.

—**Mari Cummins,** Retired Vice-President of Operations Excellence, Cardinal Health; Coach for the Master of Business of Operational Excellence at Fisher College of Business at the Ohio State University

The Power of Process

The Power of Process
A Story of Innovative Lean Process Development

Matthew J. Zayko and Eric M. Ethington

Routledge
Taylor & Francis Group
A PRODUCTIVITY PRESS BOOK

First published 2022
by Routledge
600 Broken Sound Parkway #300, Boca Raton FL, 33487

and by Routledge
2 Park Square, Milton Park, Abingdon, Oxon, OX14 4RN

Routledge is an imprint of the Taylor & Francis Group, an informa business

ISBN: 9781032113913 (hbk)
ISBN: 9780367690304 (pbk)
ISBN: 9781003219712 (ebk)

DOI: 10.4324/9781003219712

Typeset in Garamond
by codeMantra

Matthew J. Zayko Dedication:

For Kris, Sam, and Henry, who make each day even better than the last

Eric M. Ethington Dedication:

For my family & bedrock: Caroline, Jason, Jacob and Ries

Contents

Acknowledgments

Many people have inspired and taught us related to this topic over the years. We are forever thankful to the selfless mentors and leaders that have contributed to our thinking and development. There are scores of our mentors out there and we are so appreciative for their contributions, and we will no doubt not be able to list out everyone by name. For people that helped directly with our book efforts, we would like to thank you as well.

Our biggest thanks go to our spouses: Kristine Zayko and Caroline Ethington. Both have patiently supported us as this book started out years ago as an idea on a dry erase board with no clear path and that has now blossomed into a full manuscript after countless writing and brainstorming sessions (many at the local bagel shop). While at times the road ahead was uncertain for us as authors, questioning ourselves at times whether to stop completely, Kristine and Caroline fully supported and expected a book to be the output. They never lost faith in us. And an extra thanks to Caroline for creating many of the images and figures throughout the book based on our rough sketches.

We would like to thank Jim Womack, Jim Morgan, Dave Logozzo, and John Shook for encouraging us over the past few years to write on the topic of process development. All four provided support and helped clear early hurdles to help get the manuscript moving toward the launch pad.

Our editorial team of Michael Sinocchi and Samantha Dalton at Taylor & Francis/Productivity Press cannot be thanked enough for their patience and efforts to get this manuscript completed and published.

Early feedback of a rough manuscript was critical during the "concept" phase of this cycle before we even took the manuscript to a publisher. We greatly thank the following individuals that diligently read our early work and that provided constructive feedback: Don Runkle, Deborah Smith, Jim Franchville, Andy Houk, John Drogosz, John Shook, Jim Morgan, and Jim

Womack. Plus, thanks to Rich Sheridan of Menlo Innovations for providing timely advice to help move forward in the publishing process.

Both of us were influenced early in our careers with great mentoring from dozens of tremendous people while at Delphi, and the following individuals provided inspiration for the story: Don Runkle, Dave Logozzo, Joe Rolecki, Brian Kettler, Brian O'Neill, Mary Golla, Ed Northern, and many others.

A huge thanks is also reserved for our ex-Toyota sensei over the years that challenged our paradigms and that took our thinking to another level, including Yoshinobu Yamada and John Shook. We are grateful to Yamada-san, as he spent many, many hours over several years helping to personally coach us to understand the thinking behind everything he taught. **Thank you, Mr. Yamada, for withholding all of your computer files and making us create our own.**

We also thank the dozens of organizations we have worked with over so many years. There are too many of you to list, but we are grateful and thankful to you all.

From the Lean Enterprise Institute (LEI), which has provided the means for us to test out concepts with many additional organizations through our coaching work, we thank the leadership team of Josh Howell, Karen Gaudet, Matt Savas, Lara Anderson, and Pat Panchak.

Matt is forever indebted to the late Professor Walton Hancock of the University of Michigan (U-M) in the Industrial and Operations Engineering (IOE) department for giving Matt the research opportunity to learn and develop Lean thinking capability with other world-class professors, including Jeff Liker, Mike Rother, the late Allen Ward, and Durward Sobek. In addition, Professor Hancock connected Matt as a graduate student with John Shook, right after John had left Toyota to join the IOE department faculty at U-M. John has been a mentor to Matt for going on 27 years now.

In addition, Matt thanks his former co-workers at Pall Corporation that helped in gaining an understanding of the challenges of creating and spreading Lean thinking in an organization on a global basis. Special thanks to Greg Scheessele, Derek Whitworth, David Meadows, and Tricia Meadows.

Eric would like to personally thank Deb Smith and Mary O'Neill for being colleagues, mentors, and friends for over 30 years.

Additionally, Eric would also like to thank the outstanding teams he worked with at Delphi including the mini-aircore team at Delco Electronics, who intuitively knew what Lean was long before the term was coined; Brian O'Neill and the leadership team at Flint East, including Shannon Liddell, Tim

Webster, and Larry Gilliam; Dave Logozzo and the corporate Manufacturing Support Team.

At Textron, Eric would like to thank colleagues Ted Holland, JoAnn Dies, Deb Smith, Bill Comeau, Misty Shannon, and Ron Fardell and the leadership team including John Mayer, Pete Riley, Shannon Massey, Mark Rudeseal, and Lynn Kelley.

Finally, we want to thank our fellow Lean Product and Process Development (LPPD) coaches, as we have all worked together to grow this LPPD community: Jim Morgan, John Drogosz, and Katrina Appell.

> The delicate balance in mentoring someone is not creating them in your own image, but giving them the opportunity to create themselves.
>
> **—Steven Spielberg**

Foreword

Knowing How to Make Things Well

The opportunity to work in and lead teams of experts in product design, process engineering, tooling, and manufacturing operations over the past 30 plus years has given me a rare perspective and deep respect for people who truly know how to make things well. I have learned that excellence in process creation and tool-up is the secret to bringing breakthrough product to life, and creating Lean, sustainable value streams. Unfortunately, the skill and ability to make things well is a wildly underappreciated capability in many organizations for which they pay a dreadful price. Poor product quality, soaring capital expense, painful launch delays, endless rework, and struggling manufacturing operations have become the norm at such companies. This book, written by two respected experts, provides guidance on how to break this destructive cycle.

While perhaps not quite as rare as hen's teeth, the book you are holding is a unique and invaluable contribution to our understanding of new value creation. There has been a great deal written about Lean in manufacturing and some small fraction of that about product design, but very little has directly addressed the critical practice of Lean process creation. Not only does The Power of Process provide a structured approach to Lean process creation but it also addresses many of the associated organizational challenges through the story it shares.

The 6CON model that is introduced to readers offers a proven methodology to follow for Lean process creation that can be adapted to nearly any environment. The model is shared through a case study and told from a manufacturing perspective. By utilizing this tangible, real-world example the authors teach more than Lean process creation, they provide steps toward a larger Lean transformation. Throughout the book the authors also provide specific, actionable advice that the reader can put to work in their organization.

Matt Zayko and Eric Ethington are particularly well qualified to provide that advice because they lived it long before they wrote about it which makes them fairly unique. Both are veterans of Delphi where they were part of the team that led a Lean transformation of several major Delphi plants by focusing on improving process creation. For the past 10 plus years they have shared their hard-won knowledge assisting a variety of organizations from many different industries to improve the way they create new value.

You have already set yourself apart from most by actually reading the book you purchased. But do not stop there. Read it, reflect on it, and most importantly put these concepts to work in your organization. Good luck on your journey!

James M. Morgan, Ph.D.
Old Mission Peninsula
Traverse City, Michigan;
Co-author of *The Toyota Product Development System*

Preface

All the ills of the organization show up on the production floor.

—John Shook

We remember the week clearly, almost 20 years ago at a large automotive supplier production facility. Eric was the "Lean architect" for the site, working with highly capable cross-functional partners to define the vision and set priorities. Matt and his team were the "builders," working on the detail of making the system actually come to life. It was one of emotional peaks and valleys. Accomplishment and encouragement on one hand, defeat and demotivation on the other.

We had reached a milestone in the conversion of our next generation mixed-model line. Developed from our collective kaizen experience in our operation and with the complete engagement of the front-line workforce, the line was working well on all fronts. It was ergonomically superior to earlier generations of our lines due to the attention we placed on simplifying employee motions and workplace design. With material access in mind from the beginning, component delivery was greatly simplified. In the end we improved the labor productivity on the line from 15 pieces per person per hour to 25.

Our success with both mix-model capability and higher productivity informed our overall plant vision. Instead of ten lines radiating out from a central area, we could create six lines co-located next to our shipping, receiving, and supermarket area. Overall plant flow would be greatly improved. The resulting available space would then allow the relocation of our low-volume and service manufacturing from a remote plant to space adjacent to our core manufacturing areas. This would further simplify material flows and streamline management and support functions. And the list went on. It was all good.

Then it happened. Technically it was not sudden, but mentally it was. A new manufacturing line for our next generation product began to ramp up. It was designed by smart, hard-working, and well-intentioned engineers who were not connected to our shop-floor improvement efforts. We had seen the line being installed by our construction resources under the guidance of engineering. It looked rather familiar—just like the old lines we had "kaizen-ed."

Although disappointed that the new line did not have the latest in our "Lean thinking" integrated into it, we thought, "once construction is complete and the engineers are out of the way, we will go in and kaizen it too." But it was not going to be that easy. The product on this line was critical to our business. Some aspects were behind schedule, so the ramp-up was going to happen fast.

Before we knew it, the line was beginning low rate production and problems were everywhere. All of our improvement resources were overwhelmed getting the new line to meet basic requirements (quality, delivery, and cost). Updating the line to incorporate our latest thinking was not the priority—instead it was basic survival. And converting our other existing lines from their current designs to a mixed-model concept was even further away.

If the world were kind, this would be our unique story. But it is not. In the years since, we have seen this scenario repeat in many companies and across many industries. We have seen managers with Lean experience, an improvement vision and a plan, whose efforts are torpedoed by the introduction of the next generation manufacturing process. It becomes "all-hands-on-deck" to get the new process working, and kaizen of other lines becomes the extra work the plant will get to if managers ever have time. This scenario is so common that no one blinks. This is normal.

When we dig deeper we find a basic lack of understanding by those designing the new process. Sometimes the cycle times and their relationship to a takt time have been calculated, but most often they have not. When we start asking about projected yields, changeover times, lot sizing strategies, motion paths, and balance options, the information becomes even sketchier. Essentially, the plant and its managers are about to spend money on capital but have only a vague understanding of why. Again, this is normal and will continue to be normal because no one ever asks at the end, "did we get our money's worth?" An overarching financial number may be scrutinized, but how often are the real root causes of any variances identified? Generally, never.

We are not trying to paint an overly dire picture. Many organizations begin the Lean journey in "operations." The work there is typically easier to see than in the office, as are the problems inhibiting value creation. Likewise, benefits can be realized quickly that positively impact the customer. Kaizen in operations also creates, as our sensei used to tell us, real "evidence on the floor" of improvement. It gives the organization a better sense of what the Lean vision should be. It helps to transform the Lean concepts and slogans into something tangible for customers, shareholders, and employees.

This is all good and necessary, but in the end, one has to ask, "Aren't most kaizen activities rework? Why are we expending resources designing and installing systems, only to apply more resources to fix the systems once we start using them? Why not design this 'Lean thinking' into the process right up front, and then we can begin to improve even further from there? How do we break the 'launch and rework' cycle?"

Numerous organizations have tried some version of Lean process design following a formula. But true Lean process design goes well beyond forcing concepts and slogans into every situation. It is purposeful, scientific, and adaptable because every situation starts with a unique current state. In addition, Lean process design must include both the technical and social aspects, as they are essential to sustaining and improving any system.

Observing the problem of reworking processes brought us to the conclusion that a practical book focused on the standard work of Lean process creation could be helpful to all organizations.

The Power of Process: A Story of Innovative Lean Process Development

Introduction

This book enables readers to consider the details that must be addressed to actually create a Lean process. No slogans, no absolutes. Real thinking is required. Experience has taught us that this type of thinking is best learned from an example, so we provide a case-study to demonstrate the thinking that should be applied to any process. High volume or low, simple mix or complex, manufacturing or transactional—the thinking works. Along with the thinking, we want to enable the reader to derive their own future state. This is demonstrated in the story that surrounds the case.

The case study starts as a new product is nearing the end of the design process and ends 90 days after the start of full-rate production. Many stakeholders are engaged throughout the story because this is essential for great Lean process creation. We wanted anyone reading this book to relate to the experiences of characters in the story.

The stakeholders fall into two, often interdependent, categories: (A) the team, led by a pair of system architects, is focused on the WORK of Lean process creation—actually developing the physical value stream; (B) the leadership that is focused on the PROCESS of Lean process creation—concerned with managing this new way of working and effectively spreading it throughout the organization.

Within the chapters, the leadership, or *Steering Team's*, dialogue is highlighted with gray shading.

Likewise, **Key Points** we wanted to stress are contained within boxes throughout the chapters.

Below is an organization chart showing the leadership team and the working team. Yes, we fully admit, this is quite a cast of characters for a reader to keep track of, especially in a technical book. But any time we tried to narrow the field of characters, important elements were lost:

- The realism of the complex collaboration required to do Lean process creation well
- The ability to share the thinking behind the concepts and demonstrate the logic by which one might derive their own approach

So, as a reader you are blessed with a large cast of characters, and an organizational chart as your guide (see Figure 0.1).

The overall story is structured to teach thinking, chapter by chapter, around what we call the 6CON framework of Lean process creation (see Figure 0.2):

1. CONtext
2. CONcepts
3. CONverge
4. CONfigure and connect
5. CONfirm
6. CONtinuously improve

Chapter 1 is titled, "The Situation." It introduces and establishes the background for the case study.

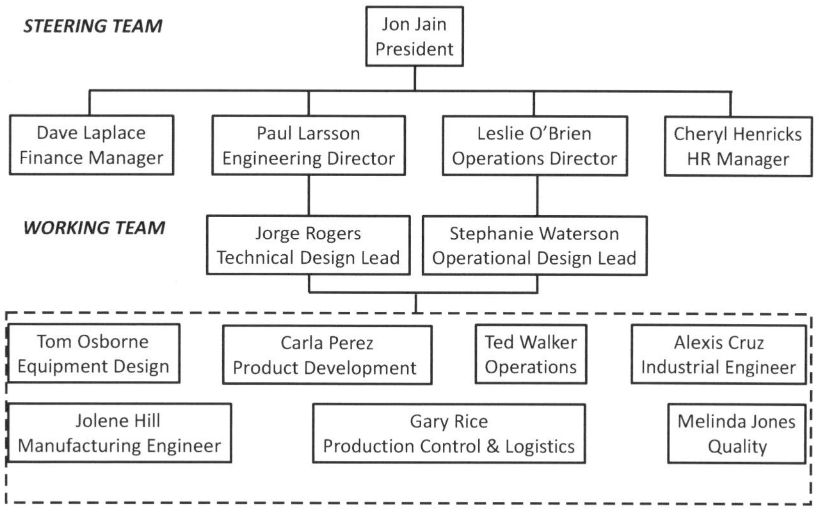

Figure 0.1 Characters.

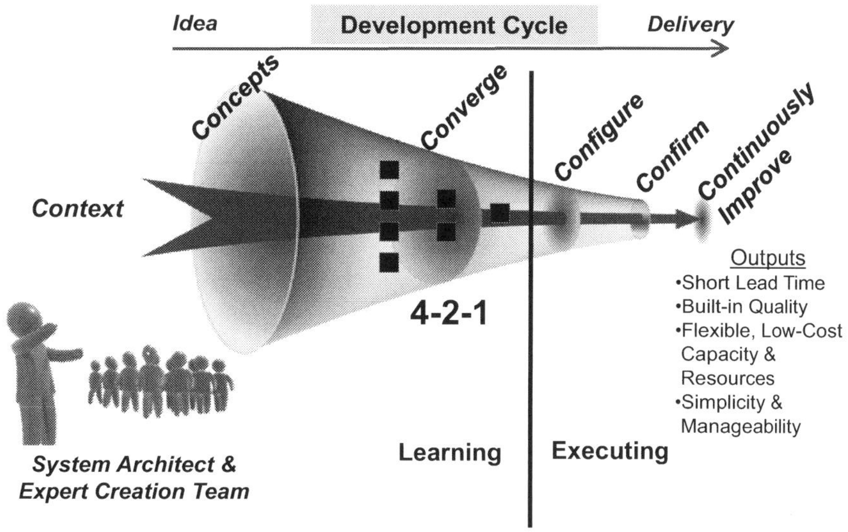

Figure 0.2 Lean process creation 6CON framework.

Chapter 2 is CONtext, where both the management and working teams develop an understanding of what all of the stakeholders' value. This understanding is translated to a vision, a method of measuring, and processes and tools to keep the team aligned and issues highlighted.

Chapter 3 is CONcepts. Multiple options are developed and evaluated.

Chapter 4 is CONverge. In this chapter, concepts morph and merge, eventually settling on a process design with the best projected payback.

Chapter 5 is CONfigure and connect. This is where all of the detailed work happens, from designing individual workplaces to figuring out how to get the materials to the right location at the exact right time.

Chapter 6 is CONfirm. Remember the stakeholders and what they value? This chapter demonstrates how to enable a smooth launch which hits the necessary targets.

Chapter 7 is CONtinuously Improve. This chapter reflects on what the management and working teams do to make the process of process improvement better. The timeframes of 90 days, 6 months, and 12 months postlaunch are considered.

Each chapter concludes with a set of Key Questions for you to consider as you start your unique process creation journey. The intended audience for this book is everyone in your organization from the process creation team members (hint, see the organizational chart above), to the managers who must lead these teams, to the top leaders who need to know enough about process creation to set the right expectations.

Finally, this book represents a "snap-shot" of what we have to share. Some content was purposely left out to make the book manageable, and we continue to learn new things each day. To ensure the conversation of innovating Lean process development continues, we have set up a website: **www.thepowerofprocess.solutions**. We encourage you to check it out and we would love to hear from you.

Matt Zayko and Eric Ethington

Authors

Matthew J. Zayko is Senior Lean Leader with GE Hitachi Nuclear, former president of his own management consultancy and a long-time Senior Coach with the Lean Enterprise Institute. Matt spent the first 12 years of his career in a variety of staff- and management-level roles under the guidance of former Toyota mentors for Chrysler/University of Michigan, Gelman Sciences, Delphi, and Pall (now part of Danaher). He has over 25 years of experience in leading enterprise improvements in numerous industries by helping to transform product development, engineering, manufacturing, service processes, and other areas. Matt has supported organizations as a globally recognized expert in process development. He has authored numerous works based on successful transformation, including articles that have been published in "Journal of Quality Engineering," "IIE Solutions," "Journal of Cost Management," a chapter in the 1998 *Shingo-Prize* winning book "Becoming Lean," and white papers for the Lean Enterprise Institute. Matt received his M.S. in Industrial and Operations Engineering from the University of Michigan at Ann Arbor.

Eric M. Ethington is President of Lean Shift, a process development and problem-solving consultancy. Prior to founding Lean Shift in 2009, Eric accumulated 27 years of work experience in front-line through executive-leadership roles. His experience in applying Lean includes most types of organizations, industries, and functional areas, and he is a recognized expert in process development and problem-solving methodologies. Eric is also a Senior Coach at the Lean Enterprise Institute (LEI) and advises LEI on the program management of their Lean Product and Process Development initiative. Eric holds a Bachelor of Science in Industrial Engineering from General Motors Institute (now Kettering University) and a Master of Business Administration from the University of Michigan.

Matt and Eric have been collaborating since 1998.

SETTING THE STAGE 1

Chapter 1

The Situation: New Process Design as Usual

A bad system will beat a good person every time.

—W. Edwards Deming

THE STEERING TEAM—STATE OF THE BUSINESS

The office was spacious and filled with nice furniture from an earlier era. At one end was a large wooden desk whose shape was reminiscent of a battleship. About 8 feet wide, fine grain maple-stained mahogany, with legs that curved outward as they reached the desktop.

Behind the desk was a worn, black leather chair followed by a wall-length credenza. The credenza looked impressive but was basically empty, except for some emergency snacks kept in one of the drawers. But as usually the case, no one was sitting at the desk. Around a table at the center of the office were four people staring at papers covering most of the surface area. Seated such that he could see his office door was Jon Jain, the divisional president of Acme Devices.

Jon had been in this role for 3 years. Simultaneously a strong promoter of Lean and a quiet, introspective student, one of his first moves upon becoming the divisional president was to set up the structure and invest in developing people to support continuous improvement (CI) throughout their operational facilities. At that time, it was not an easy decision

DOI: 10.4324/9781003219712-2

since Acme was struggling overall as a company and there was pressure from the top to cut costs in all areas, including training and people development.

Jon decided to take the short-term hit on the Acme Devices budget in order to develop a stronger operational model that would provide far greater returns in the longer run. To date, the CI teams had made tremendous progress in developing a core operating system model at all their plants and were frequently cited as a leading Lean manufacturer.

Seated to Jon's right was Leslie O'Brien. Hired by Jon about 1 year before, Leslie had previously worked as a plant manager for a tier-one global auto supplier. It was this background, coupled with her previous industrial engineering experience, that made her a great candidate to be Acme Devices' director of operations. Leslie's deep knowledge of Lean and skills at motivating teams made her the ideal person to take Acme's operations to the next level.

Throughout her career Leslie had been honing a process for designing processes properly, from the start. Her previous employer had even adapted this process to its nonmanufacturing areas as well. Leslie had made some recent tweaks to the model in anticipation for the right moment. And today's meeting was that moment.

Standing to Leslie's right was Paul Larsson, arms crossed, deep in thought. Paul hired in around the same time as Leslie. In fact, they met in Jon's waiting room as their paths crossed during the interview process. At the time they were cordial, but both thought they were competing for the same job. Little did they know they were to be partners.

Paul's extensive engineering background and deep understanding of Lean product development concepts made him Jon's ideal person to fulfill the director of engineering role. Paul and Leslie became thought partners immediately. Partially because they were both the new "kids," but more importantly, they discovered they could learn so much from one another.

Rounding out the room, seated to Jon's left, was David Laplace, Jon's finance manager. Jon had selected Dave for this role based on his ability to fulfill his financial duties while understanding the shortcomings of the accounting system especially as it related to Jon's Lean vision. Dave was a no-nonsense guy, frequently making statements like "Explain to me what you want to do, and I will help you get there if it passes the sniff test." In Jon's ideal world, Dave would have been up to the task of revamping the accounting system itself, but Jon decided to save that effort for another day. For now, Dave could be the bridge between accounting and reality.

They were meeting as Acme's Lean Steering Team (LST). With the ink barely dry on the human resources (HR) paperwork which created the CI structure, issues started escalating to Jon. Who was responsible for what? Who has decision authority on this? Jon realized that he could not make all the decisions, and he did not want to.

The early LST was formed to be a governing body and a think-tank for Acme's Lean deployment. They would own the Lean transformation as well as any necessary supporting processes—architects of sorts. The team started small with the idea of growing it organically as additional leaders had their "aha" moments with lean. "No sense in having a bunch of distracting nay-sayers in this meeting," thought Jon.

The steering team was debriefing a meeting they had all attended the week before at Acme Enterprises corporate headquarters. It was a business plan review in which Jon did most of the talking while Acme Devices entire leadership staff sat in the room listening and answering the occasional question.

"So, it looks like corporate is counting on us for a significant part of their growth strategy," said Dave. "In total, Acme has about $3 billion a year in revenue, of which our device business makes up $750 million—or 25% of the total. If we're not successful, Acme's not successful" (Figure 1.1).

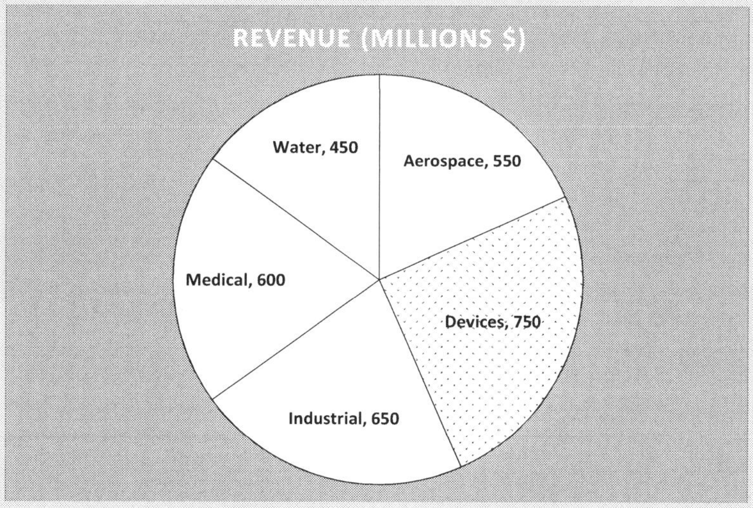

Figure 1.1 Acme enterprises annual revenue.

Along with a slide showing this breakdown were other slides highlighting that Acme Devices specialized in designing, manufacturing, and servicing products for the electrical power industry and that they were a mid-range player in the expanding market. Deregulation and growth around the world were making the new high-voltage switch (HVS) product vital for developing countries. The company was looking to expand their international presence in the coming years in response to a changing customer base.

"To achieve the growth we signed up for, execution on this next program is critical," Jon said. "Not only does the product have to be great, we need to deliver on all fronts. Innovation and customer relationship management isn't going to be enough this time."

As Paul was listening, he wished he had joined the company earlier. Their next generation product was largely designed. He was reminded of a study he read that determined about 70% of a product's ongoing cost is locked in as soon as an engineer put a line on the drawing. Well, life is rarely a green-field, and his job was to make the best of the situation.

"Project Franklin, the next generation High Voltage Switch, has been designed at our Ann Arbor, Michigan technical center," said Paul. "Although we are committed to much of the design, I believe there is still time to influence the remaining development stages and make the product a success."

Leslie asked, "How committed are we to the design?" Paul added, "Most of it is complete and we've built some prototypes on the low volume equipment in the tech center's model shop. Also, the engineering team has a concept for the production system, but it is only a paper concept."

Leslie gave Paul an uneasy look rooted in an earlier conversation between the two. They agreed that the product development team had made tremendous improvement in past years using modular-based architecture to design a simple and more robust next-generation HVS device, as well as integrating advanced software capability with the new hardware. But that seemed to be where progress stopped.

"Paul, remember our conversation last week?" said Leslie. "Great strides in the product's design, but every time a plant gets a new product, it is a bear to build. Our CI teams have job security fixing each new launch. And just when we think we are starting to make progress, along comes the next generation product…and it's like someone threw a turd in a punch bowl and walked away. Our Adrian plant makes the current generation switch, and it has taken them years to get the processes stable and meeting cost targets."

"I'm with you," said Paul.

"So how do we leverage this new product?" asked Jon. "Timing can't slip. We're committed to a product design."

Leslie interrupted, adding, "We have 4 years of experience improving the production process and building the current generation switch in the Adrian facility."

"Is it produced at any of our other three U.S. sites?" asked Jon. "No," said Leslie.

Jon continued, "If we didn't intervene in any way, what would happen next?"

"There would be a design review of the proposed process concept—probably in Ann Arbor," said Paul. "This is something Leslie and I were discussing the other night after work. We would like to move ahead with the design review but change the location to the plant. We agree this is a great opportunity to teach the organization how to do process creation better, around an actual project. Learning, while getting the work done."

Paul continued, "Jon, you brought Leslie here based on her lean process development experience and teamed us together. I think this is the opportunity we've been waiting for to introduce a new way of working."

This last statement brought a smile to Dave's face. He was very vocal about the low return on investment of typical training classes, and most people just ignored his rants as those of an out of touch finance guy.

"I'd like to hear your thoughts, Leslie," stated Jon.

Leslie shared, "Paul and I are in strong agreement. This is as an opportunity to instill the thinking we bring from our previous roles into Acme Devices. When I started working here, I was impressed with the CI teams, but frankly their progress has plateaued. They are eventually limited by the initial process design, and eventually, the product design. I think we can change that."

"I think we have the beginnings of a plan then," said Jon. "I also have a half-baked idea. I know your team is going to eventually come back to me for money. Dave, I'd like you to start thinking about how we measure success for this project. Think holistically and link it back to the assumptions in appropriation request. I'm not expecting you to do all the work, just think about it. Leslie, Paul, and the rest of the team are going to need your help."

As the meeting broke up, Paul and Leslie made plans to schedule a design review for the following week, but in Adrian rather than Ann Arbor. Dave collected all of the papers scattered on the table as he had brought most of them and left the room. Jon sat there alone for a moment, stared across the room at his useless desk and credenza and continued to work from his table. "Maybe I will treat myself to a new big table some day and get rid of these monuments," he thought.

The Design Review

KEY POINT

Create a steering team of top leaders to support the activity at the working-team level and to look for opportunities to eventually spread the lessons learned from this example throughout the organization.

Carla Perez's train of thought was broken by the chime of a new meeting request in her email inbox. She was thinking about a chapter she had just read in the book, "The Machine that Changed the World."[1] Yes, it was an old book, but Carla wanted to understand this thing called "Lean" from the beginning. "How does this really apply to engineering?" She wondered. Turning toward her computer she saw a meeting notice for next week, sent by Paul Larsson. "Project Franklin Design Review" scheduled for the following week at the Adrian plant. "That's odd, at the plant," Carla thought. Yet at the same time, it was intriguing for Carla. Carla was the leader of the product team for Project Franklin, and although a senior engineer, she was always looking for better ways of working. It was Carla who first suggested the use of modular development at Acme Devices and against a tide of engineering inertia, persevered. She usually persevered as she was often described as "steady, unflappable, and focused on facts." Paul Larsson had seen this in Carla within a week of starting at Acme and thought she would be key in bridging this new way of thinking and working with Acme's current engineering approach.

[1] *The Machine That Changed the World,* James P. Womack, Daniel T. Jones, and Daniel Roos, 1990 & 2007, Free Press.

Attached to the meeting notice was the standard design review invite list, which included:

From the engineering center:
  Carla Perez, Project Franklin Product Team Lead
  Tom Osborne, Equipment Design Engineer
Resident in the Adrian plant:
  Stephanie Waterson, Technical Design Lead
  Jolene Hill, Manufacturing Engineering
  Jorge Rogers, Operations Design Lead
  Ted Walker, Operations Supervisor
  Alexis Cruz, Industrial Engineer
From the Executive Staff:
  Leslie O'Brien, Operations Director
  Paul Larsson, Engineering Director
  Dave Laplace, Finance Manager

"This must be a big deal for Leslie and Paul to attend at this stage," Carla thought. Then she hit "accept" and went back to her book as her calendar was now blocked from 8:00 am to noon.

About a month earlier, in preparation for the Acme Enterprises Business Plan Review, Leslie O'Brien and Paul Larsson walked process flows similar to the proposed new HVS in the workplace (the "gemba"). On the walk through one plant, substantial improvement activity that was led by capable people was evident and part of a larger improvement infrastructure. The Operations team was well versed in using value stream mapping as their blueprint for process improvement efforts. Additionally, the plant had heavily invested in training and certifying specialists to use various tools and techniques for improvement in an efficient manner.

Weekly kaizen and "2P" (production preparation) events were held according to a plant action plan. The Operations team members were very skilled, knowledgeable, and enthusiastic about working in teams and developing countermeasures to problems that had been identified. There was no shortage of improvement opportunities and the plant saw this as a competitive advantage for even more efficiency gains going forward.

It was this gemba walk that led Leslie and Paul to conclude that something different needed to be done on Project Franklin if Acme was going to be able to meet its growth objectives. "On one hand, I'm impressed with the continuous improvement culture in Adrian. On the other hand, it's nothing more than a bunch of engineering rework," Leslie told Paul privately as they drove to dinner that night in Ann Arbor.

Over a couple of Reuben sandwiches at Zingerman's Deli, Leslie and Paul strategized on how they should proceed. Step one was to get the steering team's buy in. They knew to do this right; it was going to be bigger than engineering and operations meeting a few times a week. It would have to be cross-functional to be successful. Some people would participate willingly. Others would participate because Jon had endorsed the approach.

Step two would be an initial design review of the proposed process flow. This would begin the fact-based journey to both a better way of working and a successful Project Franklin. At the design review, Leslie and Paul would have to take care to guide the discussion yet keep project ownership with the team. Due to Leslie's experience, she would take the lead role with Paul's support. What was Step Three? That would become clearer during the design review, once they had a better understanding of the current situation. But it would be an opportunity for Leslie to further evolve her model of process design with help from Paul and the Project Franklin team.

Alexis Cruz did not choose to be an Industrial Engineer; she was born an Industrial Engineer; or at least that is what she told her understanding husband when purchasing new laundry baskets sized to match the capacity of their washer and dryer. When initially exposed to Lean over a decade ago, she quickly embraced it. Lean helped to explain some ideas she had intuitively developed on her own. Especially the ideas of value and lead time.

KEY POINT

The important ingredients for the team are cross-functional membership, defined roles and responsibilities led by a capable system architect.

Alexis was very in-tune with the concept of time as though she could somehow pick up that fabled atomic clock in Denver. And that is why she was the first one in the Plant Manager's conference room on Wednesday morning for the design review. As everyone meandered into the room and said their casual hellos, Alexis took deep breaths as the actual start time would be 10 minutes after the hour. "Typical," she thought.

Actually, Leslie and Paul were less than thrilled with the meeting starting late as well, but they made the conscious decision to let this meeting play out as typical, until the moment was right. This was their current state, and they needed the whole team to experience it together. This was not just about creating a new process for Project Franklin—it was about creating a new way of working together. Leslie noticed one additional attendee in the room who was not on the invite list—Melinda Jones.

Melinda was the quality manager at the plant, and she heard about the meeting through the grapevine. It always bothered Melinda that quality was an afterthought at Acme. Not that people did not care about quality, but most people viewed the quality organization as an auditing body, not an active partner. Melinda always believed if her team could only be involved earlier in the process design, many of the issues they encountered after launch could be avoided.

On the day before, Melinda caught Leslie in the hall and asked if it would be okay to crash the design review. "Absolutely," exclaimed Leslie. Leslie left that exchange with a slight grin on her face, muttering to herself, "If only everyone else at the design review would be that anxious to attend."

High Voltage Switch Product Overview—Concept 1

At the front of the room were Carla Perez and one of her engineering co-workers, Tom Osborne. Tom was the equipment design engineer for Project Franklin. Although part of the engineering technical staff, he actually sat in a cubicle in the Adrian plant, as most of his other work was focused on their equipment. Many referred to Tom as a "willing worker"— always there to help. Most people called him "Ozzy," because he usually wore a black concert t-shirt. Today's shirt was Tom Petty. Give Tom Osborne some direction and he was always willing to come up with a creative and simple way to make it a reality. He had a knack for simple, elegant equipment solutions.

On the projection screen was an agenda for the meeting. Carla would provide an overview of the new product design, then talk about the life cycle and basic process flow. Tom would provide more detail on the process flow and share the proposed process design. Paul Larsson asked that the attendees hold questions until the end, unless they needed a fact clarified such as a term or acronym.

Carla shared that this next-generation HVS was redesigned using modular architecture to comprise three primary subassemblies: A Device, a Plate, and a Case.

In addition, this was the first Acme Device product that integrated hardware and software design upfront in development, given the increasing industry software requirements and capabilities. The new modular design of the product allowed the team to evolve each subassembly at different rates to meet market and technology conditions (Figure 1.2). The core technology of the HVS product was found in the Device subassembly. The HVS product team evaluated past field service complaints and identified key features in

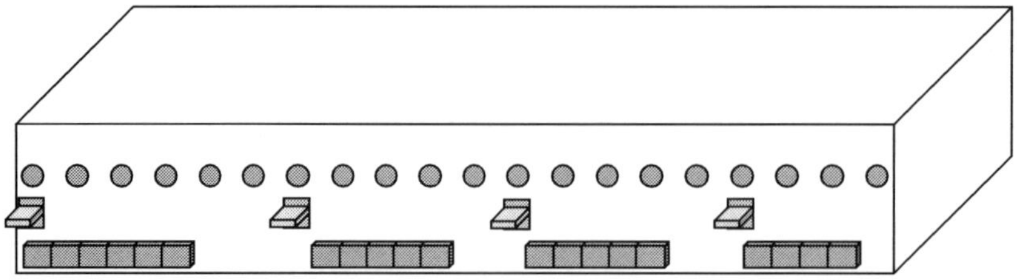

Figure 1.2 HVS product family.

this next-generation HVS product design that would improve quality, reliability, and warranty issues.

The product lifecycle for older versions of the HVS was 10–12 years of high-volume production, followed by up to 5 more years of low-volume spares with slight seasonal variability. This next-generation HVS would only have high-volume production of 5–7 years and the uncertain number of spares after that period. Peak volume was forecasted to be 900,000 units per year for high volume production (Figure 1.3). The start of production for the new HVS product would be in 6 months.

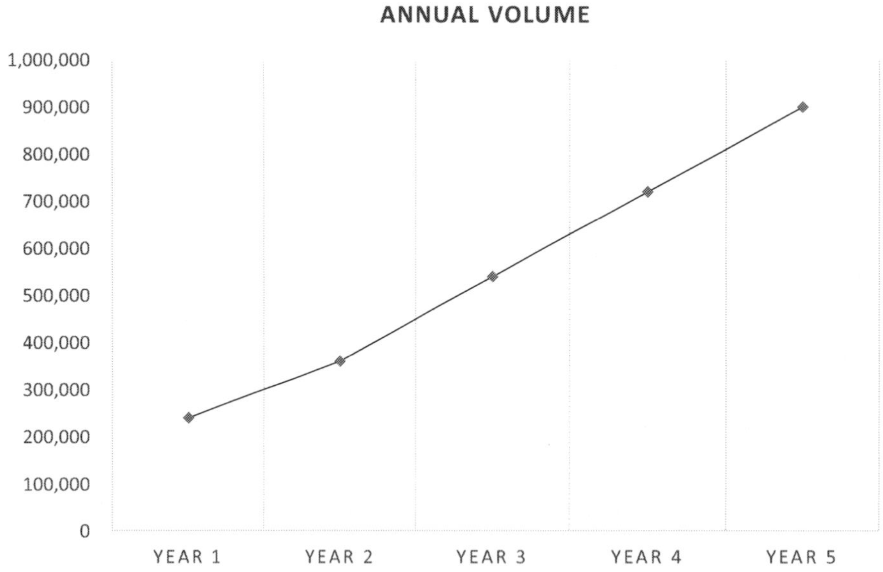

Figure 1.3 HVS ramp-up plan.

Next, Carla introduced the plan for manufacturing the HVS in Adrian (Figure 1.4). The HVS product requires 12 different operations, which were listed out in the proposed build sequence as stations:

Station (X* = Manual)	Station Description
10*	Device Sub-Assembly 1 & Press Tab
20*	Device Sub-Assembly 2 & Press Tab
30	Device Heat Weld
40	Device Label
50*	Plate Sub-Assembly 1 & Crimp
60*	Plate Sub-Assembly 2 & Crimp
70	Plate Bolt Driving (2)
70	Plate Bolt Driving (2)
80	Plate Label Press
90*	Switch Assembly
100	Bolt Driving (4)
110*	Case Assembly & Overweld / Leak Test
110*	Case Assembly & Overweld / Leak Test
120	Packout

Figure 1.4 HVS build sequence.

Carla stated that since the Adrian plant had high direct labor costs, it was decided that an automated conveyor line with minimal labor would be the best option for the facility and to meet cost targets.

At this remark, Ted Walker, the operations supervisor for the current HVS, leaned over to Alexis and whispered, "Our costs are high because we have to support all of this engineering overhead that doesn't do a darn thing for us." Alexis slowly nodded but kept listening to Carla intently.

It was Tom's turn to present the processing plan (Figure 1.5). As a speaker, Tom was not as polished or organized as Carla. He would rather be working on that upgraded fixture for the current HVS production system. The tool room had it ready, they just needed to get the line supervisor, Ted, to provide them an installation window on the line and they could have it running in 30 minutes. "Oops, not good to daydream in my own meeting," Tom thought.

Tom began, "Here's the process flow that we're proposing. And we estimate a capital spend of $1.8 million with a staffing of seven people that will be required to achieve the planned line cycle time of 16 seconds per unit. Stations 70 and 110 will need to be duplicated since their individual cycle times ended up being slightly greater than 16 seconds. Station 70 will run in series, with each station doing two of the four bolts. Station 110 will be in parallel—a HVS part will either go to one or the other, based on the conveyance logic. The plant will need to run the line on three shifts at peak

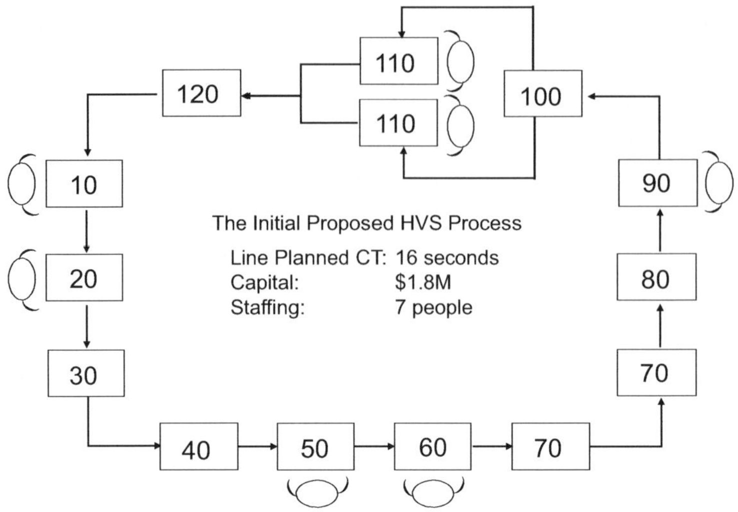

Figure 1.5 Proposed HVS process flow.

demand. The calculated internal rate of return (IRR) is 18%, which is higher than the minimum required rate of return (RRR) of 15% that was set by Dave Laplace and his finance team. So, Dave should be happy for a change."

No one laughed at the attempted humor, and Tom did not notice, as he was staring at the screen for the entirety of his remarks.

Ted was thinking, "Oh great, we'll have to add a third shift in assembly just for these engineering geniuses! Who's going to volunteer to manage that?"

"Thanks, Tom," said Carla. "Are there any questions?" The room was awkwardly silent.

Although he did no let it show, Jorge Rogers felt like he died a little inside. He wanted to say, "it's like deja vu all over again," but that would not be in Jorge's character. Jorge was cooler than most. His experience with Lean was deep. Not just book smart, but real experience.

Jorge actually worked for Leslie O'Brien at their prior company but left for Acme a few years before Leslie. He had been intimately involved with Acme's CI initiative. Jorge was always careful to bring all of the team members along during any improvement effort, making certain that they actually understood what was going to happen and why.

Jorge would often say, "We can't improve faster than our organization's ability to learn," and he actually meant it. When he received word that Leslie was coming to Acme, Jorge thought, "This will be great for all of us, she'll understand and support the changes we need to make to move to the next level." Unfortunately, that did not happen immediately. It took a year for the conditions to be right, but the time had finally arrived.

Jorge needed more time to digest the information at this point. So did the rest of the operations team. They just spent the last month, including weekends, reconfiguring a line in the south end of the plant that was similar to this new proposal. The reconfigured line was finally making money after struggling for a few years. And now they were going to get to do it all over again?

Sensing the tension in the air, Leslie intervened and said, "I think we should take a break. Here is what I would like to propose. Take 10 minutes for an actual break and then take 30 minutes to go observe the current HVS production system, but I want you to do the observation in pairs. Try to avoid observing with someone you frequently work with."

Leslie added this stipulation to get operations and engineering to observe together, "Just observe. Don't interrupt the team members doing the work—they have important work to do, and I don't want to see any of you identified as the root-cause of a quality issue on my morning walk-about. When we return, we're going to talk about your observations and how they relate to the design review so far."

Carla and Tom were confused by this suggestion. They wanted to get into more of the technical design details. They needed approval to begin machine builds for the long lead-time new capital. But both Paul and Leslie encouraged everyone to use this as an opportunity to check on the current operating system model and how their process design concept would fit.

Leslie and Paul had a good idea of where the next segment of the meeting was going to take the group and they were the knowledge leaders on this topic. But it was important that everyone involved was part of the discovery. If the team were simply told the answer and what to do about it, the long-term capability of the team would be compromised.

During the break, Paul and Leslie agreed that it would be best if Paul led the next portion of the discussion. Some of the

KEY POINT

Before designing the next generation processes, Project Teams need to *"go & see"* past process areas for similar products, in order to learn and reflect on how to be "better next time" in both the design of the process and the product. Even more valuable is *"go & do"*—performing the actual work in the process to make the product, in order to closely understand the current situation and provide higher value in the future.

discoveries were going to put the current engineering direction into question and that might be best facilitated by an engineering leader.

Lessons from the Factory Floor

At 10:30 am everyone was back in the room and had taken their original seats. "So, does anyone want to start?" asked Paul. "What did you notice as it relates to our process design conversation this morning?"

Jolene Hill, a manufacturing engineer, was quick to give an answer, "The plant is going to need more operational discipline if they are going to be successful. I saw extra inventory piled between stations, people chatting, and no one was using the standard work documentation we supplied to them."

Although these were rather basic observations and technically accurate, this was not what Paul was looking for to move the team forward. He did not hold that against Jolene. She was fairly new to this site and was just beginning to understand the basics of Lean. Jolene was in that critical stage of knowing a few tools, but not fully understanding how everything fit together in a system. "No problem," he thought, "she is more than willing to learn."

Jolene arrived in Adrian about 14 months before, from another Acme plant that had been closed for a variety of reasons, exacerbated by a workforce and leadership team that was not willing to change as the competitive world passed them by. The plant was one of Acme's older plants and the workforce almost had an air of invincibility—they had been around 68 years and they would be around another 68 years. This had always frustrated Jolene during her 15 years in manufacturing engineering at the facility. The entire experience left her a bit jaded, especially toward the frontline workers. When she saw issues in the plant, she almost always attributed them to the worker doing the work, versus digging for the real root cause.

Nevertheless, Jolene was a capable engineer and that was exactly the reason she was transferred to Adrian instead of being laid-off during the plant downsizing. "Let's dig into that a bit more," remarked Paul. "Remember, manufacturing is *the result*. The result of all of the upstream and support processes coming together and yielding the process you saw today. And what we saw has underlying root causes and we will eventually need to identify and address those, so we do not have the same conversation when Project Franklin is launched."

Paul asked the team, "What else did you see?"

Stephanie Waterson, or Steph as she liked to be called, shifted in her chair. In her kind voice she said, "There is a mismatch."

"What do you mean?" inquired Paul.

Steph elaborated, "Well, what we saw in the plant was a manufacturing approach using U-shaped cells with a mixture of manual and machine work. The older HVS production started on lines like the concept shown this morning, but over half of those lines have been changed to the cells. And the plant has plans to convert the rest of the systems to cells in the next 16 months. There is a mismatch in process design approaches."

Paul asked the group another question, "Why is the plant going through the effort to convert all of these production systems?"

Alexis raised her hand and started speaking simultaneously, "They just perform better—on all fronts. Quality, delivery, cost, uptime—you name it. This is not just me saying this, the results are hitting our bottom line. Dave Laplace has become a real fan of Adrian, dare I say."

Quiet up to this point, Ted spoke up, "They're a heck of a lot easier to manage as well. A lot less finger-pointing when something goes wrong. We can do a lot of our own problem solving right in the cell itself."

Paul was struck by Leslie's poker face. She had to be smiling inside, but she looked very neutral on the outside. "So, let's build on this thought," proposed Paul. "Over the next hour I'd like everyone to work together and update the numbers for the Project Franklin's proposed process concept. Use the actual experience data from the plant—a lot has been learned over the past few years."

Ninety minutes later, the group was ready. Carla had created a spreadsheet that summarized their estimates as well as the capital costs (Figure 1.6).

The proposed process concept would have an estimated cumulative line uptime of 63% (A) based on multiplying the uptimes of all the individual stations. The line cycle time of 16 seconds per piece (B) would result in an effective line cycle time of 25.4 seconds (C). The uptime losses at stations would be a mix of machine downtime, bowl feeder jams, changeover losses, tool changes, and more.

In effect, if this line design was to go forward without any improvement in performance before the peak volume was reached, the plant would have to purchase an additional line at $1.8 million and find the necessary floor-space. **The true project IRR (internal rate of return) would actually be 11%—and this would be below the RRR (required rate of**

(B) Line Cycle Time of 16 seconds

Concept-1: 16s Planned Cycle Time, Power & Free Conveyor System with Semi-Automatic Stations

Station	Description	Station Time	Uptime	Capital Cost	Notes
10*	Device Sub-Assembly 1 & Press Tab	12	100%	$30,000	
20*	Device Sub-Assembly 2 & Press Tab	10	100%	$30,000	
30	Device Heat Weld	10	97%	$150,000	
40	Device Label	4	99%	$80,000	
50*	Plate Sub-Assembly 1 & Crimp	14	99%	$100,000	
60*	Plate Sub-Assembly 2 & Crimp	12	99%	$100,000	
70	Plate Bolt Driving (2)	13	94%	$120,000	Bolts 1 & 2 of 4 total
70	Plate Bolt Driving (2)	13	94%	$120,000	Bolts 3 & 4 of 4 total
80	Plate Label Press	5	99%	$50,000	
90*	Switch Assembly	16	100%	N/A	
100	Bolt Driving (4)	14	87%	$200,000	
110*	Case Assembly & Overweld / Leak Test	28	96%	$180,000	Parallel operation
110*	Case Assembly & Overweld / Leak Test	28	96%	$180,000	Parallel operation
120	Packout	7	96%	$300,000	

(C) Effective Line Cycle Time 16 seconds / 63% = 25.4 seconds

Cumulative Uptime = 63%
Capital Cost = $1,640,000
Misc Controls = $160,000
Total Capital = $1,800,000

(A) Multiply this column to get the cumulative uptime of 63%

Figure 1.6 HVS proposed process flow operator/machine matrix.

return) of 15% and well below the 18% promised just hours before when the meeting started. These were exactly the type of results and operational surprises that had occurred in similar new process flows in the past.

Leslie stood up and walked to the front of the room. "Great work. And I'd like to thank everyone with letting the facts speak and not getting defensive. While you were working on this, Paul and I were discussing what we might do next. We are going to bring in lunch and extend this meeting until 5:00 pm. Let's take a 15 minute break so you can get your afternoon commitments rescheduled. I've seen this before. We are on the verge of a key discovery."

During the break, Steph pondered Leslie's final remark of "key discovery." What was up? "Key" might be good. Although stationed in the Ann Arbor technical center, Steph spent much of her time in the HVS plants. She was the engineering manager who caught the ball once it was thrown over the design wall. Go build this, make it hit these numbers, and by the way...

here are the assumptions that went into the numbers. Good luck. In spite of this situation, Steph always delivered. She was actually a second generation engineer at Acme.

Steph's father, who had recently retired, was well respected within the company. Over the years, her father rose in the engineering ranks but wanted to stay an engineer. He inadvertently caused HR to create a technical track for promotion as Acme strove to keep him working as an engineer, balancing his desire to get his hands dirty with having the ability to award him through promotions.

Steph, as they say, did not fall far from the tree. The primary difference between her and her dad was that she did choose to go into management, but sometimes questioned her own sanity in doing so. Steph was a natural bridge builder between her home department of engineering and operations. Her objectivity and lack of excitability were the foundation to her bridge building.

Once the group returned from their short break, Leslie continued the meeting. "Paul and I have been discussing Project Franklin for quite a while. It's important to Acme device's future—our future here and our future around the world. **It's so important that we can't allow business as usual to be our mode of operation**. Likewise, as an organization we have all learned something about the concept of 'Lean.' Different parts of the organization are at different levels of maturity, but fundamentally we are learning that lean can help us reach our business objectives."

Leslie paused to scan the room. It looked like everyone was paying attention. No passive-aggressive body language either—good.

Leslie continued, "One consistent discovery in our lean journeys is that lean is best learned through practice on an actual example. Books can get you the knowledge, but you need to add experience to that knowledge to make it into wisdom. So, we have an alignment of the planets occurring—an important Project Franklin and lean as a way of thinking to enable our business results. Paul and I think the time is right to use Project Franklin as that example to learn how to work differently and create lean processes simultaneously....and there is no time like the present to get started. Thoughts?"

Carla spoke up, "In spite of being told my baby is ugly this morning, I am really excited about this. I've been trying to study up on lean as it relates to product and process design, but there is not a lot out there to really learn from. Only a couple of books, which are more focused on the product end of the development process. That said, what's the scope of this project? Are we going to revisit the product design?"

"No," answered Leslie. "Timing won't allow us to revisit the product, although that would be the ideal scenario. We will stick with the new design as-is and focus on how to best develop the production process. But in the spirit of continuous improvement, Paul and I are going to ask that we capture any discoveries along the way that could make us even more effective next time."

When Leslie was talking, Paul was connecting his laptop to the projector in the room, and then he added, "Here is a classic chart that I like to refer to, based on early Munro and Associates work in the automotive industry.[2] Although there is a perception that up to 80% of the cost of the product is incurred at Operations, the majority of cost is actually committed early on during the Development cycle when the Product Design and Process Design takes place – *70% of the cost is on the print"* (Figure 1.7).

KEY POINT

As John Shook frequently says, *"It is easier to act your way to a new way of thinking, than to think your way to a new way of acting."* The best way to build sustainable capability in your organization is to select a "learning laboratory" where you may experiment and test out new ideas in a controlled environment, which will yield dramatic performance improvement results in process and people, and then cascading the appropriate learning wider and deeper. And to ensure focus, pick something sufficiently important. This experiment may take several months, and if you select an area that is not critical, other priorities will get in the way.

Kaizen or Touzen?

The Operations team in Adrian had worked very diligently the past 5 years to put in place a stronger operating model for performance increases, but every new product that launched in that same timeframe required significant improvements to incorporate the learning and operational standards. Leslie O'Brien explained that much of the improvement or *kaizen* activity the past 5 years had been valuable and necessary, but a good portion of it was actually engineering rework or *touzen* due to poorly created process flows. *(Touzen is commonly referred to as "kaizen that should not have been necessary" if an activity or item was designed properly in the first place.)*

[2] Leandesign.com/history_of_lean_design, Who Casts the Biggest Shadow? Sandy Munro, 1989.

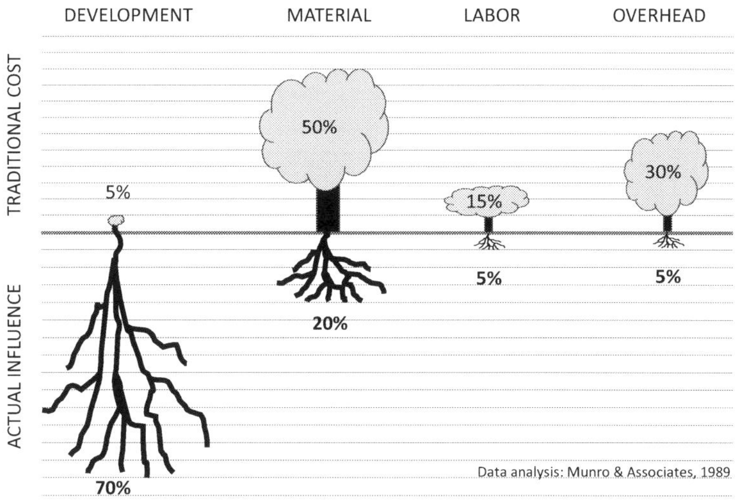

Figure 1.7 The cost forest: development's actual influence on cost.

Leslie continued, "So we are going to run an experiment with dual purposes. First, to develop a lean process for Project Franklin and second, to develop a better method for creating these new processes at our organization—a new way of working together leveraging what we can learn about lean. Let's be clear, working differently or using lean slogans is not the goal. We actually need to learn to work *better*. Thinking about our example this morning, what, in our way of working, is causing the need to re-work new processes?"

Leslie quickly added, "Before you answer that out loud, I'd like you to jot your thoughts on to post-its. We are going to go through an affinization exercise, and we'd like to hear from all of you, not just the loud people in the room." This last remark made Alexis grin.

Although there was an initial flurry of writing, it subsided in about 10 minutes. Team members were asked to read one of their post-its, explain it briefly, and place it on the wall. Others were encouraged to add their similar ideas around the newly placed post-it. Several categories emerged on what looked to be a confusing swirl of thoughts.

Paul asked the team, "So what do we do with this? For example, there is a bucket about ASSUMPTION OF AUTOMATION."

"Assume a manual process?" Alexis said hesitantly.

"I hear some apprehension in your voice, and that's well placed," said Paul. "Doing that would only lead to other problems on this or other designs, and that would be addressing the symptom. We need to think about the root cause of assuming automation." Paul briefed the team on the Five-Why process, but with the added dimension of allowing the answers to branch.

Ted found this refreshing. When he went to his introduction to Lean training, it taught Five-Why as a linear concept—as though there was only one answer to the question "why?" He had argued with the instructor that when you get into the real world in the plant there is always more than one answer. The instructor brushed him off as the typical argumentative operations guy in the class, who really did not want to be there. And although there was a bit of truth in that, Ted was bringing up a valid point.

Paul's demonstration showed the first why branching into three possibilities. And each of those branched into two or three more. But a strange thing happened, as why was repeatedly asked (not always exactly five times!)—some of the answers were starting to repeat at the ends of the various branches. Paul explained it was those repeating items that we wanted to countermeasure.

After much dialogue and guidance from the directors, they narrowed the root causes down to three, and gave them both titles, and in the Acme tradition—acronyms:

- **Too Much, Too Early (TMTE)**: Critical operational decisions are made too early with incomplete knowledge or input
- **Too Little, Too Late (TLTL)**: No upfront process thinking and limited process design for new products before their final design
- **Penny-Wise, Pound-Foolish (PWPF)**: Functional or area decisions are made that may lead to local optimization but frequently lead to overall performance reduction

Next the group was asked to brainstorm countermeasures in order to minimize future process flows needing to be reworked. With guidance from Paul and Leslie, they settled on these critical items for their experiment:

- **System Architect**: Find a *System Architect* who will be responsible for thinking about the whole value stream and its processes in conjunction with the product design
- **Responsible Experts**: The System Architect will lead a *team of responsible experts* who have a mastery of available/emerging technical and operational knowledge

- **A Process for Creating Lean Processes**: Develop a *Lean Process Creation methodology* that becomes standard engineering work in the "Development Factory" for all new products
- **Rapid Learning Cycles**: Utilize the Set-Based Concurrent Engineering methods that *"test before design"* for multiple alternatives before converging to the optimal process design that needs to be configured

There was some debate arriving at these countermeasures, but a simple diagram (Figure 1.8) that Paul sketched out helped the group reach a reasonable level of comfort with the ideas.

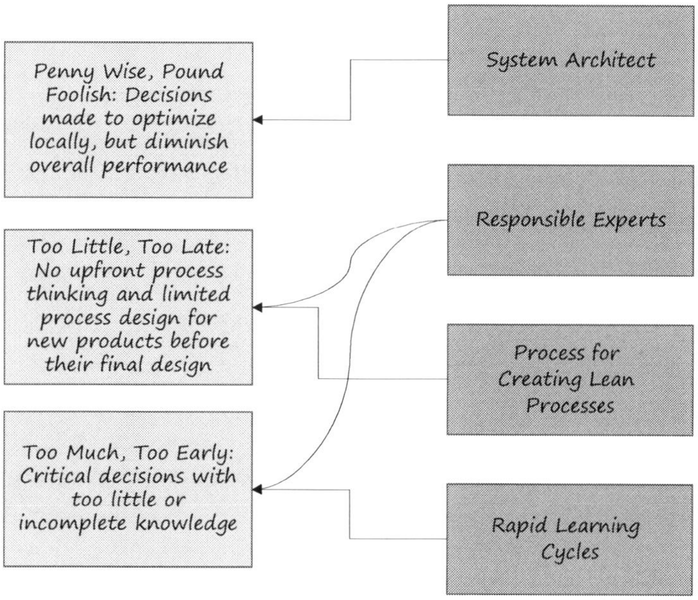

Figure 1.8 Countermeasures for better process design.

Once the group had consensus on the countermeasures, it was now time to select the people that would actively take part in this experiment to test the hypothesis that there was a more effective and efficient method for creating new process flows in a value stream. The people did not feel that there was one person who could play the role of the System Architect yet, so it was decided that both a process engineer with the technical understanding, Steph, and an industrial engineer with the operational understanding, Jorge, would co-lead this experimental Lean *Process Creation Team.*

The dedicated team also included experienced members from production assembly (Ted Walker), manufacturing engineering (Jolene Hill), industrial engineering (Alexis Cruz), product development (Carla Perez), quality (Melinda Jones), and equipment design engineering (Tom Osborne). Gary Rice of production control and logistics would also be added to the team. Dave Laplace from finance would support the team when needed.

If one could read minds, they would have noticed that Ted Walker was the most skeptical person in the room. Ted was a street-smart operations guy. If he had applied himself in high school, he might have gone on to college and become an engineer. But that did not happen. Manufacturing jobs were plentiful when he graduated from high school, and he began working on a production line at 19 years old. One of his early supervisors recognized Ted's smarts and encouraged him to apply for an apprenticeship as a mold maker. This was a turning-point for Ted and led to him earning an associate's degree, making the jump to management, and then going back to school to earn a bachelor's degree in operations management.

Ted looked at production through a unique lens of operator, skilled trades, and management. This made him valuable, especially in the early Lean production efforts. He was able to understand, support and sustain changes that were the result of the kaizen activities. Ted was so successful that, 3 years before, the company leadership thought it would be a good idea to have Ted participate with engineering in the development of a new production process. The experience that followed was the source of Ted's doubt today.

It turned out that engineering really wanted Ted's buy-in, not his input. He was quickly an island of one, attempting to share with engineering the lessons learned in operations. Engineering was not listening at the time. "Hopefully this time would prove different," Ted now thought.

The Process Creation team would need to launch a Lean process flow within 6 months, as well as develop the initial standard methodology for all future process designs. This would support one of the long-term development goals of creating profitable operational value streams starting from launch throughout the entire product lifecycle. Carla had read that in one of those Lean product development books, and as a lens for product development, it was a game-changer: CREATE PROFITABLE VALUE STREAMS.[3]

With the team and its purpose defined, Leslie thought everyone could use a break. It had been a long day, and she was mentally drained as well. "Great job everyone. We have the foundation for successful experiment.

---

[3] *Lean Product and Process Development*, 2nd Edition, Allen C. Ward and Durward K Sobek II, 2014, Lean Enterprise Institute.

I'd like to propose we break for now. Jorge and Steph, I'd like you to take the action item to get everyone back together tomorrow and define a vision by answering the question, 'what *is* a Lean process flow?' During these early meetings, be sure to include me and Paul. The team is going to do the work, the thinking if you will, but we will act as roadblock removers and guides."

The Stages of Lean Process Creation

The Process Creation Team started off their work together with a dialogue around the question, *"What exactly is a Lean process flow?"* Now that the team understood the current situation, it was important to create a shared vision of the ideal condition before embarking on the long work ahead of them—the "true north" that Leslie had asked for. Based on the team's experiences with Lean, they knew that one key fundamental was to only build at the rate that customers buy. Informed by these experiences from the CI efforts, the team listed out four vital characteristics that any process flow would have to meet:

- Short Lead Time
- Built-In Quality
- Flexible Capacity and Flexible Resources
- Simple and Manageable

Ted had argued to include "low cost," which was understandable. As an operations manager, he was grilled about costs daily. Jorge was able to explain that if these other factors were present, cost would be low as a result. On the other hand, the wrong focus on cost will drive the "penny-wise, pound-foolish" behaviors described the day before.

Earlier that morning, Steph and Jorge had met to discuss just what they wanted to accomplish in today's meeting, including a frank reflection on the team members. They met in Steph's office, which was actually a desk in the corner of the tool room hidden behind some rolling toolboxes. Steph commandeered the desk a long time ago as her unofficial office in the plant. Although noisier than most offices, the din of the tool room created a wall of sound that allowed Steph to think. And secretly, the smell of cutting fluid relaxed her.

Their meeting started with the ritual of getting coffee. Hidden inside one of the tall toolboxes was a coffee setup that rivaled Starbucks. "The best coffee for miles," thought Jorge as he poured himself a cup.

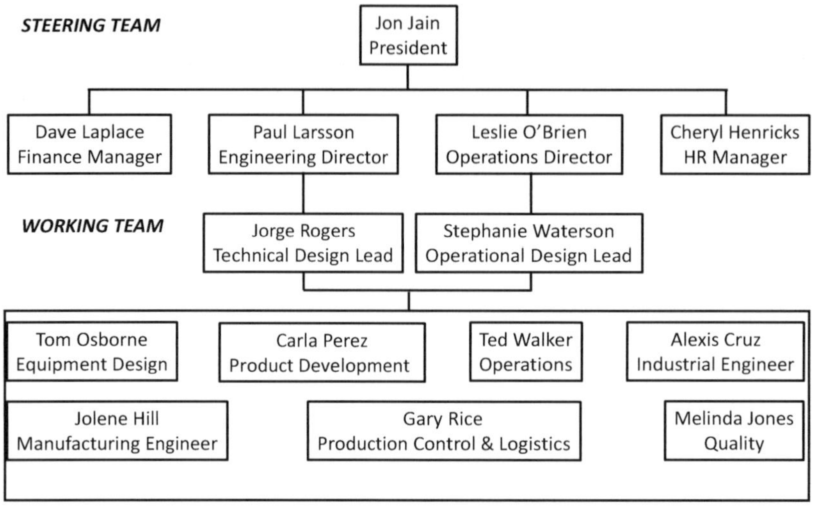

Figure 1.9 Process creation stakeholders.

The two returned to Steph's desk. "Before we get started with our assignment for today, let's do a quick inventory of all the stakeholders," said Steph. Pulling a sketch that she had drawn the night before from her desk, Steph and Jorge studied the diagram (Figure 1.9).

"What do you think of Ted?" asked Jorge.

"Early on, he'll challenge the process at every step", said Steph. "History has given him some reasons to be skeptical, but he's also experienced the real improvements from the kaizen activities, so he'll be open to trying things, just not super patient. But if we can get him to be a believer, he'll convert another 20 people."

Jorge said, "I agree. Moving on to Jolene and Tom–I look at them as a working pair."

With an eyebrow raised, Steph asked, "More?"

Jorge continued, "I'm glad Leslie and Paul placed them both on the team. Tom's willing to try anything and despite his odd social skills, he comes up with some of the most creative and simple equipment and fixture designs of anyone at Acme. Meanwhile, Jolene is a capable manufacturing engineer, and we need her talents to stitch Tom's equipment together, but we'll have to help her gain confidence in the Adrian operations."

"I agree", said Steph, "the last site she worked at was a caustic environment, especially between management and the production team members."

Jorge asked, "Do you know Carla very well?"

"I've not worked directly with her on any past projects, but everyone always speaks highly of her, even the biggest product engineering critics in the plant. Carla's known to be willing to try new things, even if it might mean some additional work for her", said Steph. She continued, "We both know Alexis and I'm thrilled you brought her to this experiment, Jorge."

Jorge said, "Alexis is the best person on my team and this effort needs a strong, detailed oriented industrial engineer to be successful."

Steph then asked, "What about Melinda and Gary?"

A small grin shot across Jorge's face.

"What's so funny?" asked Steph.

Jorge said, "Well, it's kind of funny, sad, and telling that we're talking about them last. Both of them are excellent, but both feel like their functions are always an after-thought when it comes to process design. Melinda has been pushing to get quality a seat at the table early on, so they can shift their role from reporting to actually driving quality improvements. She had to actually invite herself to yesterday's meeting. And I've heard Gary say he's tired of people thinking that PC&L stands for People Cursing & Lecturing."

"I get what he's saying," said Steph thoughtfully. "If you think about it, a well-structured Production Control and Logistics department is the only organization that can see the whole value stream from raw material to the value being placed in the customer's hands. Yet we typically design a whole process and then tell PC&L to figure out how to get materials in and out at the eleventh hour. Anyway, I smiled as we even chose to talk about them last, like they are still an afterthought. We'll have to take care to watch ourselves."

They sat for a brief minute in silence. In the background was the soft whir of the high-speed machines, doing their work of the morning inside their individual sound enclosures.

"Mind if we switch gears to our task this morning?" asked Jorge.

"Not at all, but I need a refill before we continue" said Steph.

A few minutes later, fresh coffees in hand, they quickly agreed they had better develop an answer to Leslie's "true-north" question, but then what?

"Once we define the characteristics of a lean flow, we'll have a high-level vision for the process characteristics of our profitable value stream," started Jorge, "but we still need a vision for the process creation work itself."

"Why not start with our current state?" asked Steph. "We could use our current milestones as a starting point for discussion with the team, map it out for a recent process development that was completed, and talk about what works, what doesn't, and create a high-level improved framework to test."

"Sounds like a plan," said Jorge, "but we will have to limit the whining–there are a couple of folks in the room who could really take us into the weeds."

Steph rocked back in her chair, looked at the ceiling and said, "I agree, but you're better at facilitating than I am. So, you take the lead and I'll support you all the way."

"Deal," said Jorge. Jorge was happy with this approach. Based on his past work with Leslie he felt like he knew what she was looking for and he was confident it would work. But he did not want to be the sole owner of this new approach. To be effective, it needed to be cross-functional and he knew he needed to bring everyone along.

Armed with a definition of a Lean process flow, it was now time to define what a process might look like that would yield such a flow. Jorge reminded the group that they were going to define the high-level flow. Their actual work, and what they learned doing it, would help to define the details.

To jumpstart the discussion, Steph had drawn a diagram of the process creation steps that Acme currently utilized. It included:

1. Receive product design and process concept from product team
2. Design, spec, and purchase equipment and tooling
3. Install and debug
4. Ramp-up and manufacturing sign-off
5. Start of regular production

Once it was verified with the team that these were the major steps, the team was asked to map out all the product and process design activities for the last new process development activity, another HVS product (Project Edison) for a different market. They took 1 day using the product development value stream mapping format with swim lanes to document all the key work, information flow, design changes, program scope changes, and more, as well as the consequences of changes to timing, resources, and start of production (Figure 1.10).

At the end of the day, the map was complete, and different colored post-it notes represented key milestones and timeline (lime), information flow (orange), work tasks (yellow), and delays/rework/unplanned interruptions to the process (pink).

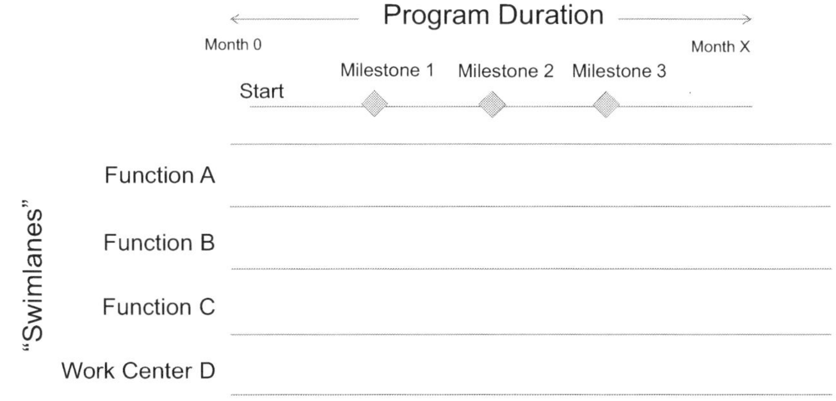

Figure 1.10 Value stream mapping swim lane framework.

Mapping out the product and process development work for Project Edison revealed the following:

- The original development plan called for 18 months from idea-to-start of production for the product and process development cycle; actual time was 24 months to the acceptable start of production (6 months late or 33%).
- Five major product design changes impacted process development timelines, leading to rework and over 6 months of delay to the real start of production. Additionally, there was an ongoing quality/warranty issue, and an operating margin that was only 67% of target.
- The plant that received this product continues to struggle with consistent quality and delivery to the customers from an underwhelming production process that they are working diligently to improve to this day.
- Twenty-nine risks and opportunities identified with this recent program specific to improving the way process development work is done.

Once the team agreed the current condition map was informative and complete for Project Edison, the team was asked to voice issues with each step. For structure, Jorge asked the team to start closest to the customer first.

"I want to keep our conversation focused, as this could quickly spin out of control. So, let's keep our issues strictly to things we have observed," said Jorge. "We aren't ready for solutions. We aren't here to point fingers. So, think about what you've experienced or observed, that was an issue at each of these phases. Let's start at the end, start of production."

"The start of production date never moves, even if we aren't ready," blurted Ted, his operation's scars clearly showing.

"Go on," encouraged Jorge.

Ted continued, "Well, what I am saying is I always have to add a load of people to the line, because things aren't really ready. There's a quality problem, so we need an inspector. A machine isn't quite right, so an extra operation is added to make up for it. Something is wrong with the parts like the packaging isn't what we thought it would be, so we toss in another person. As far as the customer is concerned, they're getting what they expect. But we're burning hundred dollar bills every hour and I'm the one that gets put under the magnifying glass." As Ted spoke, Jorge summarized his comments on post-it notes and placed them on the board between the start of production and ramp-up milestones.

"Anything else in this area?" asked Jorge. "If not, what about in the area of ramp up and manufacturing sign-off?"

"Thought you'd never ask," said Gary.

Gary Rice was the manager of Production Control and Logistics, or PC&L. He was a high-potential industrial engineer strategically placed in the department as both a developmental assignment for him and to change PC&L's role at Acme. Prior to the start of Acme's Lean journey, PC&L was an organization which existed in the backwaters of Acme to serve others. Gary would often lament that, "The primary job qualification was the ability to dial a phone and yell." Typical of many organizations, Acme learned about the idea of value streams and how to map them. More importantly, they had the epiphany of the importance of information flow.

It was Gary's experience that most organizations exposed to value stream mapping would understand that information flow is part of the map. But then they would slowly stop showing it on the map or they would throw a few casual lines on top of the material flow but not really understand exactly how each process step was really determining what work to do next. The net result was the overemphasis of process changes and cutting inventory without regard for the scheduling process. Gary's personal mission was to change that. He wanted PC&L to become the "conductor of the orchestra" they would not play the instruments, but they would work to make them play together and make beautiful music.

Gary continued, "With every new production system, we have to go back and change how we present the materials to the team member or operator. It's difficult to introduce materials to the line without interrupting the team member, the amount of space for materials on the line is never correct—always too much or too little, and..."

"Before you go on, could you elaborate on what you mean by too much or too little, how do you know?" asked Jorge.

Gary responded, "Sure, our material handlers provide parts to all the lines on a cadence, currently every 30 minutes. They know what to bring back to the line based on the kanban cards they receive, which are pulled from the containers as soon as an operator starts consuming them. So best case, there needs to be at least 30 minutes of material on the line to cover the lead time between material handling routes. This is best case, assuming the person who delivers the materials also pulls their own materials from the central supermarket. If we have a market attendant, then the quantity required on the line doubles."

Gary continued, "But what I actually see is rack space on the line that has nothing to do with the timing of the delivery routes. Some components have space for 3 hours of inventory and others have 10 minutes. We design racks based on the leftover space available, not to facilitate material delivery."

"Any comments?" Jorge asked of the team.

"If shorter route times result in less inventory on the line, why not go to 15-minute routes?" asked Jolene.

Jorge jumped in, "Great question, but let's parking lot that. I think our takeaway is we need to be thinking more proactively about materials & information flow and its impact on the production system." Jolene was satisfied with that for now, but why not 5 minutes?

While smiling, Ted was thinking, "Perhaps PC&L was changing for the better." As long as Ted could remember, operations both ran the operation and scheduled their production. And although PC&L was trying to take over the scheduling of production, operations had resisted. Frankly, they did not trust PC&L to know the nuances of the production process enough to make good scheduling decisions. This rant by Gary was starting to change Ted's mind.

"Let's move on to install and debug. What are your thoughts here?" asked Jorge.

Although Steph wanted to answer the question, she remained silent. "Better to have the team reach a collective conclusion versus me telling them," she thought.

Jolene spoke up, "Let's start with what we saw on the floor the other day. Steph, I think you called it a mismatch. The process that was selected for implementation didn't leverage anything we learned doing improvements in the plant. I don't understand how that happens."

"I have an idea but let me put it in the form of an observation so Jorge doesn't yell at me," said Carla jokingly. Carla had always taken pride in her relationship with the plant and everyone who supported operations. As a product engineer it was easy to get caught up in designing the next new thing. Early in her career, Carla intuited that to be a great product engineer she would have to learn to work well with production.

Carla continued, "We pretty much settle on a process design direction right up front and then keep tweaking it here and there to get the numbers to work out. All the numbers—the financials, the cycle times, the quality levels. And then we do something I'm not proud of, we send everything to process engineering at the plant and tell them this is what they are getting, and it better hit these numbers. The irony is what we send to process engineering lacks a lot of detail."

"What do you mean?" asked Jorge.

Carla answered, "We may tell them that station 10 should take 10 seconds, but that is an estimate—we really haven't designed the work station at that point…so is 10 seconds reasonable?" Jorge was capturing Jolene's and Carla's thoughts on post-its and adding them to the map.

Alexis added, "I find myself going back to engineering and marketing multiple times to better understand the product's value proposition to our customer. I've always thought if I understand the value, I can make better decisions as we refine the process."

"Go on," prodded Jorge.

Alexis continued, "For example, if I know Project Franklin is for emerging markets and will require the ability to produce a large variety of final assemblies, I may add more changeover flexibility into the process design. But if I don't understand the value proposition, I may just do what I did before."

Melinda Jones had been quiet up until now. She was enjoying this conversation because it was making her think beyond her own role in the quality organization. Melinda said, "I may be jumping around here, but does anyone check to see that we actually achieved what we promised? We have all these assumptions built into spreadsheets: the uptime of the equipment, yield by process, cycle times by stations. And I am sure there is more. These assumptions are worked and reworked until the project is financially viable on paper. So, I am wondering—no, in fact I know—we don't go check after launch to see if we hit our targets."

This exercise continued a while as one person's thoughts inspired another's. Although it was not the clean customer-back flow that Jorge had started with, the team was on a roll and that was good enough. Everyone grouped the post-its on a white board and through discussion the following issues emerged:

Milestone	*Key Issue*
Receive product design and process concept from design engineering	Unclear value proposition
Design, spec, and purchase equipment and tooling	Forcing THE ONE early concept to work
Install and debug	Over-the-wall with little detail
Ramp-up and manufacturing sign-off	Production starts on time, even if the process and material flow is not ready
Start of regular production and de-bugging/improving	Process targets are not verified Resources scatter

"Indulge me—let's reflect on what we just did" said Jorge. "Using our current process model as a starting point, we discussed our observations about what we've seen that doesn't quite work. We affinitized these into themes—themes that are really familiar to both Leslie and me, in our past lives." Jorge added a column to their whiteboard and titled it, "Phase." Underneath, he printed a memorable list of the phases, taken from his work at his last employer.

Jorge continued, "At my last job we had the same universal issues we have here at Acme. We found by understanding each phase, and its purpose, it made it easier to come up with a robust process to guide us. Then we came up with a hypothesis of sorts—the steps we believe could lead us to design a Lean process flow. We had four phases of process development at my old company: CONcepts, CONverge, CONfigure & CONnect and CONtinuously improve."

"You said four phases, but I see five words," commented Jolene.

"Yeah, it wasn't perfectly clean," said Jorge, "We found that configure and connect were so interdependent that we considered it a single phase but kept both of the words."

This kind of talk was giving Gary goosebumps, and he was almost embarrassed about it. Finally, someone taking the connections or information flow seriously while designing the system!

Jorge continued, "But you can see, we've identified two additional areas of opportunity; two more phases if you will. It would be cool if we could come up with words to describe each of these phases that start with the letters C, O, and N."

Milestone	*Key Issue*	*Phase*
Receive product design and process concept from design engineering	Unclear value proposition	?
Design, spec, and purchase equipment and tooling	Forcing THE early concept to work	CONCEPTS
Install and debug	Over-the-wall with little detail	CONVERGE
Ramp-up and manufacturing sign-off	Production starts on time, even if the process and material flow is not ready	CONFIGURE & CONNECT
Start of regular production and de-bugging/improving	Process targets are not verified	?
	Resources scatter	CONTINUOUSLY IMPROVE

It only took the team a couple of minutes of discussion to fill in the two missing phases. The final list was:

- Context
- Concepts
- Convergence
- Configure
- Confirm
- Continuously Improve

"Is this making sense so far? So, what do we do next?" asked Jorge.

Quiet until this point, Steph said, "Let's start the experiment, and be sure to reflect and learn as we go."

"These steps imply a sequence, and I just want to go on the record and say that to be most effective, the steps of Configure and Connect will have to be worked out together. They are just too interdependent to treat otherwise," said Gary.

Alexis nodded in violent agreement. "Point taken," said Jorge. "Let's put a little more definition around each category or CON."

6CON Model

The Process Creation Team referred to this as the *6Con Model*. The description for each stage was the following:

- **Context**: understanding each customer's value proposition, the high-level value stream design, and the value stream's key attributes
- **Concepts**: discovering the key knowledge gaps and exploring multiple process design options to facilitate learning in the converge phase
- **Converge**: testing/modeling the initial design concepts and narrowing them down to select an optimal design through rapid learning cycles
- **Configure**: engineering and arranging the selected process concept to create value and minimize waste with a reasonable management system, while linking the material and information flow system to upstream suppliers and downstream customers
- **Confirm**: leveraging a robust launch readiness approach to finalize the process while ensuring it meets the targets set in the business plan
- **Continuously Improve**: making and sustaining consistent improvements over time that will produce even higher levels of performance while providing upstream feedback

The stages were meant to be overlapping and were also seen as a logical flow for creating any new process. With help from the team, Ted sketched out an image (Figure 1.11) of how they viewed Lean Process Creation based on these stages and characteristics.

One major challenge for the Process Creation Team was that they were not used to designing Lean processes for new products. In the past 5 years the operational teams had been able to take the existing lines, and with

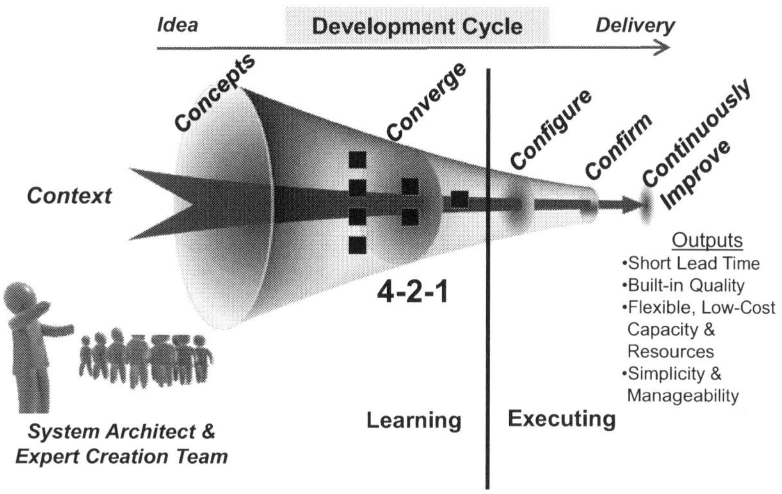

Figure 1.11 Lean process creation framework.

good knowledge of their strengths and weaknesses, redesign and improve them using a standard improvement approach. They essentially made the best of the hand they had been dealt, slowly getting better, step-by-step, visually shown in the chart below (Figure 1.12) as they moved from phase 1 (instable) to phase 2 (stable), and if the organization stayed focused, to phase 3 (step-change improvement) before the end of the product lifecycle.

Now, by working upfront in the development cycle, the team was expected to not only have an improved condition, but this HVS process flow should be closer to its ideal condition (phase 3) from the start of launch, in order to leverage the performance results for the majority of the product lifecycle. Although the Lean concepts would be the same in either case, the approach that was used for improvement of existing processes was probably not going to work for the design of new processes.

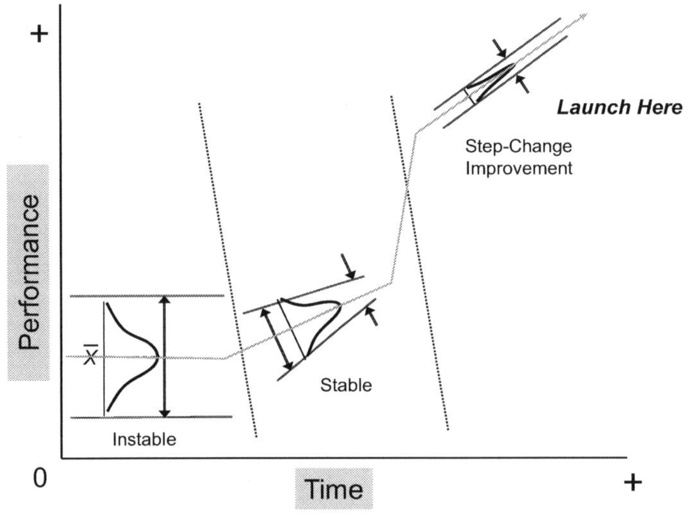

Figure 1.12 Improvement curve for systems.[4]

Since development is a matter of learning rapidly before converging to a selected design, the Process Creation Team decided that the best way for them to learn was to come up with a core set of questions that would guide them through each of the proposed stages of the 6Con Model. It was time to get to work.

After the steering team broke up, David Laplace returned to his office and called Melinda Jones. "Melinda, Leslie just gave the Lean steering team

[4] Based on thinking presented by Dave Logozzo, "Your Role as the Architect" presentation, slide 17, Lean Enterprise Institute 10th anniversary, 9/18/2007.

a debrief that included what she called a 6-CON model. She specifically mentioned that you brought up the issue that spawned the phase called CONFIRM. Can I stop by tomorrow to better understand your thinking?"

"Absolutely, I'm open all afternoon," Melinda said. "Why are you interested?"

Dave responded, "Jon had given me an assignment last week to think about this very subject, so I'd like to hear your thoughts." After hanging up the phone, David sent a meeting notice to Melinda for 2:00 pm tomorrow and Melinda's email inbox made that annoying chiming sound almost instantly.

THE STEERING TEAM—ESTABLISHING A CADENCE

It was 4:55 pm and Paul Larsson was sitting at the table both talking and solving an Acme-branded Rubik's cube created by marketing as a handout at trade shows and to customers. Also present were Leslie O'Brien, Dave LaPlace, and Cheryl Henricks. They were all waiting for Jon Jain to arrive at their LST meeting. Project Franklin was now underway with a new approach, and Jon thought it was best for the steering team to begin meeting weekly.

Jon was a big proponent in the power of cadence, and he believed this project needed a leadership cadence to support it. Jon also thought the time was ripe for Cheryl Henricks, his HR manager to join the steering team. "A change in process might begat a change in roles, and I need you to understand and guide us on those changes," Jon coached Cheryl. She was all too happy to be part of this change.

Cheryl transferred to Acme from the auto industry 5 years earlier and instantly began shaking up Acme's HR organization. She made it her goal to make HR a strategic partner at Acme, and shed its image of "the department of NO." "No, you can't hire them. No, you can't fire them. No, you can't recognize them. No, you can't discipline them."

Cheryl's experience was when HR better understood the business they could enable management's strategic and operational visions. Cheryl also understood the value of a well-developed Lean practitioner to both the organization and to other companies. During the past year she led an initiative to create clear career paths within the largest departments at Acme and recognize Lean capabilities. It was this activity that put Cheryl on Jon's radar—and now here she was.

Jon sailed into his office at 4:59. "Whew, just made it. It would be embarrassing to lock myself out of my own meeting," he said. Jon was a zealot for punctuality and respecting the time of others. "Cheryl, great to see you—glad you could make it to our soiree." "Thanks for the invite," she replied.

Jon continued, "Leslie, can you give us an update on the status of the process creation team?"

Leslie told Jon, Cheryl, and Dave about the series of meetings and the process creation model the team created for testing. She also shared the names and roles of everyone on the team and provided a little background on each person.

"Does the team have a home? A place to collaborate?" asked Jon.

"We've grabbed a wall in the Adrian plant in the old temp sensor room," said Leslie. "In fact, we're giving them use of the room for Project Franklin work."

"What are they going to do with a wall?" asked Jon.

Paul answered, "Initially they were meeting inside of conference rooms, but we asked them to begin to post information pertinent to the project on the wall so they can more readily interact with one-another and quickly see the status of the project. They are still experimenting with exactly what to post, but Leslie and I will get them there." Paul placed the puzzle on the table, unsolved.

"It sounds like a good start. What support do they need from us?" asked Jon.

Paul answered, "From my experience, they will run into some bumps as they try to engage the rest of the organization. Others will lose patience with the team as they try to understand the details of the work to be done. Unfortunately, lean is often understood in terms of seven or eight forms of waste—just make it go away. Much of the organization doesn't realize this waste is a symptom of the work, and unless we understand the work in detail, we can't make the waste go away."

Paul continued, "There will be this tendency to just jump to solutions made up of lean slogans—U-cells, one-piece flow, no inventory. And if you try patching all of those concepts together without understanding the work you figuratively end up with a Frankenstein of a process. You might have the best nose, the most striking eyes, and the greatest smile—but it's a monster when stitched together. That is a long way of saying we will have to watch for that behavior in our organization and intervene as appropriate."

Jon said, "I'd like to see this wall. When would be a good time?"

"Glad you asked," said Leslie smiling, "I want us to start holding these meetings at the wall as well. Let's hear directly from the team."

Jon countered, "I want both. Let's meet with the team on a regular cadence—you tell me what that needs to be—but I want to keep this steering team preserved as well. As a leadership team we are going to need time to reflect and learn, and we need to do that together."

Leslie took the action item to establish a 30-minute weekly meeting of the LST members with the Lean process creation team. They would call it the process creation leadership review.

Jon had one last comment, "I want each of you to be thinking about who, if anyone, we need to add to our steering team in the upcoming weeks. I don't want to add for the sake of adding more people. Who is both ready to be part of this discussion and critical to the process?"

As the meeting broke up Paul Larsson's brain returned to solving the Rubik's cube—someone had tampered with the puzzle, making it unsolvable. He wondered who else knew that trick.

Must-Do Actions for Getting Started

1. Form the Leadership Steering Team
2. Form the Cross-Functional Working Team
3. Go and See the current situation (better yet, Go and Do)
4. Establish your learning laboratory

Key Questions for Getting Started

In your organization, the following questions will be valuable to answer at the start of your Lean Process Creation learning:

- What is your current condition for creating new processes? Use a recently launched process and map out the steps taken to deeply understand the situation before jumping to solutions. Include current performance metrics to show the gaps

- Which *post-launch* process improvement work (kaizen) did you experience that could have actually been avoided with proper upfront process design (touzen)?
- What are examples of each of the following process creation failure modes that occurred?
  - Too Much, Too Early (TMTE)
  - Penny-Wise, Pound-Foolish (PWPF)
  - Too Little, Too Late (TLTL)
- What will be your new target condition for Lean process creation? Learn from the *6Con* model to link to your current Development System milestones
- Who will lead the process creation (system architect) for your next program?
- Which responsible experts will you dedicate to the team?
- How will leadership support, engage, and learn with this process creation team and their experiment? Use the Acme-style steering team in the early stages.

INNOVATIVE LEAN PROCESS DEVELOPMENT

2

Chapter 2

CONtext

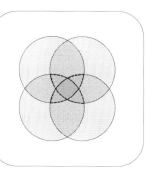

Any fool can know. The point is to understand.

—Albert Einstein

Purpose: Understanding each customer's value proposition, the high-level value stream design, and the value stream's key attributes

Chapter Prologue: *Before the team is ready to jump into developing various process concepts, they need to first align around the value stream vision and gain clarity on the objectives and targets. In addition, they need to observe the current high voltage switch processes in deeper detail to understand the consequences of past product and process design decisions on customer and company value.*

One Day Later

The next day, the process creation team reconvened at the Adrian facility in the old temperature sensor production room. About 18 months ago, the room had produced its last sensor, was cleared of production equipment, and then slowly began to fill with junk. During one of her regular walkabouts, Leslie had insisted the junk be dealt with properly and the room cleared for future use. "Every plant I've ever been in, cleared floorspace attracts junk," she thought. Yesterday, Ted convinced Leslie to let the team use the room as the basecamp for their Lean process creation experiment.

The room was currently rather sparse. It had a couple of folding tables placed together to form one large surface, about a dozen chairs, a portable

DOI: 10.4324/9781003219712-4

screen, and two rolling white boards. All of these items occupied about one-third of the room, the rest of which was wide open.

Jorge welcomed everyone. Present was the entire team along with Dave Laplace. "With the 6CONs we identified yesterday, today we are going to begin with the first one, Context," said Jorge. Gesturing to the white board, "If you look here, I've written five questions on the board to get us rolling. We can modify this list—remember the scientific method and Plan-Do-Check-Act or PDCA."

Initial Questions:

- What are the Financial Health and Factory Health Measures?
- What are the objectives and targets for this process? What is the value from the customer perspective, and how will this process exceed it?
- What may be learned from observing similar processes that exist today?
- What is the Future State Value Stream Design and Operating Plan?
- What are the takt time (demand) levels and planned process cycle times?

Jorge explained, "My thinking is, by answering these questions we will have a good understanding of the context of this new product. And context is important—it provides us with a lens to view our decisions through. Without context we are just flying blind as we make decisions. Any questions?"

Since it was early and the coffee had not kicked in, the room was quiet. Jorge continued, "To get us started I asked Dave Laplace to join us to answer the second question on the list—what are the financial health and factory health measures?"

Demonstrated in the initial program review session and further explained to the team by Dave, Acme Devices normally used a standard capital budgeting model based on internal rate of return (IRR) to help select programs and investments. "One problem with this approach is that the people responsible for organizing this budgeting model for a program are often incorrect in their assumptions, metrics, and inputs," said Dave. "This results in lower actual profits for the programs. And this leads to an unhealthy friction between the budgeting, engineering, and operations areas that has worsened over time. Each party distrusts the inputs from the others and deep down inside, no one believed that the budgeting model was really a good way to predict outcomes."

Dave continued, "I liken it to Acme's own version of the *Abilene Paradox*—no one was individually satisfied with the model, but we keep going along using the model without realizing there could be another way."

Steph was inwardly elated to hear this kind of talk from finance. She had spent years gaming the system, actually expending resources, doing what she felt needed to be done to get projects through. Steph once spent $500 in skilled trades resources to move an automated assembly machine across an aisle so it would sit in a different department with a lower burden rate. No one questioned what she did, because it was the right thing to do with the allocation methods distorting the costing, but she was not proud of having to do stuff like that. Now there might be an opportunity to fix the situation.

Jorge spoke up, "I agree with you Dave, but we can't just stop looking at the financials. What do you suggest?"

"I think Leslie and Paul have some experience in this area from their previous companies," said Dave. "Let's talk to them, or better yet, we could create what we think is a better model and run it by them." The team agreed that was the best way forward and Dave took the action item to draft a better model.

"Okay, another question," said Steph. "What is the Future State Value Stream Design & Operating Plan?"

"How are we supposed to know that?" asked Jolene. "The value stream extends backwards through shared production equipment and a multitude of suppliers. Are all of those in scope or is our focus the assembly process?"

Jolene sketched a diagram (Figure 2.1) to explain what she was asking on the second whiteboard. Alexis was nodding while the drawing materialized. "Are we looking from raw material into the customer's hands or some segment in between, and how do we decide?" asked Jolene.

"Good question," said Jorge. "Anyone have an idea?"

"I'm a bit embarrassed to ask this," said Tom, "but what do we mean by value stream? That term gets thrown around, but inconsistently. It's like the word 'inconceivable' in the movie, The Princess Bride." Only Dave smiled at this odd reference, but that was good enough for Tom. He now knew he had a kindred spirit with a finance person.

"Good question, Tom and thanks for asking," said Jorge. "Think of a product currently in production. The value stream consists of the suppliers and customers, the transportation network, the incoming, in-process and outgoing materials, and all of the processes in between. Layered on top of it is the scheduling or information system that tells each step what to work on next. And a value stream map is a visual representation of the actual value stream that allows everyone to see the waste in the system."

Jorge continued, "I want to emphasize that the information flow is just as important as the material flow. I'm saying this because, from my experience,

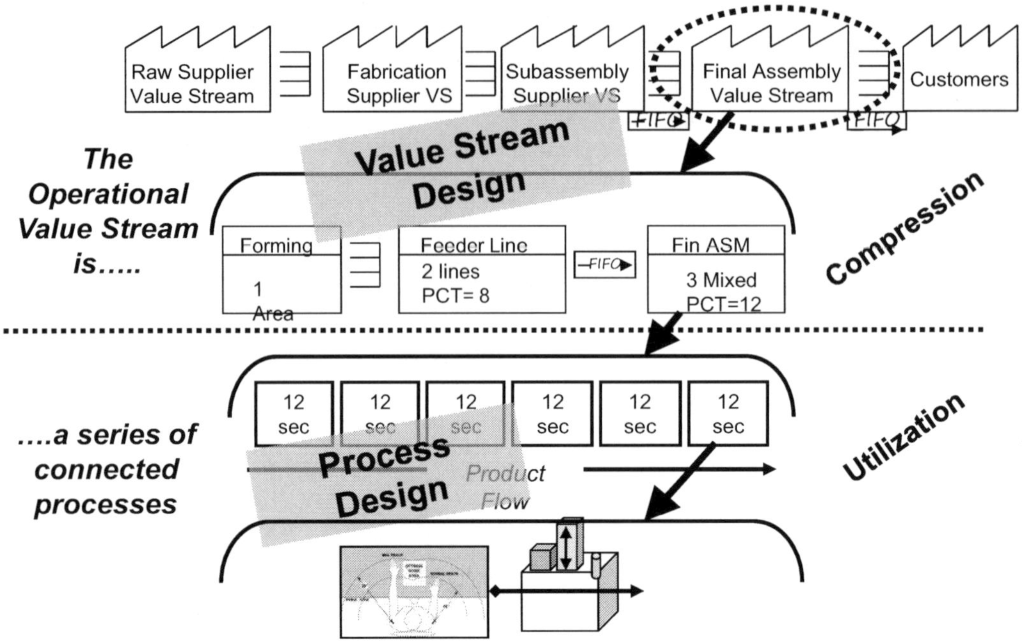

Figure 2.1 Operational value stream linkages.

the material flow gets a lot of attention and then the effort put into representing the information flow is minimal."

"I think we could make a scope decision here in this room, but how do we get others to agree with our thinking?" asked Ted.

Carla, quiet until now spoke up, "The original HVS product team used a *Declaration* to help align around the product vision. Similarly, could we create something of an Operational Declaration?"

"Can you explain more?" asked Jorge.

Carla continued, "I'm not sure of the exact content, but an Operational Declaration could be made up of the value stream design we propose, the operational assumptions based on operations capabilities, and the need of the new product and perhaps financial assumptions, tying back to Dave's model. When we wrote the Declaration for the product design, we had similar content. In fact, as I'm saying this, next time around we need more input from process engineering and operations. This would provide alignment up front in the product design phase and help to inform the Operational Declaration in a more proactive way."

"Carla, can you work with Ted and Jolene to write this Operational Declaration? I think the three of you can bring the views of product, process, and operations into this paper in a smart way," said Jorge.

Alexis interjected, "I'd like to suggest, based on the team that has been assembled for this lean process experiment, that we focus on the value stream from receiving to shipping in the Adrian plant. We can reasonably influence that segment of the value stream. I'd be happy to lead the work to develop the future state vision as input to the Operational Declaration."

"Okay", replied Jorge. "Can you take the action item to lead the balance of the team through a value stream mapping and visioning activity?"

Alexis answered, "Sure, but I also don't want to get ahead of ourselves. Something seems wrong about drawing up a future state vision without learning from our current processes. Although not perfect, there is a lot of organizational knowledge embedded in the current value stream. If the team is good with it, I'd like to start there—mapping our current state process, learning from it and then create a future state vision."

A quick glance around the room revealed expressions of agreement on everyone's faces. "Let's get to work," said Steph. "One advantage of this room is the flexibility of the rolling white boards and tables. Let's create a working space along the back wall for the Operational Declaration development and the value stream development can stay in this area." Without a word, the team got up and rearranged the room to suit the needs of their next steps.

Having the sub-teams next to each other would prove to be a necessity. Yet to be realized, they were in a *Catch-22*. The current state and future state designs were critical inputs into the Operational Declaration. Likewise, the Operational Declaration would provide critical information to inform the future state design.

The Value Stream

With the value stream sub-team, Alexis Cruz demonstrated how the value stream design is the key input that is needed before working down through all the various levels of design as part of the Lean Process Creation cycle:

- **Value Stream**: the sequence of flows of material, information, and processes required to create the value for a particular product or service to meet the customer need.[1]
- **Process**: a systematic series of operations or actions directed to a specific end.

[1] *Learning to See*, p. 1, Rother & Shook, Lean Enterprise Institute, 1999.

- **Operation**: performance of practical work steps in an orderly manner.
- **Step**: a stage in an operation where a series of elements will occur.
- **Element**: a fundamental action where a sequence of motions is carried out.
- **Motion**: an individual manual or machine movement that is required as part of a given work element.

Each level of design is dependent on the upper level, as well as being influenced by the lower level. This was valuable context to keep the sub-team focused, as there can be a tendency to dive too deep, too early. Alexis was careful to get input from everyone on the sub-team as well as pull in stakeholders working on the Operational Declaration and others not part of the Lean process creation team. She learned long ago that the "value" of value stream mapping extends far beyond the physical map. The process of creating a value stream map is a great way to achieve organizational alignment around how things are, how things actually work, and what key issues should be addressed first, second, third, and so on.

With a couple of days of effort in both the conference room and out observing the current process, the following basic current state map (Figure 2.2) was created to summarize the key learning from the detailed value stream map, with the future state[2] simply drawn over the basic current state:

The targeted lead time was determined through discussions with the Operational Declaration sub-team. As they were creating a compelling descriptive vision for the operation, an end-to-end lead time of 7–14 days was determined to be critical to success. It would support Acme Devices inventory turn targets and allow Acme to disrupt the industry by delivering products to customers in lead times never seen before.

"I'm a bit uncomfortable with a future state vision showing the control board separate from final assembly," said Gary. "Doesn't lean advocate removing inventory and connecting processes together?"

Alexis responded, "Not exactly. I think as we work through this process with Jorge and Steph, that will become clearer. Connecting processes and removing inventory is one of many possibilities. And don't worry about the uncertainty, I think Steph would tell us to create a vision based on what we know and if we learn something in the future that can enhance our vision, we can change it."

---

[2] *Learning to See*, pp. 9–34, 49–74, Rother & Shook, Lean Enterprise Institute, 1999.

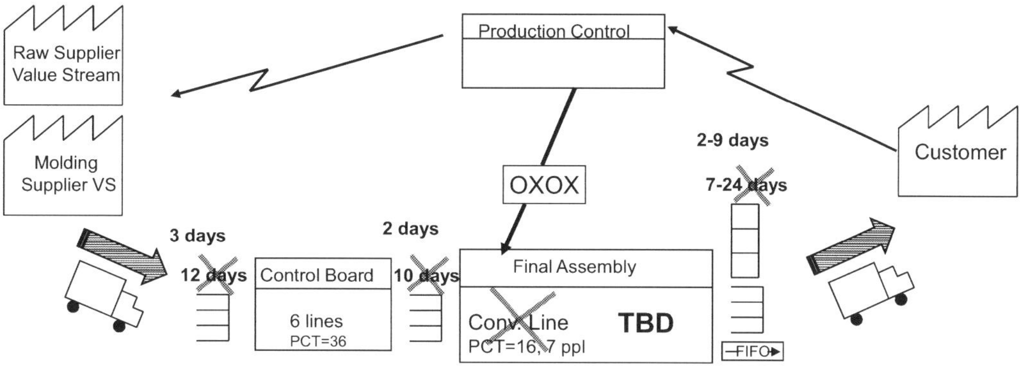

- **Current HVS Value Stream Lead Time = 29-46 days**
- **Target HVS Value Stream Lead Time = 7-14 days**

(72% value stream lead time reduction)

Figure 2.2 HVS current and future state mapping.

Objectives and Targets

Dave Laplace had invited Melinda Jones, along with Leslie and Paul, into a conference room to discuss targets and objectives. He invited Melinda since she expressed interest in an earlier conversation. Leslie and Paul were there to share any insights from experience. Usually whenever the topic of measurable objectives and targets was brought up, the discussion was unstructured and resulted in too many things to measure. Jon's assignment to Dave still echoed in his head. This time it needed to be different. What were the *critical few* items to measure?

As Dave explained the task at hand, Leslie spoke up. "To get us started, I have found it helpful to start with the stakeholder needs: the customer, our investors, and our employees." She wrote these headings on a white board. "Our customer is looking for a quality product to be delivered, on-time."

"What about price?" asked Melinda. Leslie responded, "We can add that. What are our investors looking for?"

"Most simply, a return on their investment," said Dave. "Okay, and what about our employees?" asked Leslie. After some discussion they settled on fulfillment and security. Security being both job security and physical security—being safe at work.

"This makes sense so far, but all of these are after-the-fact measurements. Are there leading indicators we can look at?" asked Dave.

"You're reading my mind," replied Leslie. "Let's look at quality first. What's a good leading indicator of the quality the customer will see?"

"First time quality at the process level," said Melinda. "If we can control quality, process by process, then the customer should see a quality product. If we cannot control the quality at the process level, then we have to rely on testing and inspection. And while those catch most of the issues, something inevitably gets through."

Smiling, Paul interjected, "You guys are getting it! That's the type of thinking we need to make a fundamental impact."

As the conversation continued the white board was filled with their logic and conclusions (Figure 2.3a). A leading indicator for the ability to meet schedule was work in process (WIP) inventory levels. The logic being that WIP was calculated based on certain demand and process assumptions. If those assumptions were violated, it would show in the WIP and schedule adherence would be in jeopardy.

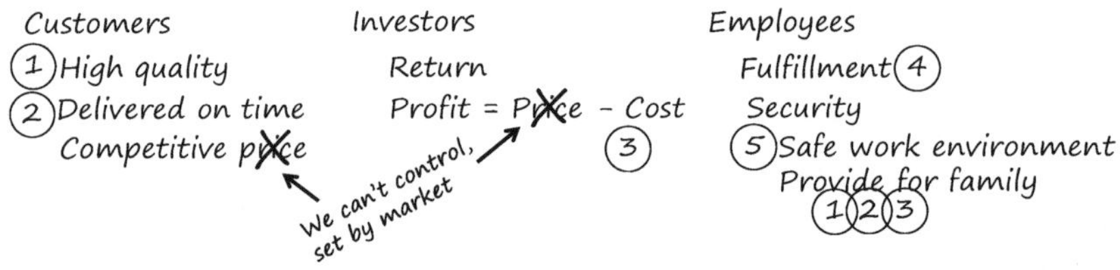

Figure 2.3a Indicators.

Price was determined to be "locked-in" either by a customer agreement or more broadly by what the market was willing to pay. Once a target price was established, it was better for the Acme team to focus on meeting a cost target to ensure a certain profit.[3] Quality and schedule had significant impact on cost, but those were already addressed.

Three other leading indicators that impact cost were labor efficiency, process efficiency, and material costs. They wanted to be clear that labor efficiency was not a matter of standard hours generation it was a measure of how loaded each operator was relative to the operation's cycle time. A measure of the manual work balance. Process efficiency was the simple product

[3] Logic established in *Workplace Management*, p. 17, Taiichi Ohno, Gemba Press, 2007.

of all of the uptimes of all of the stations in a system. Again, no relationship to traditional standard hours. Material costs could be significant as they often made up 60%–70% of the operating costs. The team determined that cost also helped to support the monetary aspect of employee job security.

This left physical security and fulfillment. Based on experience in the current process, the group concluded that good predictors of safety were job motions and audit findings. An increase in job motions was a reflection of poorer ergonomic design which could result in cumulative trauma issues. On the other hand, the findings of safety observation tours could reveal opportunities for discrete safety incidences such as cuts or contusions. With respect to fulfillment, although Acme had an annual engagement survey, this was after the fact. It was decided that a measure of employee involvement in work design and improvement would be the engagement score leading indicator.

Although reasonably satisfied with the results, Dave was not sure these measures would be helpful when selecting between options. They were helpful for defining success of a selected option, but how to compare? He so desperately wanted to get away from the idea of internal rate of return. Dave added a column to their previous work called Comparisons. He wanted there to be a linkage between how they selected between options, how they managed leading indicators of the selected option, and the ultimate results they were looking for (Figure 2.3b). They decided first time quality at each process might be hard to predict at the concepts stage, but they could at least provide a low/medium/high estimate.

	RESULT	PROCESS	COMPARISONS
1	Quality	First time quality by process	Quality proxy
2	Delivery	Work-In-Process inventories maintained	Manageability Process Flexibility
3	Cost	Labor Capital Materials	Labor effectiveness Capital utilization Material costs
4	Engagement	Job design & improvements	Configuration flexibility
5	Safety	Motions Audits	Motions & audit findings

Figure 2.3b Indicators.

Next was WIP level being maintained. Since the schedule from day to day would be variable, the sub-team decided a measure of flexibility to meet those fluctuations and a proxy of management ease would be good comparison criteria when selecting between concepts for ability to meet schedule. The cost metrics of labor and process efficiency should be somewhat quantifiable in the concepts stage, so those were left untouched.

To simplify things a bit, material costs were not going to be tracked at the concepts stage. The assumption was that all of the purchased materials would be the same for each concept. A proxy for safety audit findings would be used for comparisons. There was much discussion on whether to include motions at the concept comparison stage as well. For now, the answer was no. To make fair comparisons the motions would have to include both the direct team members as well as the indirect support members, and the indirect motions were typically not well understood in the concept phase.

Finally, the sub-team decided to include a rating of configuration flexibility as a proxy of the team member involvement in their work design and improvement. Initially, Paul thought this would be an unfair demerit for automated processes. Stephanie explained to Paul that automated processes may also possess configuration flexibility, often by how they are oriented toward one another. Lay them out one way and team members could work together with others, rotate them 180°, and the team members are now stuck in their own personal birdcage, unable to see or work with anyone. In the end, Paul agreed that this was worth tracking.

Dave closed the meeting with some comments, "I'm excited about trying these indicators. They should serve us well. Both in setting targets for the ultimate success of the program, but also in establishing leading indicators to monitor on our way to success. It is a simple balance of results metrics and process metrics, both of which are important. For a next step, I am taking the action item to share these with the sub-teams working on the Operational Declaration (OD) and value stream designs."

The Value Stream's Operating Strategy

Alexis and the sub-team created the operating strategy for the high-voltage switch (HVS) product. Prevailing logic said to get the most from every dollar spent, so run all operations three shifts, 5–7 days a week depending on the labor agreements. Unfortunately, this logic did not consider the whole picture of the factors that impact the running of an operation.

Operating Plan Strategy

Material Flow →

Value Stream Position	**Raw**	**Fabrication**	**Sub Assembly**	**Assembly**
Operating Plan (days x hours)	7 x 24	5 / 6 x 24	5 x 16 / 24	5 x 8 / 16
Direct Labor	Very Low	Low	Medium	High
Processing Time	Very Low	Low	Medium	High
Capital Investment	Very High	High	Medium	Low
Changeover Flexibility	1 – 2 parts	3 – 10 parts	11 – 50 parts	50+ parts
Types of Processes	Continuous processing	Stamping, molding	Component assembly	Manual final assembly
Focus	Uptime, Scrap	Uptime, Scrap & Changeover	Balance Operator & Machine Cycles	Balance Operators & Flexible Lines

Figure 2.4 Operating plan strategy.

Jorge had provided them with an operating strategy model based on notes he had taken years before (Figure 2.4). The model helped to give guidance on the best approach to balance capital investment, people resources, and material. Fabrication and processes further upstream tended to be high capital investment and low labor content, thus the best approach to utilize the assets was to load them with demand as much as possible up to 24 hours per day. Downstream from Fabrication, the processes tended to be lower capital investment but higher amount of direct people resources, thus managing across one or two shifts was more desirable than across three shifts.

Additionally, the cycle-to-cycle process variability introduced by manual labor, multiple processes flowing together, and changeover frequency drove the need to have the flexibility of an open shift to make up schedule shortfalls on a daily basis.

Based on the current operating plans for the HVS product, Acme's operating plan in Adrian was forecasted to look like Figure 2.5.

The team was concerned that the current assembly concept with the conveyor line had both medium capital and medium/high labor. In addition, the line would have very little capacity flexibility. The team preferred to have assembly be as flexible as possible with much lower capital and the same amount of people resources.

High Voltage Switch Device Value Stream
Current Proposal

Material Flow →

Value Stream Position	**Purchased Raw**	**Control Board** (or FLOW)	**Assembly**
Operating Plan (days x hours)	7 x 24	5 x 24	5 x 24
Direct Labor	Very Low	Low	Medium / High
Processing Time	Very Low	Low / Medium	Medium
Capital Investment	Very High	High	Medium
Changeover Flexibility	1 – 2 parts	3 – 10 parts	11+ parts
Types of Processes	Continuous processing	Stamping, molding	Mix of manual & automation
Focus	Uptime, Scrap	Uptime, Scrap, Changeover	Balance Operators & Flexible Lines

Figure 2.5 HVS operating plan proposal.

A few days had passed. Jorge and Steph thought it would be a good idea to regroup the team to make sure everyone was aligned on the status of the project. Jorge's questions were still on the white board and would serve as the structure for the meeting.

- What are the Financial Health and Factory Health Measures?
- What are the objectives and targets for this process flow? What is the value from the customer perspective, and how will this process achieve it?
- What may be learned from observing similar processes that exist today?
- What is the Future State Value Stream Design and Operating Plan?
- What are the takt time levels and planned process cycle times?

"Dave, where do we stand on the measures, objectives and targets?" asked Jorge.

Dave answered, "The metrics sub-team tackled the financial health measures along with the process objectives and targets. We wanted metrics that linked from concept comparison to leading implementation indicators to business results. For targets and objectives, we know what we want to track—we just need to work with the Operational Declaration sub-team on agreeing on the actual targets."

Jorge asked, "Can you place those metrics and their linkage at the top of the white board on the east wall? I'd like to keep those in front of the whole team throughout the duration of this activity. As we create more definition, we can update the metrics sheet."

Jorge next asked. "What about the status of learning from our current process and the future state value stream design?"

"We have both complete for now," said Alexis. Surprised, Jorge asked, "For now?"

Alexis clarified, "Yes, we created the current state map based on the current production process. When we observed the process, we noted some issues with the communication of schedules and inventory overflows. From the current state map and using input from the Operational Declaration (OD) sub-team, we created a future state map. But we suspect it will change as we learn more about our final process design and as the Metrics sub-team and the OD sub-team refine the metrics."

Jorge grinned. "You are absolutely correct. The trick will be keeping us all on the same page as we iterate through this process. To that end, will you post your findings on the same white board as the metrics?"

Alexis said, "Consider it done. And by the way, we still have to work on the takt time levels."

"What about the Operational Declaration?" asked Jorge.

"Still a work in progress, but having more clarity on key metrics will really help to focus our discussions," replied Carla. "I think we should be able to review a draft two mornings from now."

"Sounds like a plan," said Jorge. "So, the Value Stream team will continue to work on takt scenarios, and the OD and metrics teams will put their heads together to get a draft Declaration. Any questions?"

Jolene spoke up, "We are always trying to understand if a production system is ahead or behind. How do we know if we are ahead or behind? We know we have a start of production date out in the future, but there is a lot of unknown between now and then."

Steph jumped in, "Great observation, and a good way to bring us back to the dual purposes of this activity. Yes, we need to get this product successfully launched on time, but we also need to document this process we are going through and look for ideas to improve it the next time. And to Jolene's point, if we do not understand ahead or behind, identifying problems and improving them will be next to impossible. Jorge and I will take the action item to create a high-level timing plan and plaster it into the middle of the white board we are populating."

As people arrived the next morning the white board had begun to take shape (Figure 2.6).

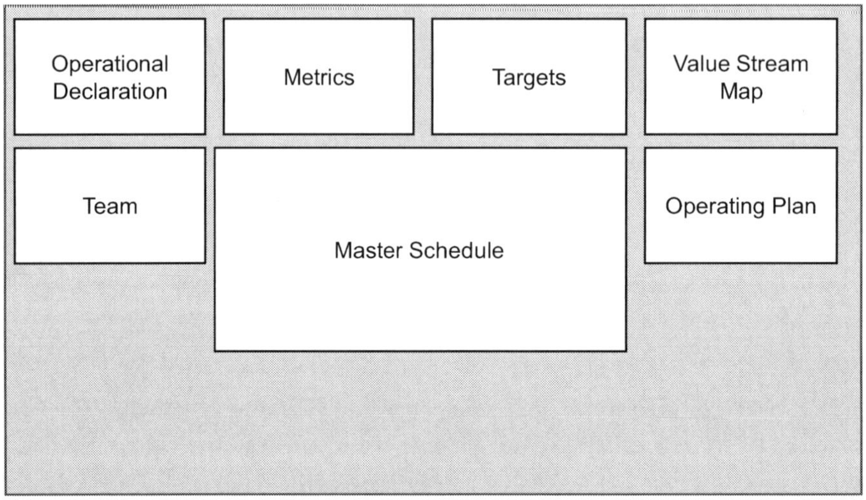

Figure 2.6 Initial HVS team visual management.

Along the top were placeholders for the Operational Declaration, Metrics, Targets and Value Stream Map. Below, on the left side, was a spot for the Team information. Additionally, down the right side was a location reserved for the details of the Operating Plan. And plastered right in the middle was the process creation master schedule, with a start date, some key milestones, and a lot of To-Be-Determined (TBD) items in between.

The team would have to work together to fill in the TBD items. Jorge could overhear a conversation taking place between Alexis and Tom. Alexis was wrapped in a heavy sweater. The room was cold because the HVAC system was designed to cool a manufacturing space full of equipment—equipment that generated much more heat than people. In contrast, Tom was in fine engineering form in a black t-shirt that said, "You've read my shirt—that's enough interaction for today."

Alexis was saying, "An A3 is a single-page problem solving story, and the work you do to engage others to write the story is just as important as the story itself. We'll use the A3 to get alignment on why Project Franklin is important to Acme, what we know about our current value stream, and where it is lacking, and then, based on what we understand to be the barriers to achieving our goals, the suite of countermeasures we're considering to overcome the barriers."

Tom said, "It kind of sounds like a summary of everything else on this board."

Operational Declaration: Bring the Compelling Vision Together

The breakthrough on the metrics snowballed into a breakthrough for the Operational Declaration (OD). Although not the only component of the OD, the metrics created the framework for a discussion. If certain quality, schedule, cost, safety, and engagements targets would have to be met, what underlying assumptions would the new production system need to incorporate? Also, what best practices were currently being utilized in operations and what process assumptions would need to be true to ensure success? Dave Laplace had joined Carla, Jolene, and Ted.

The sub-team quickly arrived at the conclusion that they would frame the Operational Declaration around the metric categories of quality, schedule, cost, safety, and engagement. But where to start?

"I want to be sure that whatever we come up with is compatible with the rest of our operation," said Ted. "It's okay to challenge operations to get even better, but we have some good stuff happening and I don't want us to set a direction in this conference room that undoes all of our good work."

"Why don't we sketch up a quick observation form and go walk the current value stream?" asked Jolene. "I've done something like this before where we make observations in each category, we then rate the observations as either best practices or something that could be improved, and then we make recommendations based on the ratings." Everyone agreed with this approach and they quickly sketched up a form and made copies for the whole team (Figure 2.7a).

FOCUS	OBSERVATION	RECOMMENDATIONS
Quality	• Alarm limits use instead of SPC • Supplier quality certification docs posted	
Schedule	• WIP actual < WIP design • Parts delivered by tugger from central area • No fork trucks in area	
Cost: Capital	• POU maintenance items • OA = 75%	
Cost: Labor	• Efficiency (balance)=75% • PPH tracked • Frequent delivery = small racks • No trash/packaging on line	
Safety	• Incidences tracked • Safety observation audits in place	
Engagement	• Std work docs in drawer • Production moves in ebbs & flows; not smooth	

Figure 2.7a Observation form detailing. (b) Observation form completed.

After an hour of individual observation in the workplace, the team reconvened back in the conference room with their individual sheet.

Individually, everyone looked at their observations and placed a "+" next to best practices and a "–" next to opportunities for improvement. Then they individually wrote down their recommendations:

Next, each person copied their recommendations to post-it notes and placed them on a white board next to the appropriate category (Figure 2.7b).

FOCUS	OBSERVATION	RECOMMENDATIONS
Quality	• Alarm limits use instead of SPC • Supplier quality certification docs posted	• Use alarm limits • Self certified suppliers • Improve FTQ BY 50%
Schedule	• WIP actual < WIP design • Parts delivered by tugger from central area • No fork trucks in area	• WIP calculated & clearly defined • Central market • No fork trucks in production • 100% SCHEDULE ADHERENCE
Cost: Capital	• POU maintenance items • OA = 75%	• POU maintenance • OA > 85%
Cost: Labor	• Efficiency (balance)=75% • PPH tracked • Frequent delivery = small racks • No trash/packaging on line	• LE>90% • Track PPH in production • <30 mins on line • Mkt de-trashes & optimizes parts
Safety	• Incidences tracked • Safety observation audits in place	• Track incidences, near misses & observation findings • Improve all by 50% yearly
Engagement	• Std work docs in drawer • Production moves in ebbs & flows; not smooth	• Workers to create standard work

Figure 2.7b Observation form completed.

Finally, they talked about each idea, eliminated redundancies, removed ideas the team decided were out of scope, added a few new ideas, and came up with the following Operational Declaration.

Quality or High Built-in Quality:

- First Time Quality (FTQ) will be improved by 50% compared to the existing production system.
- No online rework. Defects will be quarantined and tore down in a central area. Components determined to be OK will be returned to the production inventory.
- There will be no receiving inspection. Suppliers must be self-certified and provide appropriate documentation.
- Quality inspectors will collect defects every 2 hours or less and transport them to the quarantine area for disposition.
- Alarm limits will be established on critical processes. Alarm triggers must be responded to within the job cycle.

Schedule or Value On-Time:

- All schedules met 100% of the time
- Lead time from supermarket to the shipping dock to be 7–14 days
- Central supermarket to be used to store all purchased parts
- Purchased parts should be received in small lots. Lots should be sized to be less than or equal to the finished goods pack size. If less than, the lot size should be a multiple of the finished goods pack size or the line pitch
- Fork trucks will only be utilized in the immediate dock area. All materials moving from the supermarket to the line will be delivered via tugger routes.
- Tugger carts will be designed to be loaded/unloaded from either side
- Level scheduling will be used for all customer requirements. Build to order will be used in the case of low runners
- Manifests and pull cards will be used for scheduling as well as internal pull
- The final assembly line will be scheduled one finished good pack at a time

Cost:

- Process Efficiency
  - Operational Availability (OA) goal is 85%
  - WIP levels shall be clearly defined between processes

  - First-In/First-Out shall be assured through the design of material handling systems for inventory between processes
  - There will be a bias toward keeping maintenance items at point of use
  - Aisle width for tuggers shall be 9.0′ minimum. For aisles with lockers 10′ minimum
- Labor Efficiency
  - Goal is 90%
  - Pieces per person per hour will be used to measure operator productivity after launch
  - Preparation of materials for optimum parts presentation will be done in the supermarket
  - Delivery routes will be 30 minutes or less

Safety:
- Workstations will be designed to minimize operator motions outside of the 13″×13″ value-added zone
- Safety related incidences, near misses, and observation findings will be tracked and continuously improved

Engagement:
- 100% of standard work design and documentation will be developed by the team members doing the work under the guidance of a team leader or support industrial engineer

Proud of their work, Carla could not wait to share it with the larger team the next day.

Takt Scenarios

In parallel, Alexis had the value stream sub-team working on various takt time scenarios. Although takt time was an often-used term at Acme, few people really understood what it meant, let alone how to use it. At its most basic level, it was nothing more than the rate of customer demand calculated as:

$$\frac{\text{TOTAL AVAILABLE TIME}}{\text{CUSTOMER DEMAND}} = \text{TAKT TIME}$$

The trick of the calculation was to be sure the numerator and denominator referred to the same time period, and ideally the shorter the timeframe, the better to match customer demand and minimize over- or underproduction. If the available time was "per day" then the customer demand needed to be "per day."

This always seemed simple enough to Alexis, but she had seen errors related to this way too often. Alexis knew she was about to tread into dangerous territory as she wanted the team to calculate various takt scenarios, not just one. "Better to let the data do the talking," she thought.

First, the team revisited the volume projections that were provided at the start of the project. Taking into account for the operating plan target of two shifts assembly per day and 240 working days per year at 450 minutes available per shift, the team calculated the takt time by year (Figure 2.8).

Seconds available per Year = 2 shifts/day x 240 days/year x 450 minutes/shift x 60 seconds/minute

Takt Time = Available time / volume (NOTE: time duration units need to match; e.g. seconds/YEAR and units/YEAR)

Year	Shifts / Day	Days / Year	Minutes / Shift	CALC: Seconds available / Year	Annual Volume (units)	CALC: Takt Time (seconds / unit)
1	2	240	450	12,960,000	240,000	54
2	2	240	450	12,960,000	360,000	36
3	2	240	450	12,960,000	540,000	24
4	2	240	450	12,960,000	720,000	18
5	2	240	450	12,960,000	900,000	14

Figure 2.8 Takt time scenarios.

Alexis knew that takt times were not level throughout the year due to seasonality, as well as that the projected volumes were forecasts that were vulnerable to changing like the weather. "Don't like the weather? Just wait 5 minutes and it will change," she thought.

In the past, Acme Devices had gone into new process designs that set up the line capacity based mostly on the takt time forecasts. The product team would then target process flows to run faster at about 80% of takt time, calling this the planned cycle time (PCT) to incorporate in changeovers, downtime, training time, scrap, and more.

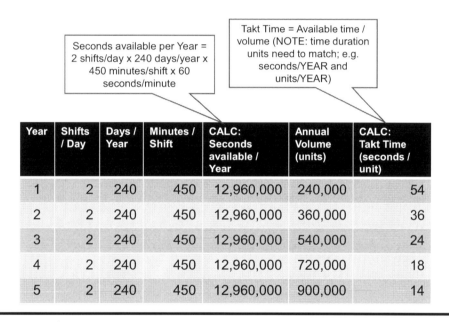

Frequently, this would result in lines needing to be re-configured post-launch when volumes changed or peaks were delayed. When volumes reached high enough levels or line performance was lower than expected, entire cells or lines were typically duplicated for increased capacity without understanding the causes for gaps in performance. Jolene and Ted experienced this in the previous year when the entire assembly department layout changed in order to squeeze in unplanned equipment for a newer product.

"So, it looks like we need to design a system that can be rearranged to get incrementally faster year after year," said Tom.

"Let's just say it needs to be flexible," said Alexis, "This is only part of the story. Gary, can you show us the information you brought to share our historic seasonality?"

Gary Rice of Production Control and Logistics had been given the task to explain the typical "order profile" for the HVS products over the course of a year, by pulling the weekly data from the previous 5 years period (Figure 2.9). Based on the order profile, the Switch products tended to have three "speeds" that they needed to be able to produce at: Low (Jan–Mar), Medium (April–June, Oct–Dec), and High (July–Sept).

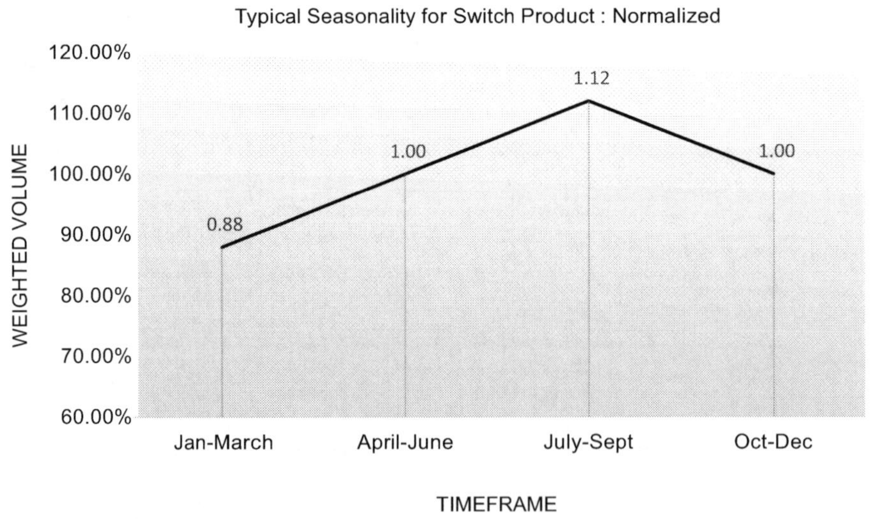

Figure 2.9 Switch demand seasonality forecast during year.

"If we extend our spreadsheet to include seasonality swings, here is our best estimate of potential takt times," said Alexis (Figure 2.10).

Alexis added, "Notice that in year-1, the takt time can swing from 61 seconds down to 48 seconds."

12,960,000 sec/yr x 88% / 240,000 units/yr

Year	Shifts / Day	Days / Year	Minutes / Shift	CALC: Seconds available / Year	Annual Volume (units)	CALC: Takt Time (seconds /unit)	CALC: Takt Time @ 88% of volume	CALC: Takt Time @ 112% of volume
1	2	240	450	12,960,000	240,000	54	61	48
2	2	240	450	12,960,000	360,000	36	41	32
3	2	240	450	12,960,000	540,000	24	27	21
4	2	240	450	12,960,000	720,000	18	20	16
5	2	240	450	12,960,000	900,000	14	16	13

12,960,000 sec/yr x 112% / 900,000 units/yr

Figure 2.10 Takt time scenarios with seasonality.

"But I thought we were supposed to design the system to run at the takt time," said Jolene.

"I'd prefer to save this for another day, with Jorge and Steph present, but for now think of takt time less as a design guideline and more of a management tool," said Alexis. There was an uneasy acceptance of this last statement around the room, but the body language was positive.

Alexis said, "Adding another variable, this takt calculation does not make any allowance for issues such as downtime, maintenance, or scrap. If we set an operational availability goal of 85%, we'd actually have planned cycle times requiring our process to run at the following rates" (Figure 2.11).

"Now for year-1, we could see the need to have a process that runs efficiently at anywhere between 41 and 52 seconds. There are a lot of levers at our disposal to achieve this, but for now, at least we have our targets," finished Alexis. The sub-team seemed satisfied yet skeptical. But satisfied for now.

After all, many of them had engineering and operations backgrounds and liked the idea of a single number to target, a takt time. Tell them the number and they would hit it. But now Alexis was introducing a lot of variables. Real ones, but the implications were pushing a lot of people out of their comfort zones. "Wow, that was just the start," thought Alexis, "We didn't even broach the subject of *natural cycle time* (NCT) yet. That'll come later and be even more upsetting."

Input data from previous table

Seconds available x 85%

Deliberately using the term "Planned Cycle Time". This is NOT a takt time as it has other factors considered in it.

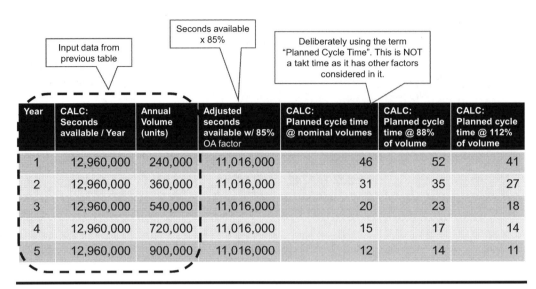

Year	CALC: Seconds available / Year	Annual Volume (units)	Adjusted seconds available w/ 85% OA factor	CALC: Planned cycle time @ nominal volumes	CALC: Planned cycle time @ 88% of volume	CALC: Planned cycle time @ 112% of volume
1	12,960,000	240,000	11,016,000	46	52	41
2	12,960,000	360,000	11,016,000	31	35	27
3	12,960,000	540,000	11,016,000	20	23	18
4	12,960,000	720,000	11,016,000	15	17	14
5	12,960,000	900,000	11,016,000	12	14	11

Figure 2.11 Planned cycle times with seasonality.

The War Room

With the entire Lean Process Creation team assembled in the room, Jorge and Steph were ready to get the meeting started. Failing to be inconspicuous in the back of the room was Jon Jain and the steering team. "How it sometimes sucks to be the boss. I just want to sit back, observe, and learn," he thought. But he knew his mere presence would change the dynamics.

"I want to thank all of you here for being on time, let's get the meeting started," opened Steph. "As I like to say, no sense in rewarding the late-comers by waiting for them. Let's look at our open items from yesterday. First, where are we on the Operational Declaration?"

"We have the first draft ready," said Carla. "We think it is a good start, but here's a copy for everyone. We'd like your thoughts. So, look it over and I will get us together outside of this meeting to refine it."

"Thanks," said Jorge. "Can you also keep the latest version of the document on our project white boards?" "Yes sir!" said Carla, with a playful salute.

"Alexis, where do we stand on the takt time scenarios?," asked Steph.

Alexis responded, "We have calculated takt times for nominal and seasonal volumes and then created options to reflect our operational availability targets. So, it is a starting point, but I want to get agreement on…wait…I see in this Operational Declaration an OA target of 85%. That's the assumption we used, so I guess we are good."

"Wouldn't be doing my job if I didn't ask," started Jorge, "Can you post the scenarios on the board?" "Will do," said Alexis.

Steph continued, "I think we've completed our due diligence answering the questions in the Context stage. Remember, this is our first attempt, and this will be an iterative process. If we learn something as we move forward, we can come back, and if we agree, adjust some of our basic assumptions. Jorge, do you have anything to add?"

Jorge added, "Of course. I want to thank everyone for the work you've put in so far. If you look at our board, you can start to see our story coming together. I'd like each of you to send me a photo as I'd like to document who has which roles as part of this core team. Think of this board and this entire room as our laboratory, or sometimes you might hear the word "obeya" used. It just means 'big room.' As our obeya, this will be the place where we can meet, work, run experiments, track progress, and whatever else you imagine. It's our skunk-works, but with a very targeted purpose."

"So, as you have changes in your respective areas, please keep your section of the board up to date. Also, see these red post-its? We're going to designate these to flag issues. If you happen to be in here and see an issue in your area, or in another area, make a note of it on the post-it and add your initials. Ideally, you can follow up directly with the leader of the work in that area, but if it turns out to be an issue that needs the extended team to resolve, we can discuss it in this meeting. Any questions or comments?" Jorge asked.

Alexis uncharacteristically raised her hand, "I have one. I'm looking at the Operational Declaration and I have a feeling we could have worked our way through the Context stage a little more smoothly."

"What do you mean?" asked Steph. Alexis responded, "Well, we sent three teams out in parallel: Metrics, Operational Declaration, and value stream design. And although we finally arrived at a conclusion, it seems to me it would have made more sense to establish the metrics first, have that feed the Operational Declaration, and have that feed the value stream design."

"You are 100% correct," said Steph, "And we should document this as an improvement for the next time. In this case, we had formed this team and thought it was important to get started now, on something. And Jorge and I decided to get everyone working in parallel rather than have a dozen people working in series. Now that we have an improved metrics framework that actually links from concept comparison to configuration and through to confirmation, I suspect we will be able to re-use that thinking on future projects. And before we form the entire team, we should be setting business driven targets for the process and use the team to create the Operational Declaration and value stream vision."

"Well then," said Jorge. "We have the whole day ahead of us. Let's move on to Concepts."

THE STEERING TEAM—LEARNING TO BE HELPFUL

Jon, Leslie, Paul, Cheryl, and Dave all quietly departed through the back door in the room. "Can we go talk in your office, Leslie?," asked Jon.

The furniture in Leslie's office was even older than Jon's, but conveyed an even more sense of grandness. The desk and table were relics of a past when ultra-high-end wood furniture graced the offices of executives everywhere.

Once they settled into the office Jon spoke up, "I'm encouraged by what I'm seeing. The team has come a long way in a short time. Is there anything that I can do to help?"

"We need to get you into that room on an interactive basis," said Paul.

"I agree," said Leslie, "And we saw how having you quietly in the back changed the dynamics. Only Alexis asked a question—and she doesn't count as she's not shy. She'd ask a question if the CEO was in the room. Anyway, the board that Jorge and Steph are piecing together will provide you with a great medium to interact with the team on a cadence. We just have to figure out what that cadence will be."

"Glad to hear that's what you think", said Jon. "I so desperately wanted to look at that board in more detail, but I didn't want to upset the team dynamics. Also, I think if I am around the team on some sort of cadence, they will get used to me being around in good times, not just when things go wrong."

"Dave," continued Jon, "I really like the work on the metrics. I'd like to link things one step further. These measures—I'd like them somehow represented in the appropriation request. **It has always bothered me that we hand out millions of dollars and don't close the loop to see if the system is actually performing to the levels assumed when the appropriation was sold**. Can you work on closing that loop?"

"Sure," said Dave with a grin on his face, "and I have some ideas on how to make this happen."

Jon continued, "Back to my cadence with this team, Cheryl, I'm going to need you to shadow me during these early reviews. I need honest feedback on my interactions with the team. You have been leading some great work in improving our employee engagement scores and the last thing we need is me screwing it all up."

"Roger, that sir," said Cheryl. She continued, "I was looking at that board and I think we can use it as a pilot to teach all of our leaders how to both lead the organization and develop the next generation of leaders."

Must-Do Actions for Context

1. Understand value from the customer's perspective before designing the process
2. Use the Operational Declaration to enroll the team around the value, the vision, and the target condition
3. Use an obeya space for transparency, focus, and alignment as learning and decisions occur
4. Make a plan for a process that will successfully deliver value and profit at any volume

Key Questions for Context

In your organization, the following questions will be valuable to answer during the Context Phase:

- What are the *Financial Health* & *Factory Health* Measures?
- What are the objectives and targets for this process flow? What is value from the customer perspective, and how will this process exceed it?
- What may be learned from observing similar processes that exist today?
- What is the Operational Declaration (OD)?
- What is the Future State Value Stream Design and Operating Plan?
- What are the takt time (demand) levels and planned process cycle times

Additional key questions that could be included:

- How will you understand and identify the operational vision and value from the customer's perspective, and how will you maintain it?
- How will you create flow, eliminate waste, and minimize variability with the actual technical work of developing the Lean process?
- How will you create and capture new knowledge early-on and during the Lean process creation cycle?
- Key tools:
  - Obeya space; Program Schedule wall
  - Operational Declaration

Chapter 3

CONcepts

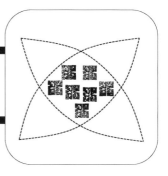

Imagination is the beginning of creation.

—George Bernard Shaw

Purpose: Discovering the key knowledge gaps and exploring multiple process design options to facilitate learning.

Section Prologue: *With the alignment created in developing a robust context for the HVS project, the team begins the work of developing multiple concepts. It will be important during this Concepts phase for team members to think outside their existing mental models, but getting them to do so will be a bit of a challenge. A little knowledge can be dangerous when it is merely used to reinforce preconceived ideas. The team will be challenged with developing four reasonable concepts, as well as a means to compare them. Although improvement is part of Acme's DNA, the team will have to look beyond making the existing system better, thinking creatively to what a new system could become for them.*

Natural Cycle Time[1]

"Okay, I will take the lead—but you may have to back me on this," said Jorge. Steph nodded in agreement. They had just spent the last hour talking over the tool room din at her desk. The subject was Natural Cycle Time, and

[1] Concept introduced to the authors by Y. Yamada during a May, 1999 project review of Cruise Control Modules.

DOI: 10.4324/9781003219712-5

it was always controversial. One of the first topics in Lean education is takt time. Unfortunately, takt time as typically taught is only half the story.

For engineers, it is the attractive half. Take a number, divide it by another number, and as long as you make sure the units are consistent, you have a target. And engineers can always hit a target, end of story. To make progress in the concepts phase, the team needed to understand natural cycle time (NCT) and how it relates to takt time as well as planned cycle time (PCT).

Jorge and Steph had agreed that there is value in the team seeing their paradigms about takt time deconstructed and then reconstructed into something slightly different, but more useful. If they just told the team the definition of NCT, and that they had to consider it in their designs, people would just go through the motions without understanding.

As Steph and Jorge entered "Franklin's Tavern," the name given to the former sensor room by the team, everyone was scattered about the room in small groups working feverishly. Steph was particularly happy about a meeting that had materialized in front of the obeya. That was a sign that the board contained at least some of the right information. "Can I get everyone to come to the big table?," said Jorge. "We want to get started on the Concept phase, but before we start, we want to have a discussion."

With everyone seated around the table Jorge started, "I want to do a little reflection on the calculations behind our first concept—the one shared by Carla a few days ago." "Although we know there are some flaws in the concept as it stands, I want to talk about the thinking–our thinking–that created the concept." Jorge turned towards Carla, "How did you know you needed one line running at 16 seconds?"

"We started by calculating the takt time," Carla said. Alexis always appreciated Carla. She was one of the few product engineers that understood takt time, although she was pretty humble about it.

"Can you elaborate?," asked Jorge. "Sure, Alexis correct me if I misstate something, but takt time is total available time divided by customer demand. We assumed three shifts of run time because we want to maximize the use of our capital investment. But I have to be honest, we then applied an efficiency factor to account for the historic performance of production."

"Let's just stick with the equation," said Jorge "When calculating takt time, which volume did you use?" Alexis answered, "The peak—we have to plan to meet the peak." Jorge responded, "Agree, but does the customer guarantee they will purchase peak volume?"

There was an awkward pause in the room. "No," said Ted. "So, we're going to calculate a takt time, and then design our system for that time, based on a number that we may not see?," asked Jorge. "I'll add another variable," said Alexis. "Why three shifts? Why not two? Why not a 24/7 shift pattern?" Steph listened from the back of the room, satisfied with the direction of the conversation.

"Wait a minute!," said Jolene. "I was taught that we calculate the takt time and then design our process to it. And now you are saying that the number can be highly variable depending on which scenario we choose. This feels like a *Catch-22*." Whispers broke out around the table.

"Let's just look at this logically," said Jorge. "Yes, we want our processes to be able to produce at the takt time because it represents customer demand and producing what the customer purchases reduces waste throughout the system. But we need to acknowledge that the takt time is a moving number. We can predict some of the variance, such as the new program ramping up. But we can't predict the customer's actual demand. Have you ever heard the first law of forecasting—*the forecast is always wrong?* Yet we're often using a forecast to calculate a takt time. So, the message isn't to abandon takt time, it's to understand its limits and think differently on how to manage those limits. Alexis, I noticed that you took your sub-team through a series of takt time calculations. I think they are posted here on the obeya" (Figure 3.1).

Jorge continued, "They vary from 61 seconds to 13 seconds, depending on the volume. Why calculate the ranges, Alexis?"

Year	Shifts / Day	Days / Year	Minutes / Shift	CALC: Seconds available / Year	Annual Volume (units)	CALC: Takt Time (seconds /unit)	CALC: Takt Time @ 88% of volume	CALC: Takt Time @ 112% of volume
1	2	240	450	12,960,000	240,000	54	61	48
2	2	240	450	12,960,000	360,000	36	41	32
3	2	240	450	12,960,000	540,000	24	27	21
4	2	240	450	12,960,000	720,000	18	20	16
5	2	240	450	12,960,000	900,000	14	16	13

Year	Adjusted seconds available w/ 85% OA factor		CALC: Planned cycle time @ nominal volumes	CALC: Planned cycle time @ 88% of volume	CALC: Planned cycle time @ 112% of volume
1	11,016,000		46	52	41
2	11,016,000		31	35	27
3	11,016,000		20	23	18
4	11,016,000		15	17	14
5	11,016,000		12	14	11

Figure 3.1 Time scenarios.

Alexis answered, "If we don't consider the spectrum of times, I think we set ourselves up for failure. We effectively design a system to operate efficiently at a single sweet spot we may never see. Unfortunately, I've never figured out how to fit this all together. You can see we also calculated planned cycle times as well. This is the takt time, but adjusted to consider set-up, machine reliability and other factors affecting output."

"This is a great segue to the idea of natural cycle time", said Jorge. "NCT considers the product characteristics, process knowledge, and more to suggest a least common multiple to design processes and balances to. **We want our natural cycle time to be *as low as reasonable*. Let that soak in. The lower the NCT, the lower the increments of process times we will have to mix and match to meet varying planned cycle times. And these varying planned cycle times allow us to meet multiple takt times**. Let's consider an example (Figure 3.2). Here is a cell with two stations, each at 60 seconds. The material flows from left to right. The takt time is 60 seconds so everything matches, and we give ourselves a check mark and walk away happy. But what if the takt time shifts to 40 seconds?"

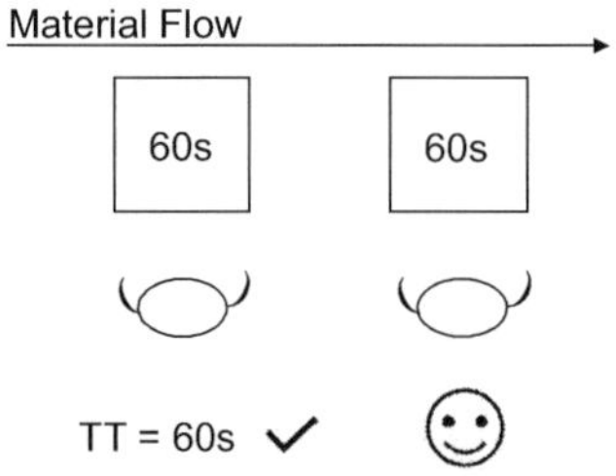

Figure 3.2 Two stations, 60 second takt.

"That's easy," said Ted. "We do what we always do, we add a second cell?"

"That right! We double the people, and we double the investment," replied Jorge. "But if we had designed the process from the start, looking at a range of takt and planned cycle time scenarios—and considering aspects of the process—and arriving at a NCT of 20 seconds, the line arrangement might have looked like this" (Figure 3.3).

Jorge continued, "The total work content is still the same, but you have smaller building blocks, Legos if you will, to mix and match. Now the only variable is people. Little to no additional investment is required. And the beauty is the standard work at each process step always remains the same, the operators adjust the number of processes that they work. Anyone have an idea of how you hit a takt time around 30 seconds in this system?"

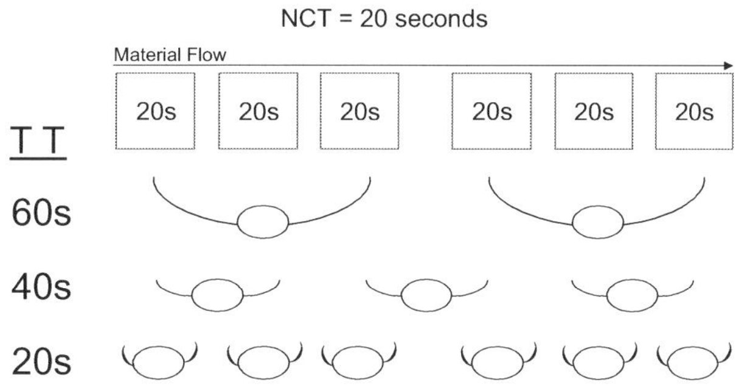

Figure 3.3 Cycle time flexibility.

"Have first shift run at 20 seconds and second shift run at 40 seconds?," said Alexis reluctantly. "Exactly!," said Jorge. "That'll get you to around 27 seconds for the weighted average."

"I still feel like we're violating some core principle of lean," said Tom. As an equipment design engineer, Tom learned about takt time a few years ago and had been hard-designing machines to takt time since then "We've been using takt time to target our process cycle times for years. On the other hand, this makes logical sense."

Steph jumped in, "That's why we wanted to have this conversation. Jorge and I went through the same consternation years ago. We're not suggesting abandoning takt time, just better understanding how to really use it. Lean is often credited with starting in the auto industry. Anyone know the time they set a typical vehicle assembly plant at?"

"60 seconds," said Tom. "I just took a public tour a few weeks ago." "Correct," said Steph. "Do all cars sell at the same volume?"

There was silence as everyone glanced around the room at each other. "Of course, not," said Steph. "They have learned that around 60 seconds is a good natural cycle time for vehicle assembly. As you go higher the operator needs more work, therefore, more materials—and you can only fit so many materials near the operator. So, now they start to walk more and more, adding waste to the process. If you start reducing the cycle time, the size and weight of the parts begin to present a problem. Before we realize it, the operator just has time to get the materials to the vehicle but not enough time to complete any actual assembly work. So, the size of the parts and the style of the work have come together to suggest a natural cycle time of around 60 seconds" (Figure 3.4).

The opportunity with NCT would be to use the knowledge and experience of the process creation team members to select the time at

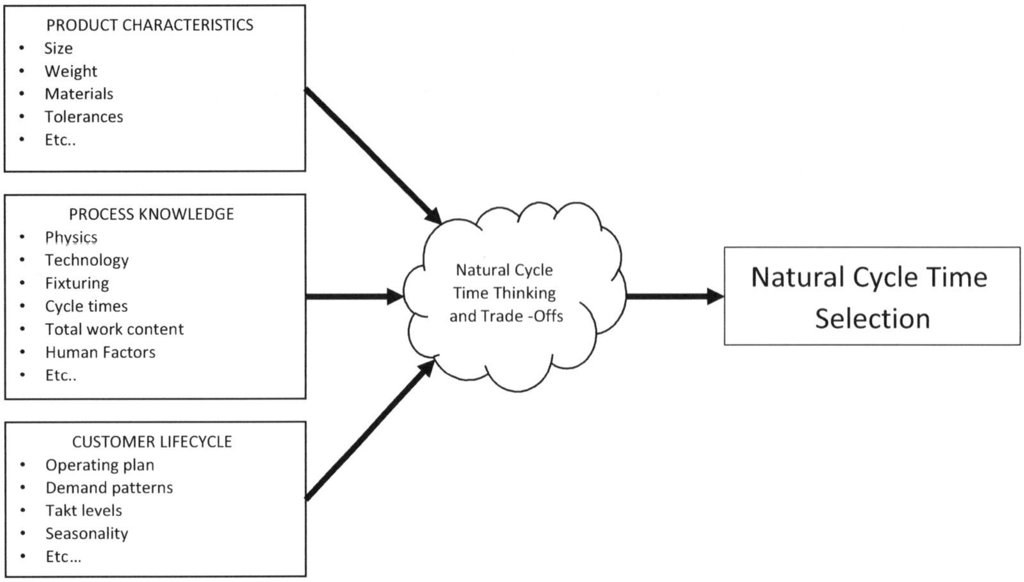

Figure 3.4 Natural cycle time selection factors.

which a process would most effectively operate. Once the NCT would be selected, the engineering challenge becomes balancing the workstations to this cycle time, resulting in flexible capacity to meet varying demands with zero or minimal changeover and setup time between product types. As improvements are made to individual stations, the NCT may be changed.

This would be a key shift in how Acme designed all new process flows. And this shift would not be an easy one since engineering was conditioned to create new process designs to a takt time. The team understood the thinking behind the concept but members were not sure what it really meant. Nevertheless, they agreed to give this thinking a try on Project Franklin.

To determine the NCT upfront for the new high-voltage switch (HVS) process flow, the team needed to also look at the processing cycle times that were currently in place for the HVS.

NCT Determining Factors for HVS:

Product Characteristics

- Medium size product with small components
- Weight=1.2 pounds fully assembled
- Circuit Board Device, Metal Plate, Plastic Case

Process Knowledge

- Mix of lightweight assembly and test stations
- Total Work Content about 180 seconds per assembled part
- Peak station cycle time is 28 seconds per piece (Case Assembly and Overweld/Leak Test)
- Human Factors include drill operations and twists/turns

Customer Volume Lifecycle

- The team referred to the earlier discussion of takt time and estimated volumes per year from the *Context* section (Figure 3.5)

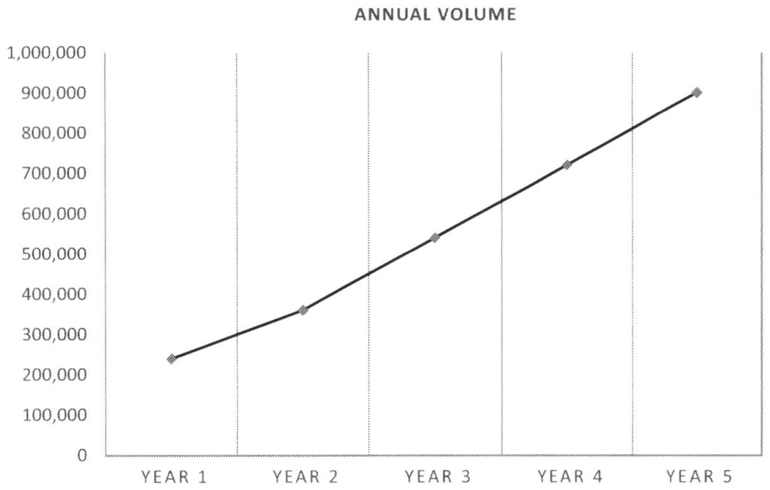

Figure 3.5 Customer volume ramp-up plan.

Based on the various factors above, the team decided that an NCT of around 30 seconds would be the lowest that could be achieved without any radical changes to the current processing method. This would be a question that the team would be re-visiting many times as the process design matured further. Nevertheless, this gave them a target to use to get started.

Steph walked to the front of the room. "Now that we have a basic grasp of the product, value stream, and performance

> **KEY POINT**
>
> It is imperative to design production systems that are responsive to variable takt times based on customer demand fluctuations. This leads to the need for fast changeovers, flexibility across product mix, and scalability to ramp-up or ramp-down effectively and efficiently. The Natural Cycle Time is a key enabler in creating effective processes.

targets, it is time for us to deeply understand the actual process of building the HVS product," said Steph. "And from this understanding we will develop multiple concepts to compare and learn from."

Concept 2

The Process Creation team already had one concept (Concept 1) from the initial HVS product team meeting using the conveyor system (Figure 3.6).

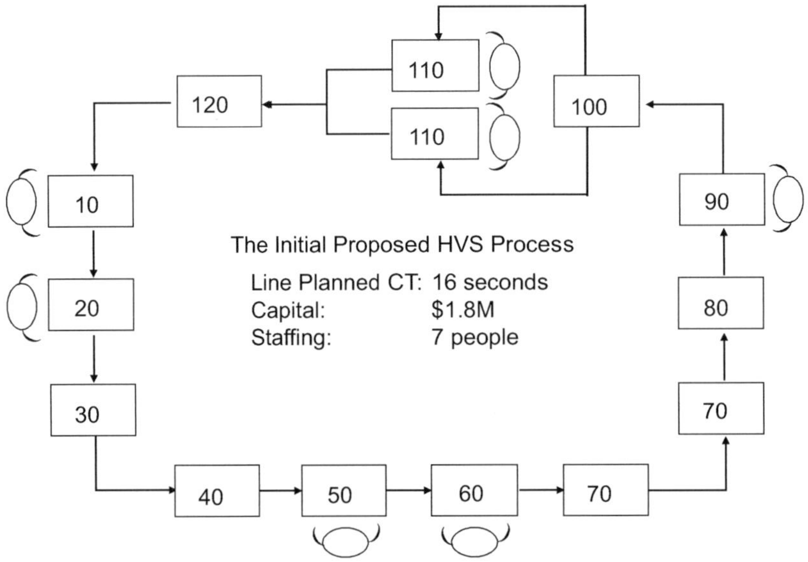

Figure 3.6 Concept 1: the initial proposed HVS process.

"Can we share something?," asked Jolene. The current HVS production area in Adrian was converting all legacy lines to U-shaped cells, which could serve as the model for the new process. Jolene had combined her process knowledge with Ted's operational experience and created a second concept. "This is something Ted & I put together, a second production concept for Project Franklin." Jolene shared a layout (Figure 3.7) that included stations and walk paths.

Based on the experiences of converting the legacy conveyor lines like Concept 1 to cell operations using the chase-style build like Concept 2, Ted and Jolene estimated that they could improve the capital investment by 30% and people resources by 10% running at a 60-seconds per part PCT, based on the operator/machine matrix data.

Operation	Description
10	Device Sub-Assembly 1 & Press Tab
20	Device Sub-Assembly 2 & Press Tab
30	Device Heat Weld
40	Device Label
50	Plate Sub-Assembly 1 & Crimp
60	Plate Sub-Assembly 2 & Crimp
70	Plate Bolt Driving (4)
80	Plate Label Press
90	Switch Assembly 1 & Bolt Driving (2)
100	Switch Assembly 2 & Bolt Driving (2)
110	Case Assembly & Overweld / Leak Test
120	Packout

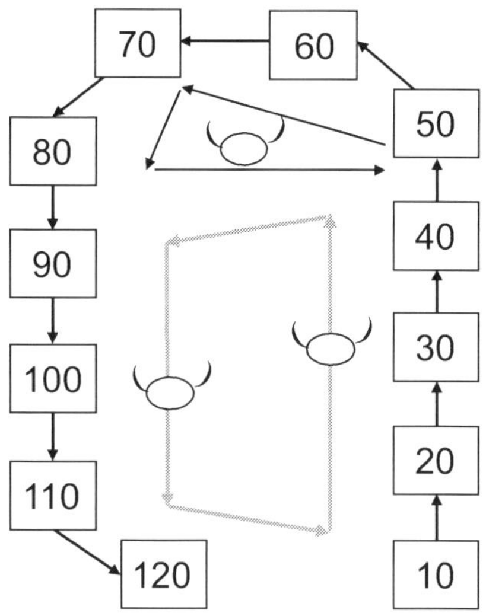

NOTES:

1. Manual pack-out, bolt driving and labelling
2. Layout and team-member work paths can be changed to optimize walk paths

Figure 3.7 Concept 2 summary.

"How many cells would be required in total?," asked Jorge. Jolene did a quick calculation on the white board (Figure 3.8).

$$\frac{\text{60s planned cycle time}}{\text{14s TT @ peak volume}} = 4.3 \approx 5 \text{ cells}$$

Figure 3.8 Determining the number of cells required.

"Five cells," she replied. Tom was smiling, along with most of the room. "Why don't we start to configure this process? This looks much better than our original concept," he asked (Figure 3.9).

Sensing the room's mood, Jorge cleared his throat. "This is definitely an improvement, but let's not get ahead of ourselves. We currently have two concepts based on a limited knowledge of the actual work required to build a high voltage switch. Additionally, they both incorporate versions of our current way of thinking, which might be limiting our improvement potential. If we look at the investment on our operator-machine matrix, almost $500K per cell, are we ready to invest $2.5 million without fully exploring our options? Once we spend those capital dollars, we *have* to earn against them. Steph

Operation	Description	Operator Time	Machine Time	Total Operation Time*	Equipment Cost
10	Device Sub-Assembly 1 & Press Tab	14 sec	6 sec	20 sec	$30,000
20	Device Sub-Assembly 2 & Press Tab	12	6	18	$30,000
30	Device Heat Weld	4	7	11	$150,000
40	Device Label	4	0	4	$0
50	Plate Sub-Assembly 1 & Crimp	13	4	17	$35,000
60	Plate Sub-Assembly 2 & Crimp	11	6	17	$35,000
70	Plate Bolt Driving (4)	26	0	26	$0
80	Plate Label Press	4	2	6	$35,000
90	Switch Assembly 1 & Bolt Driving (2)	21	0	21	$0
100	Switch Assembly 2 & Bolt Driving (2)	25	0	25	$0
110	Case Assembly & Overweld / Leak Test	21	16	37	$180,000
120	Packout	3	0	3	$0

Total Manual Work per Part = 158 seconds
12 Stations
Capital Cost = $495,000

Total Operation Time = Operator Time (load, internal prep work, unload) + Machine Processing Time*

Figure 3.9 Operator/machine matrix for Concept 2.

and I have talked—we'd like the team to develop four concepts during this phase of process creation, detailed down to the operation and step level."

As he said this, Jorge pointed at the list that Alexis had written during the value stream visioning activity.

- **Value Stream**: the sequence of flows of material, information, and processes required to create the value for a particular product or service to meet the customer need
- **Process**: a systematic series of operations or actions directed to a specific end
- **Operation**: performance of practical work steps in an orderly manner
- **Step**: a stage in an operation where a series of elements will occur
- **Element**: a fundamental action where a sequence of motions is carried out
- **Motion**: an individual manual or machine movement that is required as part of a given work element

Ted interrupted, "I'm glad you pointed at that list, it's been bugging me. I get the idea of a value stream, but what are examples of the other things on this list?"

"Good question, what do the rest of you think?," said Jorge.

Alexis started, "Here in the plant, a process could be a sub-assembly line, the final assembly line, or an injection molding area. In the office, say in Human Resources, a process might be interviewing, candidate selection, offer generation, or on-boarding. An operation, on the other hand, might be a station on the final assembly line or in HR it could be, say within candidate selection, perform analysis of candidates."

Jorge commented, "I like how you are giving both manufacturing and office examples, but does someone want to try to describe a motion in both cases?"

Carla said, "I think a motion in operations is very basic like reach, twist, and grab, and in the office, it could be key-in, reach, place—perhaps not that different, as I say it out loud."

"That's great!," said Jorge, "What about an element?"

Jolene spoke up, "I expected you to ask about steps next, but I'll still answer your question. An IE told me that an element is work that isn't easily broken apart—once you start the motions you tend to see them through. So, a motion might be grab, but the element would be grab, rotate and place. It's impossible to grab and have someone else do the rotate and place. And in the office, an element might be *key-in data* and *press enter*. It would be kind of silly to have one person key-in the data and another person hit the enter key."

"So then, what's a step?," asked Ted.

Alexis answered, "It is just a grouping of elements that take place in an operation. So, if you go to the first assembly station at any line and describe to someone what is happening you will most likely talk in steps: first we get the base, then we add the sensor, then we add the connector and finally we test it. In the office you might tell someone: first we receive all of the files, then we enter the data into our selection matrix, then we calculate scores, sort scores high to low, and then discuss the results."

Jorge said, "Ted, thanks for asking. And the point isn't to perfectly define every level, it is to understand that various levels exist, and like atoms are the building blocks of matter, motions are the building blocks of work. The only way to truly create great concepts, and ultimately great processes, is to understand the motions and manipulate them for the better."

Steph added, "Before we jump into developing entire concepts, we need to understand the basic operations that are required to transform the HVS components into a finished device. Don't worry about details such as part transfer methods, line shape, etc. Just the operations for now."

Jorge wrote a list of questions on the board. "You may not understand all these questions for now, but you will later on. These need to be answered as we develop our concepts."

1. What are the fundamental operations and precedence?
2. What is our *3D* learning? (scaled, physical model)
3. What is our *4D* learning? (same as 3D, but with the work motions)
   a. Data
   b. Facts
   c. Ideas

Jorge and Steph made a decision earlier—let the team dive in and if they became stuck, throw them a lifeline.

The first task for the team was to breakdown the process into each fundamental operation. The team was encouraged to begin by taking the Concept 2 operations as a starting point (Figure 3.10a).

Operation	Description
10	Device Sub-Assembly 1 & Press Tab
20	Device Sub-Assembly 2 & Press Tab
30	Device Heat Weld
40	Device Label
50	Plate Sub-Assembly 1 & Crimp
60	Plate Sub-Assembly 2 & Crimp
70	Plate Bolt Driving (4)
80	Plate Label Press
90	Switch Assembly 1 & Bolt Driving (2)
100	Switch Assembly 2 & Bolt Driving (2)
110	Case Assembly & Overweld / Leak Test
120	Packout

Figure 3.10a Concept 2 operations.

Before the team began brainstorming operations and alternatives, Jorge asked Alexis to introduce the precedence chart to the team (Figure 3.10b). Alexis gladly obliged saying, "Borrowing from my old Ed Polk methods book,[2] a precedence chart was described as displaying all possible sequences in a series of work elements or operations."

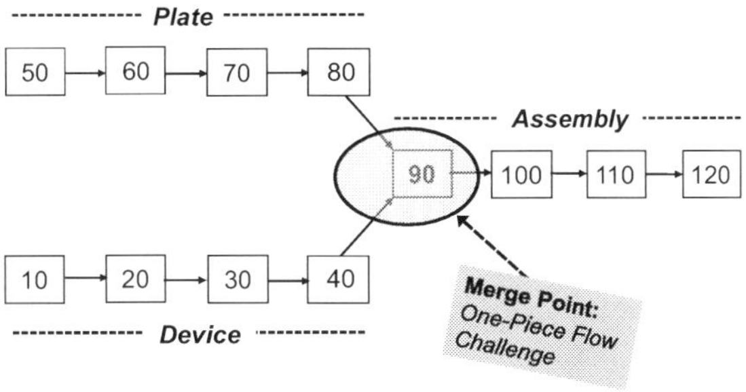

Figure 3.10b HVS precedence chart, Concept 2.

She continued, "It's useful for determining many aspects, including the complexity of a flow, the flexibility in moving specific operations, the impact of product design changes to flow, and more. Plus, as further details are decided, the precedence chart may incorporate the basic data and facts for each operation. But for now, it will allow us to all see which operations flow into others."

For the HVS precedence chart, the team could see the challenge in having two sub-flows (Device 10–40 & Plate 50–80) feed into one process (90–120) in a balanced, one-piece flow manner. It also showed that the Concept 2 approach with a U-shape cell would require a double-handling step in either the Device or Plate operations unless there were product design changes (Figure 3.11).

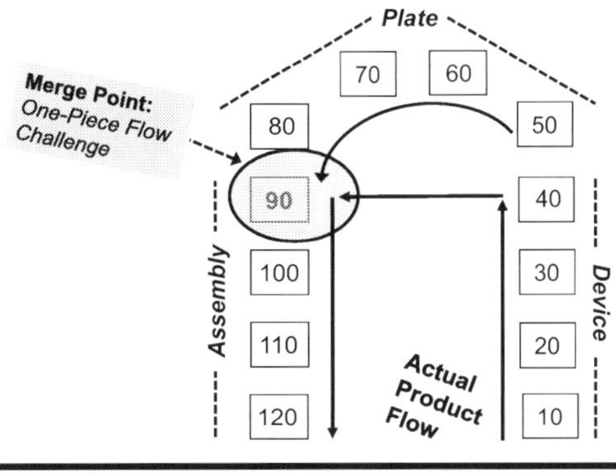

Figure 3.11 Concept 2 product flow challenges.

[2] *Methods Analysis and Work Measurement*, p. 34, Edward J. Polk, McGraw Hill, 1984.

Operations?

Jorge asked the team how many total operations were necessary in the current situation for the new HVS, to which they responded 12 (operations 10–120). Jorge then asked Steph the same question, to which the answer was "More than twelve."

"I'm not following you," said Melinda.

"I want everyone to think about operation 10, which was called Device Sub-Assembly 1 and Press Tab on the operator/machine matrix," said Jorge. "What manual work can be done while the Press Tab machine was cycling, and what machine work can be done while the manual work was being completed?"

"One of our current practices is to have the operator move to another station to do other work while the machine in operation 10 completes its cycle," said Ted.

Steph jumped in, "It's like we own a car wash and decided to collect the money inside the actual washing area. Most car washes *decouple* the two operations of paying and washing by meeting you outside before you go into the wash area. **The decision whether or not to combine steps into a workstation should only be made after first breaking the process down into its fundamental operations**."

> **KEY POINT**
>
> Use physical parts or prototype parts to help visualize the operations and steps during brainstorming. Break operations down to their fundamental level before combining together.

Steph added, "In reality, both of our initial flow concepts failed to start with the basic, fundamental work required to build the end product. So, let's rewind and start there now." The team understood that Operation 10 was really two separate operations—a manual subassembly group of steps followed by a machine load/cycle/unload group of steps.

This same discussion was repeated for each of the initial operations list and the team settled on the revised list of operations for the HVS. The estimated number of operations went from 12 to 18 (Figure 3.12).

Operation	Description
10a	Device Sub-Assembly 1
10b	Press Tab1
20a	Device Sub-Assembly 2
20b	Press Tab2
30	Device Heat Weld
40	Device Label
50a	Plate Sub-Assembly 1
50b	Crimp1
60a	Plate Sub-Assembly 2
60b	Crimp2
70	Plate Bolt Driving (4)
80	Plate Label Press
90	Switch Assembly
100	Switch Bolt Driving (4)
110a	Case Assembly
110b	Overweld
110c	Leak Test
120	Packout

Figure 3.12 Eighteen actual operations.

Now that the team had a better understanding of the foundational operations, it was time to develop various process concepts by breaking down each operation into more detailed work steps (Figure 3.13).

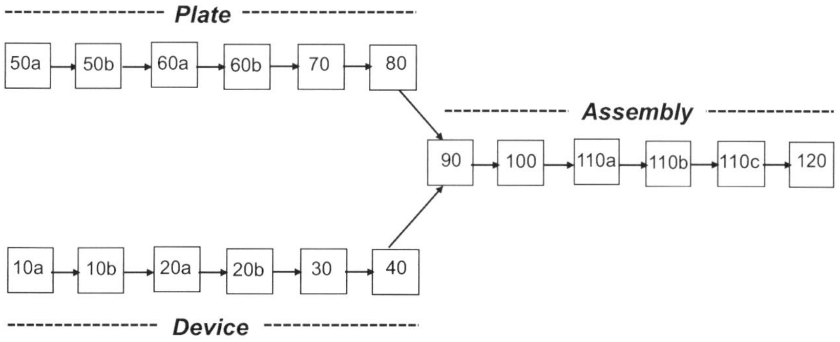

Figure 3.13 HVS precedence breakdown.

Concept 3

"If our two initial concepts are built on flawed assumptions of what constitutes an operation, why continue to even consider them?," asked Alexis.

"We need to think beyond our team here," started Steph. "We understand the flaws, but beyond our war room is an organization that's still set in its ways. We need to bring them along and let the process inform them as well. Even if concepts 1 and 2 are flawed, I've learned over the years that it's much more valuable for people to see their paradigms logically deconstructed and then reconstructed into a better way of doing things rather than trying to convince them to abandon their old thinking and jump to something new. Also, there might be something in these concepts that will help to create a better future state."

"And how are we going to objectively do those comparisons?," asked Alexis.

"I have an answer for that," said Dave Laplace. "We've already done a lot of work in defining key attributes to define success. Remember, we rolled it up into our Operational Declaration posted over here on our planning wall. I was asked at the start of this project to figure out a way to measure success. Initially I was overwhelmed because there are so many ways that success could be defined. But our earlier exercise that started with our stakeholders and their needs, and backed into our Operational Declaration, gave me an idea."

KEY POINT

From the start, think about how you are going to spread what you learn from your initial Lean process creation pilot to the rest of your organization. Great results are not enough, you need to be able to change how people think. And most of those people will not have the benefit of experiencing what your pilot team did.

Dave continued, "What if we came up with comparison measures that were appropriate for the current stage of process development? The Operational Declaration provides the value stream end-state to meet the business case targets, but some of those numbers are impossible to measure until production has started. But there have to be leading indicators we can measure just before start of production (SOP) that can give us a good idea of how well the launch is going to perform. Likewise, these leading indicators are hard to measure earlier in the development cycle, but they too have leading indicators – all the way back to where we are right now" (Figure 3.14).

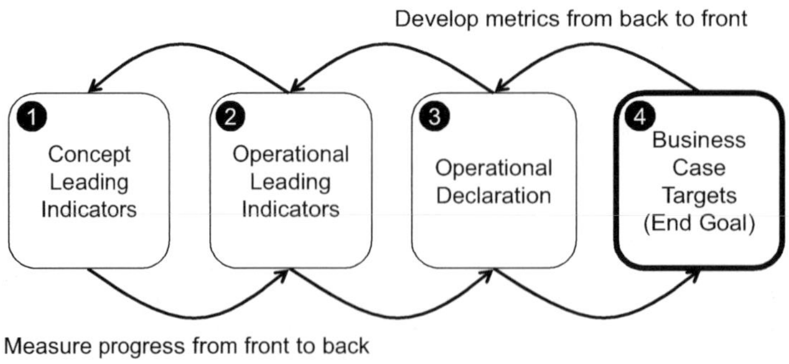

Figure 3.14 Operational leading indicators "Discovery."

Dave finished, "So, leveraging the buckets of Safety, Quality, Schedule and Cost, I'd like to propose the following comparison model for now:"

- **Effective Labor Efficiency:** Proxy of safety and ergo, which is using labor in an efficient and balanced manner, calculated by multiplying the base labor efficiency by the base process efficiency.
- **Capacity Flexibility:** Proxy of schedule, which is flexibility of the concept to process at different line rates.
- **Lifecycle Cost per Unit:** Proxy of cost, which is total operational cost for x years divided by total number of units produced in x years.
- **Manual Work per Unit:** Proxy of cost, which is total seconds of manual work in a single unit.
- **Total Lifecycle Labor Investment:** Total labor required to produce the total units produced in x years.
- **Total Lifecycle Capital Investment:** Total capital required to produce the total units produced in x years.
- **Total Lifecycle Operational Cost:** Total Lifecycle Labor Investment plus Total Lifecycle Capital Investment.

Dave continued, "I have entered the information for our first two concepts into a scorecard spreadsheet (Figure 3.15) using these criteria and I think you'll find the results interesting."

Concept	Effective Labor Efficiency	Capacity Flexibility (sec / unit)	Lifecycle Cost per Unit	Manual Work per Unit (sec)	Total Lifecycle Labor Investment	Total Lifecycle Capital Investment	Total Lifecycle Operational Cost (Labor + Capital)
1	51%	16	$2.26	120	$6,150,000	$3,600,000	$9,750,000
2	86%	60, 90, 180	$1.88	158	$5,642,857	$2,475,000	$8,117,857
					Cost Avoidance:		**$1,632,143**

Figure 3.15 Initial scorecard.

Concept 2 would be 17% lower cost per unit over the 10-year lifecycle ($1.88 versus $2.26), yielding an expected cost avoidance of $1.63 million. There were probably additional savings associated with Concept 2 as it had better capacity flexibility that would translate into better matching capacity to demand and ultimately lower lifecycle operational costs.

"Thanks for doing this Dave," said Jorge excitedly. "If the rest of you don't mind, let's work with this model for now. We can tweak it if we need to. I also like what you said about having the success metrics essentially be layers of leading indicators. We used a similar approach at one of my old jobs and it helped us to minimize surprises when we started production."

The team agreed. The Lean scorecard was added to the obeya (Figure 3.16). For now, they would have to develop the other alternatives before moving to the next stage of Converge. The team felt like they had enough understanding of the data for the initial two concepts, since they were so similar to the existing processes in Adrian. It was now time to start clean-sheet and think of a better way of working and producing this next generation of HVS for the other two concepts—Concept 3 and Concept 4.

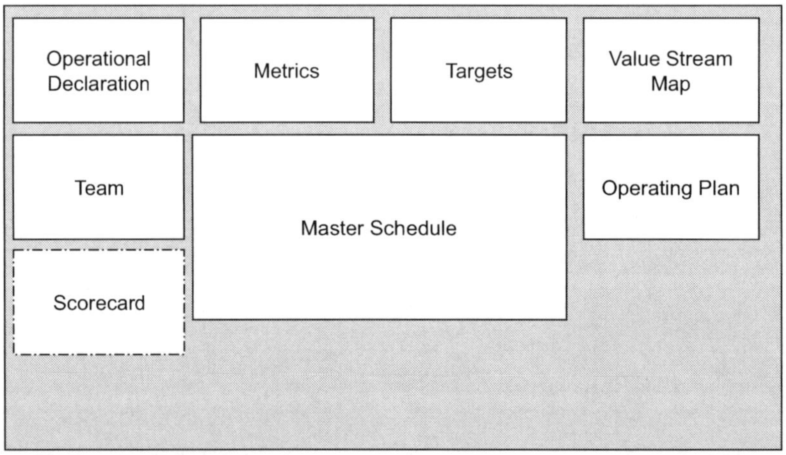

Figure 3.16 Updated obeya.

"Tomorrow I want to start with a teaching exercise," said Steph. "As we consider additional options, we need to be able to quickly develop ideas at the work-step level. We are going to create some table-top mock-ups. Ted, will you and Jolene collect all of the components that would be needed at Operation 10 of Concept 2? Just a few of each."

KEY POINT

There is tremendous value when having a physical, tangible mock-up of the process for team members to focus around. "A mock-up is worth a thousand design reviews."

The next morning when the team entered the room there were a couple of additional tables in the open space just inside the door. Steph and Jorge had set up a couple flip charts nearby. Tape, markers, empty cardboard boxes, and component parts were sitting on one of the tables.

For each operation, the team had to get into the detail at the work step level.

Starting with the first two operations, Device Subassembly 1 and Press Tab, the team needed to do a table-top mock-up to determine the work steps. For a starting point to practice the table-top mock-up, Jorge and Steph worked with the team to create Operation 10 from concept 2 as initially proposed. This meant having Device Subassembly 1 and Press Tab steps combined.

"We are not looking for perfect, this is just a mock-up," said Jorge. "But it is amazing how a simple mock-up enriches the discussion and flow of ideas."

First, the team used tape to identify the location of the working fixture in the machine. They added another outline of tape to indicate there the safety guarding would typically be. Next, they placed the actual component parts around the "machine" in their proposed position. Once the table-top mock-up was complete, then the team listed out the basic work steps and sequence on a flip chart before estimating the times for each step.

Work Combination Table

Steph took a few minutes to show the team a simple and scalable tool called a work combination table (Figure 3.17). It was similar to a Gantt chart at the work detail level. A work combination table can help everyone see the interacting work times of team members, machines, and if scaled up, with each other.

Next, Jorge and Steph worked with the team to look at the two operations separately. They came up with the following table-top mock-up, sequence of steps, and time estimates (Figure 3.18).

For this situation, the revised Operation 10a and 10b each had a total operation cycle time of 10 seconds. Initially in Concept 2, these two operations combined gave a total operation cycle time of 20 seconds. By simply decoupling the operations, the installed capacity was effectively doubled without additional manual work (14 seconds of total work in each case). Although initially there was confusion over the perception of an extra handling step being in place now, the team was confident in these operations of 10a and 10b and decided to make them the basis for Concept 3.

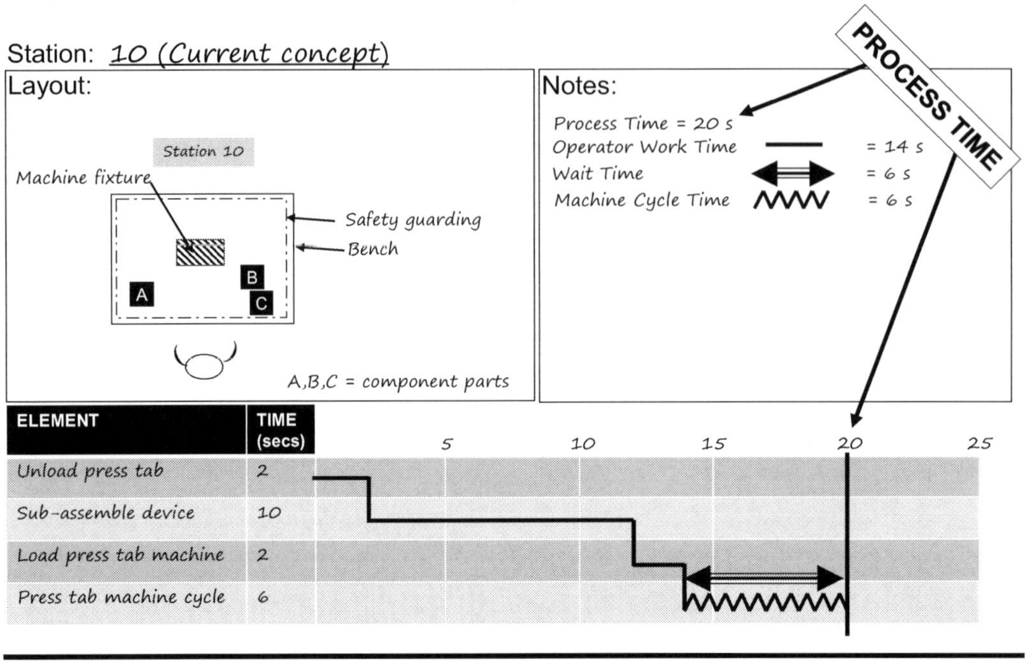

Figure 3.17 Station 10 work combination table.

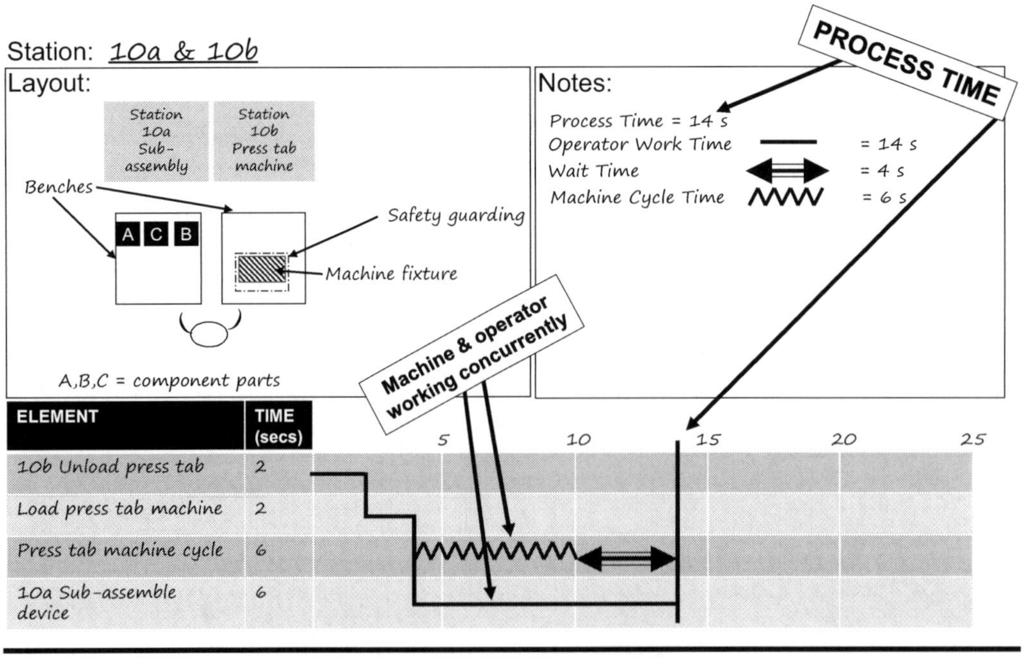

Figure 3.18 Stations 10a and 10b work combination table.

KEY POINT

Capacity: When you hear the word capacity, what do you think of? Often it is something like, "How much can we process in a given time period." But when we hear conversations that involve the concept of capacity, we often observe that people have subtly different definitions that make a big difference (Figure 3.19). Although your organization needs to have its own vocabulary on this subject, here are three basic concepts of capacity:

Actual Capacity: This reflects the current process performance. The available time is reduced because of scrap, equipment down time, supplier interruptions, etc., that are in excess of the planned assumptions in the system design. It is important to understand all of these factors separately to aid in problem-solving.

Designed or Planned Capacity: This reflects your current plan to meet your demand. It includes allowance assumptions, but they may not reflect what is actually being experienced.

Installed Capacity: This is a raw number. The available time divided by the measured cycle time of the process. No allowances. This is important to know as it defines your maximum potential.

Closure of the first gap should be led by operations. Closure of the next two gaps should be led by engineering—the product and process designers.

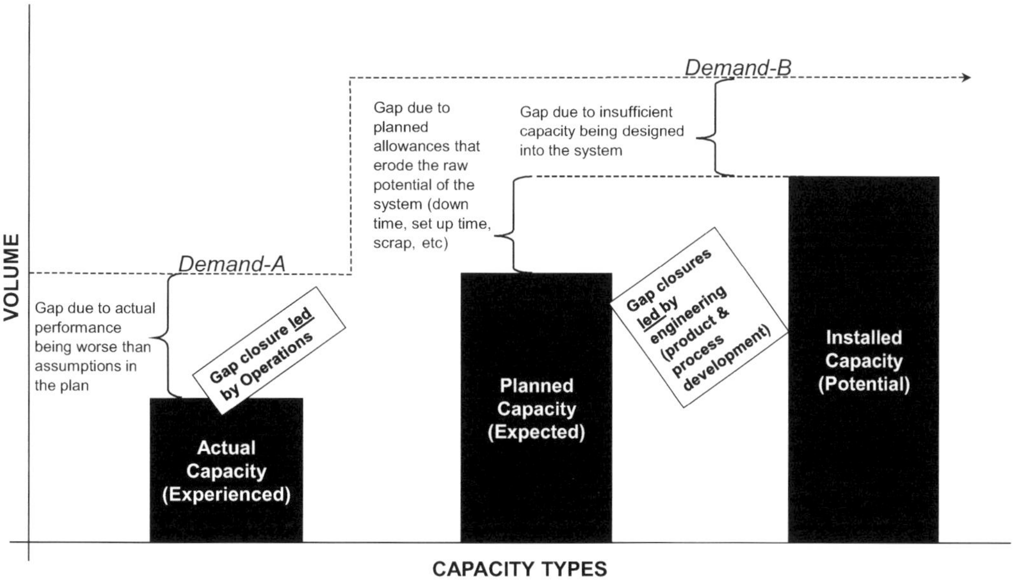

Figure 3.19 Capacity types.

The team did related work for each operation in the list. Station 110 (Figure 3.20) required special attention because it was the bottleneck and was ultimately dictating the natural cycle time of the line.

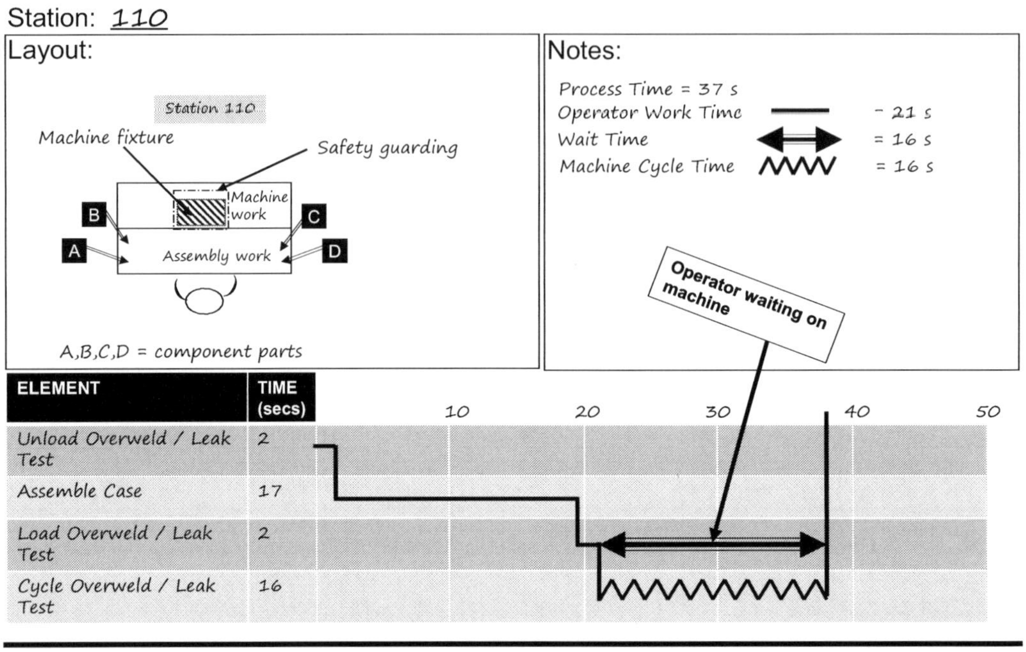

Figure 3.20 Station 110 work combination table.

By choosing to decouple the manual prep work required before the machine operation part of station 110, the team came up with a table-top mock-up. They also decided to leave the operation of Overweld and Leak Test coupled at this station (Figure 3.21). They felt there was not a benefit in separating them since they were both machining-style steps and it would save a handling step. This would be included in Concept 3.

The original Operation 110 cycle time of 37 seconds was now reduced to two stations (Operation 110a and 110b) with cycle times of 17 and 20 seconds, respectively. Since Operation 110 was initially the bottleneck in the process, this effectively improved the capacity at this Operation by 46% (37 seconds to 20 seconds per part). Again, the estimated manual work time was the same total.

After lunch, the team reconvened in Franklin's Tavern. Tom had suggested having "tavern" in the name as a nod to Ben Franklin's love of beer. "So, what did you learn this morning?," asked Jorge.

"I really saw the benefit of understanding operations at the element level," said Tom. This made Steph smile. As an equipment design engineer Tom's

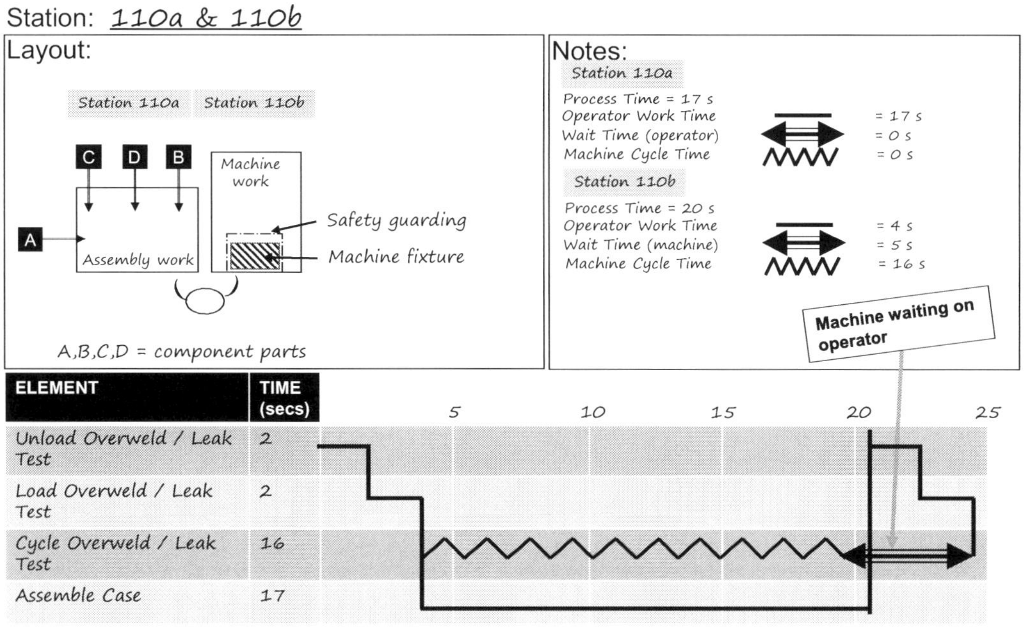

Figure 3.21 Stations 110a and 110b work combination table.

work creates a lasting impact on a production system. Assume the manual work is done inside the machine fixture and you have pretty much combined those cycle times for good. Or until someone is willing to spend the money to rectify the situation.

"Glad to hear that," said Jorge. "What else?"

"I really appreciated the simple, table-top mock-ups," said Gary. "I don't want to sound like I'm whining, but I feel like the integration of the materials into the workplace is always an afterthought. I could see how decoupling, in certain cases, simplified material flow into and through an operation."

"You aren't whining Gary," said Steph. "And as we continue into mocking up the entire process, we will all see, in 3D, better ways to integrate the materials, machines and people. In fact, this is a good segue into the next topic."

"It's not enough to understand each individual operation in isolation. We have to learn to see how the whole process might work or flow," said Steph. "Could a few of you run to the cardboard crushing area and bring back a bunch of large boxes—boxes large enough to act as the base of a workstation? We will also be using the packaging tape and other supplies already in the room."

Within a matter of a few hours, all of the operations for the full-sized mockup were complete.

The team members were anxious to start arranging the operations into a U- and other various shapes as well as determining work allocation between people, but Jorge guided the team to keep everything in a straight line initially with the assumption that only one person would operate the process. The team summarized the learning and updated the time estimates in an operator/machine matrix as they developed Concept 3 (Figure 3.22).

Operation	Description	Operator Time	Machine Time	Total Operation Time*	Equipment Cost
10a	Device Sub-Assembly 1	10 sec	0 sec	10 sec	$0
10b	Press Tab 1	4	6	10	$25,000
20a	Device Sub-Assembly 2	8	0	8	$0
20b	Press Tab 2	4	6	10	$25,000
30	Device Heat Weld	4	7	11	$135,000
40	Device Label	4	0	4	$0
50a	Plate Sub-Assembly 1	9	0	9	$0
50b	Crimp 1	4	4	8	$30,000
60a	Plate Sub-Assembly 2	7	0	7	$0
60b	Crimp 2	4	6	10	$30,000
70	Plate Bolt Driving (4)	26	0	NCT 26	$0
80	Plate Label Press	4	2	6	$35,000
90	Switch Assembly	20	0	20	$0
100	Switch Bolt Driving (4)	26	0	NCT 26	$0
110a	Case Assembly	17	0	17	$0
110b	Overweld / Leak Test	4	16	20	$160,000
120	Packout	3	0	3	$0

Total Manual Work per Part = 158 seconds
17 Stations
Capital Cost = $440,000
Simplified Guarding Reduces Capital Cost

Total Operation Time = Operator Time (load, internal prep work, unload) + Machine Processing Time*

Figure 3.22 Operator/machine matrix for concept 3.

When compared to Concept 2, the team estimated that Concept 3 would require less capital, due primarily to needing less guarding from smaller machine footprints (Figure 3.23). Additionally, Concept 3 had a faster potential process cycle time of 26 seconds, versus 37 seconds for Concept 2. For peak volume, this would require investing in only three lines versus the five lines for Concept 2. This resulted in an additional $1.1 million in capital spending avoidance.

Concept	Effective Labor Efficiency	Capacity Flexibility (sec / unit)	Lifecycle Cost per Unit	Manual Work per Unit (sec)	Total Lifecycle Labor Investment	Total Lifecycle Capital Investment	Total Lifecycle Operational Cost (Labor + Capital)
1	51%	16	$2.26	120	$6,150,000	$3,600,000	$9,750,000
2	86%	60, 90, 180	$1.88	158	$5,642,857	$2,475,000	$8,117,857
3	86%	30, 45, 60, 90, 180	$1.61	158	$5,642,857	$1,320,000	$6,962,857
						Cost Avoidance:	**$2,787,143**

Improved capacity flexibility

Investment reduction of $1,155,000

Figure 3.23 Scorecard w/concept 3.

The NCT for Concept 3 was estimated to be around 30 seconds per device, based on the predicted process characteristics. Concept 3 also had flexibility to run at five different cycle time rates to better match variable takt times.

At this point, the team did not feel comfortable with assessing the manual work time differences, but they were confident that it would not be increased from Concept 2. Steph and Jorge planned to address this confidence gap in the development of Concept 4.

Next, the team was challenged to come up with a fourth concept. Reflecting on the three concepts so far:

- Concept 1 had higher automation (larger capital investment) and machine content, but also high manual requirements and a single line rate option of 16 seconds.
- Concept 2 was developed, and it had much lower automation, simplified machines, and higher manual content, similar to many of the U-shaped cells that the Adrian plant was using as their current operating model.
- Concept 3 was more innovative in that the team started with the basic operations and separated the manual work from machine work. But Concept 3 was essentially a derivative of Concept 2.

"True innovation yields 30% or more improvement in capital and resource efficiencies along with increased effectiveness in delivery and lead-time," said Steph to the team. "We haven't seen that yet."

"That's kind of deflating," remarked Carla. Steph added, "It's not meant to be a criticism, think of it as a challenge. Look how far you've already come in such a short time."

"Looking at Concept 3, what are you uncomfortable with? What risks do you see?," asked Jorge.

"The biggest issue I see is challenging the workforce to work at a faster cycle time than they are accustomed to," said Ted. "We have been doing kaizen for years, implementing U-shaped cells, removing chairs and all the hassles that went with it. Early on we nearly had a revolt. The workforce is used to making high voltages switches at 50 seconds per part, and now we are jumping to 30 seconds."

"And I don't understand why you wouldn't let us arrange Concept 3 into a U-shape," added Alexis. "I've read the books and watched the YouTube videos. The 'U' allows you to control the in and out of the cell, it moves the workers closer together as a team, it minimizes walking, and it allows you to balance the cell to different demand levels—in fact, the chase-style we use is simple and self-balancing."

"I understand what both of you are saying. In fact, several years ago I had this very same conversation with my mentor," said Jorge. In an attempt to alleviate some of the concerns and create a teaching moment, he continued, "And although this will be clearer as we proceed through our lean process creation activity, it's important to let the work suggest the shape. Everything you mentioned about U-cells, that you had read in the literature, is also possible with other shapes. In the end we may come up with a U-shaped configuration, but we're going to let all of the work tell us what the optimum shape is."

Jorge continued, "Independent of shape, but often seen in a U-configuration is the use of a chase-style method of operating. When you have current processes with fixed, known operations, the chase is one countermeasure to help balance out manual work in a pre-engineered, imbalanced process. To rely on the chase as your method of balancing for new processes is attune to engineering taking the easy way out. In fact, engineers aren't really needed to design a chase. Again, at this point I'm not ruling out a chase, but we need to stress that balance across operations is critical and must be done before deciding on the people and material movement methods. The work motions are the same, but the means by which it is allocated across workstations influences capital and resource efficiencies."

It was at this point that Steph interjected, "Jorge, I also want to talk a bit about the faster cycle time." "Oh, yeah" said Jorge, "I almost forgot about that."

Steph continued, "The goal is to develop a simple, manageable processes that will flow smoothly. We want the work to be at a reasonable rate. So far all we have changed is the targeted cycle time for each operation, we haven't even addressed how much work each person will do. This ties back to Jorge's comment about balance. We need a target to balance to and our NCT will be that target. As we have said before, we want it to be as low as reasonable, but we will need observation and improvement of individual operations to zero in on what it actually needs to be."

Steph glanced around the room. There were still a couple of looks of uncertainty. "Let's do a quick thought experiment. If we were to set the NCT at three minutes, what are the implications to the workstation design." No answers. "To keep a person busy for three minutes, what would happen to the amount of incoming material as compared to the current process?"

"It would triple," said Alexis slowly. A look of epiphany crossed her face as she continued. "And that would expand the amount of walking and reaching they'd have to do to get all the materials assembled in the station. The process would have more waste built into it—not to mention how complex the actual machine process would get with all of that assembly occurring at one point."

"You got it!," said Steph. Steph continued, "Let's go in the other direction. What if our target were 5 seconds?"

Ted jumped in, "You'd only have enough time to do one thing at most and then you'd have to pass on the part." "Exactly," said Steph. "So, the real NCT is somewhere in between, and we need to find it. Once we zero in on it we can design a balanced system in which we can use varying labor plans to produce efficiently for a broad range of takt times."

Concept 4

For Concept 4, the team reflected on the observations from the Concept 3 mock-up. One frequent comment was that certain operations were not as repeatable as others. In particular, Operation 70—Plate Bolt Driving—was the least repeatable. The total HVS product portfolio had three different styles of base plates. Operation 70 had a tooling changeover time of 10 minutes if the final product required a different plate.

Additionally, Operation 70 required installing four bolts to secure the Plate subassembly. In Concept 3, the method was for a person to manually install four bolts using a power driver, one at a time from a part presentation bin. The most repeatable time for this process was 26 seconds, but the cycles ranged anywhere from 21 to 36 seconds. "Isn't there a team looking at automating this process?," asked Jolene. "There was," said Tom, "But it cost too much."

Motion Kaizen

Another observation was that the work performed by the operator involved a lot of long reaches and awkward movements. It was as though part presentation and work methods were thought about after the machine was purchased. "This is a good time to introduce everyone to the idea of motion kaizen," said Jorge.

"Let me warn you, once you learn this technique, workplaces you've casually walked by in the past will suddenly bother you very much! The basis for motion kaizen is the idea that *time is the shadow of motion* in operations. To actually reduce the work time, you really need to reduce the motions of both the people and the equipment."

Jorge then drew a quick sketch on a whiteboard (Figure 3.24). "Long motions drive the team member away from where the value-added work takes place, adding cycle time. This includes reaching, walking, bending, eye motions—everything. In general, one motion equals 0.6 seconds of time when we develop a good eye for counting motions."

"No better way to learn than by doing," said Steph. "Let's start with the first station of Concept 2." Starting with Operation 10a, the team was taught how to count all of the nuances of motion: reaches, twists, flips, snaps, and

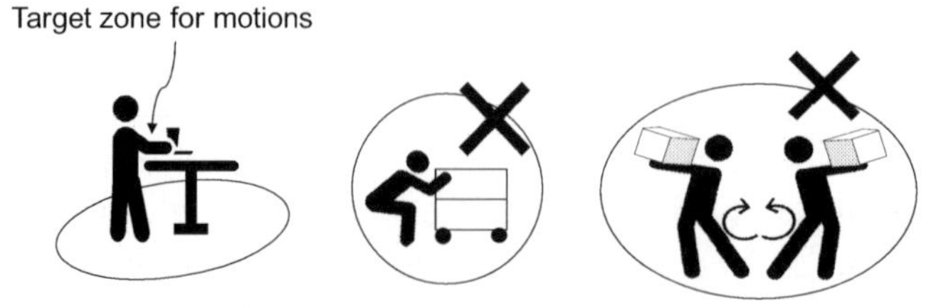

Figure 3.24 An eye for motions.

so on. Then Steph pointed out extra steps and eye movements that were unseen by the team.

KEY POINT

Time is the shadow of motion. To reduce actual work time, you need to reduce motions for both the people and the equipment.

Alexis could not keep quiet any longer. "I've time studied jobs like this for years and haven't noticed these things before—I'm kind of embarrassed."

"Don't be," said Steph. "During time studies we try to get a time for a sequence of work. A common approach is to find something easily identifiable, like pushing the cycle start button, and using that to start and stop your watch by. In the end you get a time, but your observation is focused on that one thing—cycle start. You miss seeing all the details in between."

Ted chimed in, "What I am liking is that I can see possibilities in using this technique to engage the team members. If I approach a team member about reducing their cycle time by 5 seconds, what they actually hear is *you need to work faster*. But if I suggest we figure out how to remove motions from their job, they'll show me how because that sounds like we are making the job easier. And we actually are. In fact, I'd like to get a team member and try this again, to see their reaction, but better yet, to get them involved."

Ted left the room for a few minutes and returned with one of their more senior and outspoken team members. Ted thought, "If we can make her happy, we'll make everyone happy." Although Ted's experiment started out slow, as the team member thought it was odd for people to just observe without stop watches, once the dialog began on reducing and simplifying motions, Ted had the buy-in he was looking for.

Continuing, the original Operation 10 (from Concept 2), the workstation design was larger, and the components had to be presented from the sides of the machine due to the safety guarding blocking access from in front of the worker. This led to longer reaches to get each of the three component types (Base, Board, Four Tabs).

Using this station layout, the team counted 17 motions (equals 10.2 seconds) to load the components as part of the subassembly at Operation 10 (Figure 3.25).

By decoupling 10a from 10b, this enabled a much smaller machine design footprint and more access for presenting components into the "green zone" or target zone—an imaginary 13″×13″ square right in front of the operator.

Using this improved station layout, the team was able to present the components into the target zone, allowing the worker to use simultaneous motions of the left and right hands. The estimated total work was ten

Station: 10 (Original)

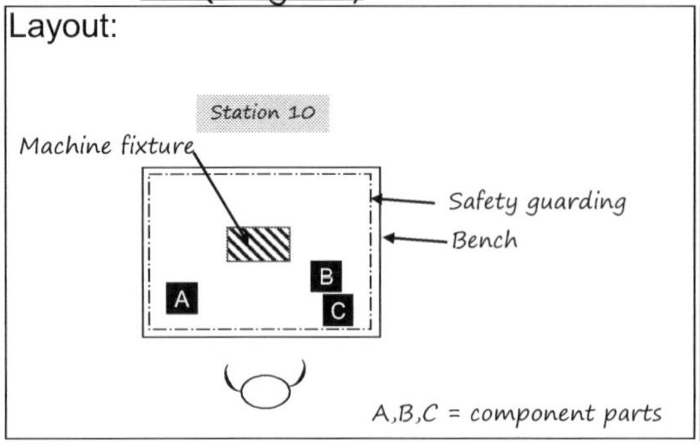

Description	Left	Both	Right
Get & place device base (A)	4		
Get & place circuit board (B)			5
Get & insert 4 tabs (C)			8
TOTALS	4		13

17 motions in total

Zero motions performed simultaneously

Cycle time = 17 motions x 0.6 s/motion = 10.2 s

Figure 3.25 Motion analysis original station 10.

Station: 10a & 10b

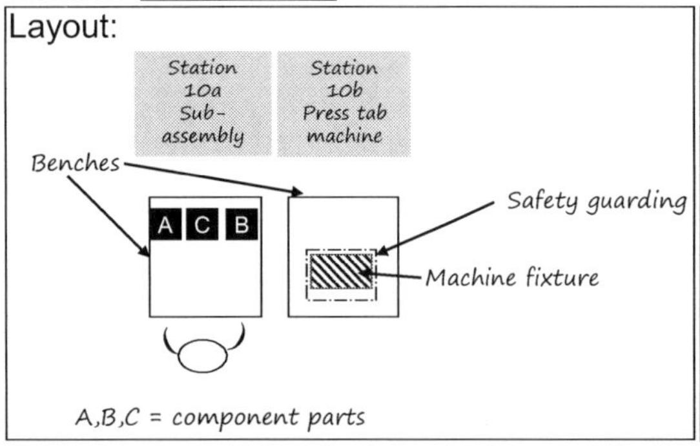

Description	Left	Both	Right
Get device base (A) & circuit board (B)*	3		3
Place device base (A) & circuit board (B)*	3		3
Get & insert 4 tabs (C)*	4		4
TOTALS	10		10

20 motions in total

10 motions performed simultaneously

Cycle time = 10 motions x 0.6 s/motion = 6 s

* Simultaneous motions

Figure 3.26 Motion analysis stations 10a and 10b.

motions performed by each hand in parallel, which equated to 6 seconds for the improved Operation 10a (Figure 3.26). This was a 41% reduction in motions, hence, a 41% reduction in work time.

This same approach using motion kaizen was used for Operation 20a, Operation 90, and Operation 110a, resulting in motion improvements.

There was definitely a buzz of excitement in the room. The team was seeing the potential for improvement by applying some simple, logical thought, and being careful about blindly following dogmatic slogans. "Great work, everyone," said Steph. "This is the level of improvement I knew you could achieve with some tweaks in your thinking. I genuinely want to thank you to being open to learning new approaches but doing so with a critical eye."

"I'd like to second that," said Jorge. "After lunch let's tackle Operation 70."

$O^1S^2I^3$

After lunch the team returned to the obeya and discovered the following writing on a whiteboard (Figure 3.27):

Observe

Standardize & Stabilize

Improve	$	Risk
• Methods / part presentation	o	o
• Machines / equipment	++	++
• Layout / system	++++++	++++++

Figure 3.27 O^1-S^2-I^3.

Once everyone was in the room, Jorge started talking, "I want to introduce all of you to a simple but powerful hierarchy you won't find in books. O^1-S^2-I^3…easy as 123. We've talked about some of the elements before."

Jorge continued, "The O^1 stands for Observe—and that is the basis for all improvement. That's why we've been stressing going to the gemba and that's why we've located the obeya near the gemba as well. We need to observe the processes or better yet, work them ourselves. Some we can observe directly, others we will mock-up. But that first-hand observation of the processes, how they flow, the motions involved, the locations of the equipment, materials and operator all relative to each other—that is the foundation for us to begin improvement."

Next, Jorge said, "S^2 refers to standardize and stabilize. To truly improve, we need a baseline for comparison—a standard method. Don't fret about it being perfect. Just settle on the best-known method for doing the current job, document it and use it. This will help to stabilize the process and allow us to truly understand if an improvement idea is actually better. So far I think you've already heard all of this."

Jorge noticed nods of agreement around the room. "This is most likely the new part, I^3, or three levels of improvement. The first level to be explored is methods & parts presentation. Then you move on to the second level, machines & equipment and finally reach the third level, layout or total system. Any guesses as to why this sequence?"

Dave Laplace spoke up, "I'm embarrassed to say this being the finance guy, but I think it has to do with money. Workplace and part presentation improvements are much cheaper than laying out the entire department."

"You are spot-on, Dave," said Jorge. "At my last company we went through a phase of changing the layout of a department to move workstations closer together, removing the inventory in between, and calling it Lean. But to the people doing the work, they were still stuck doing the same awkward motions on the same poor processes. And this won't shock you, Lean got a bad name. It wasn't until our mentor taught us this hierarchy that we really started making a bottom-line difference along with keeping the people engaged every step of the way."

KEY POINT

Creativity before Capital. The Improvement hierarchy of O^1-S^2-I^3 can be utilized for existing processes as well as when designing new processes. Following the logic of the steps builds "muscle-memory" for a simple yet powerful mental model that helps minimize both complexity and unnecessary investment while unlocking value.

Jorge continued, "Another nuance, and related to money, is the relative degree of risk. A workplace change can be quickly simulated or tested to determine the true benefit. Not too risky. But changing a departmental layout is not easily done, or undone. One more point, and then I will get off my soapbox, this hierarchy allows one level of improvement to inform the next level. So, the workplace & parts presentation design can inform the equipment design. And the equipment design can inform the overall layout. Next time you walk through the plant, look at how many workstations could be significantly improved with small tweaks to the equipment design, only if someone had thought about the methods and parts presentation before starting to weld steel together."

"That's a great lead-in to our next task," said Steph. "How do we improve Operation 70? And to paraphrase Jorge, remember, *creativity before capital.* Spend money as though it is coming out of your own pocket." Dave Laplace grinned inwardly. In his eyes, this was breakthrough thinking.

The team decided the best place to start was to go to the Concept 3 rough mock-up for Operation 70, observe the work steps, collect data and facts, and develop countermeasures (Figure 3.28). The total repeatable manual work time for Operation 70 was 26.4 seconds.

For each of the four total bolts, it took ten motions or an average of 6 seconds to get one bolt, position the bolt, and then use the power driver at the proper torque setting to install the bolt onto the plate.

These three basic steps each had variability from cycle-to-cycle, but the majority of variability, about 80%, was found at the initial step of getting one bolt, since bolts were jumbled in a box from the supplier. In addition, this operation had a major ergonomic problem that was never noticed before. The type of power driver used was a hand-held, pistol-grip style. This forced

Station: 70

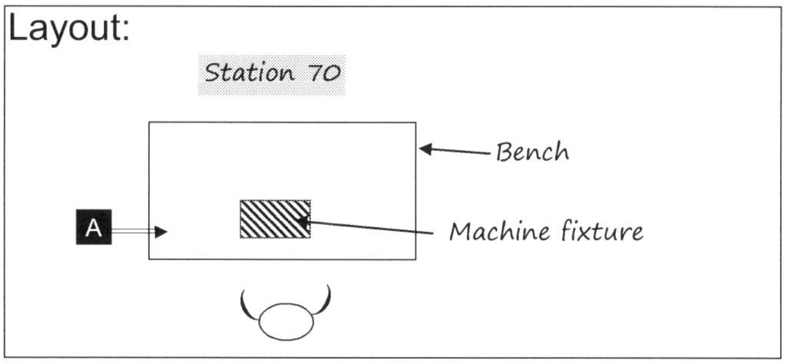

Description	Left	Both	Right
Load part to fixture	2		
INSTALL 4 BOLTS Get & place bolt (A) Get & position drill Drill bolt into place	5		2* 3 2
Unload to station 80 WIP			2

10 effective motions X 4 cycles = 40 effective motions

52 motions in total
8 motions performed simultaneously

Cycle time = 44 motions x 0.6 s/motion = 26.4 s

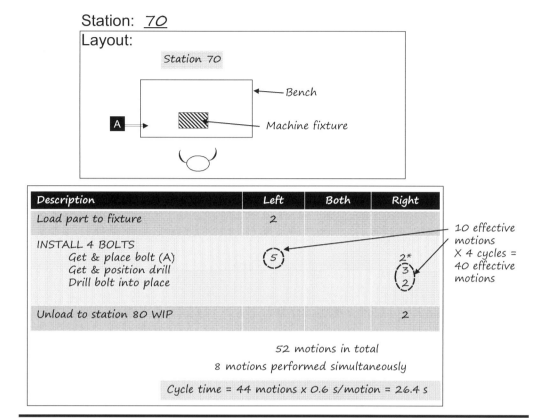

Figure 3.28 Motion analysis station 70.

the worker into awkward body postures and could lead to longer-term ergonomic concerns and injuries with high repetitions.

For the variability problem, the team brainstormed numerous ideas for eliminating the inconsistency of this operation. One idea was to get parts delivered into Acme from the supplier in the right orientation. But since these bolts were a standard type and available off-the-shelf, the team knew that this option could come with a higher purchased part price. Still, it was an option worth pursuing since the idea was estimated to save about three motions per bolt, or 1.8 seconds. If that were extrapolated across the production volume for year-1 it equated to 25% of one person's time.

Another idea was to use inline bolt bowl-feeder technology. The technology used compressed air systems to position screws or bolts through an inline tube into place for a drill to simply apply the torque and move to the next hole. This idea would involve some capital investment but recent progress in bowl feeding technology had made these types of systems cheaper and more commercially feasible for production with improved uptime performance.

Tom Osborne formerly worked in the window industry and shared the experience of using this technology for delivering screws into the power drivers for the high-usage hardware, saving about 3 seconds per screw. The cost of bowl feeders at the time was about $15,000 per machine.

The team simulated the effect that an inline bolt feeder may have on the Operation 70 using the rough mock-up by having a team member play the part of the feeder bowl. By eliminating the step of manually getting the bolt and much of the step of positioning of the bolt, the team estimated that one bolt could be installed with five motions, a reduction of 50%. This would give the Operation a total of 20 motions, or 12 seconds, for installing the bolts, plus 2 seconds for the load/unload (Figure 3.29). This would be the Operation 70 plan that they would use for Concept 4.

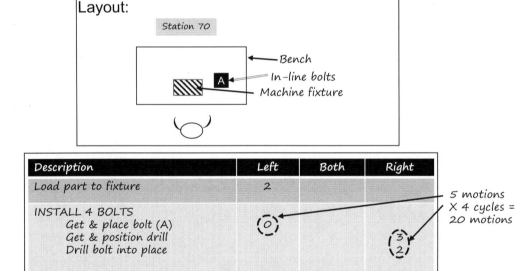

Station: 70 Improved

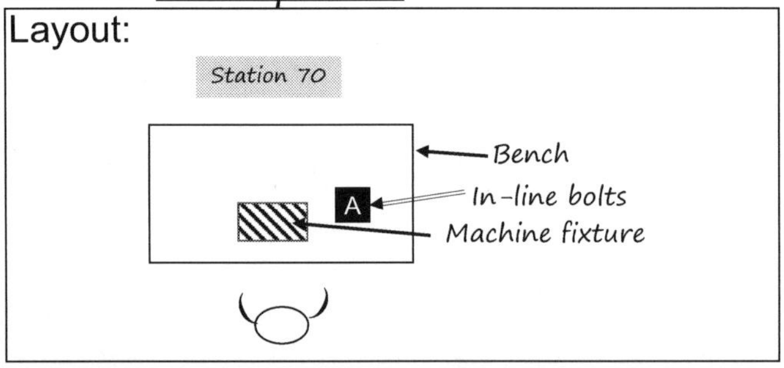

Description	Left	Both	Right
Load part to fixture	2		
INSTALL 4 BOLTS			
Get & place bolt (A)	0		
Get & position drill			3
Drill bolt into place			2
Unload to station 80 WIP			2

5 motions X 4 cycles = 20 motions

24 motions in total

Zero motions performed simultaneously

Cycle time = 24 motions x 0.6 s/motion = 14.4 s

Figure 3.29 Motion analysis station 70 improved.

For the bigger ergonomic concern, the team targeted using a drop-down style, hand-held power driver. This would lead to a simple up-and-down motion for the worker to align and drive each bolt into place.

Operation 100 of Switch Bolt Driving had similar challenges with cycle-to-cycle variability and ergonomics. It also required four bolts to be installed at its operation. The team used the same approach for this operation that they used for Operation 70. It seemed very reasonable that an inline bolt bowl-feeder could also be used at Operation 100. The overall cycle time was estimated to reduce from 26 seconds down to 14 seconds. The team would use this as the Operation 100 plan for Concept 4.

After all the planned improvements at Operations 10a, 20a, 70, 90, 100, and 110a, the team realized that the new bottleneck on the line became the combined Overweld & Leak Test Operation at a time of 20 seconds. The next highest operation was Operation 90 at 15 seconds, with many of the other operations balanced close to this. Steph sketched out the machine balance chart for the current process concept.

Now that many operations had been simplified and broken down to their fundamental steps, Jorge asked the team what the natural rhythm of the process was from their perspective. For this process, with combined Overweld and Leak Test, the answer was almost unanimously 20 seconds. "Something doesn't seem right to me," said Alexis.

"Go on," said Jorge. Alexis continued, "So far, we've been asked to look at the basic elements of work, yet we have a machine—the Overweld & Leak Test—that isn't broken into its elements."

"That's why I'd suggest the natural rhythm, or natural cycle time for this process is actually 15 seconds," said Steph. Steph explained to the team that it was risky to combine Overweld with Leak Test given that in the past, the Leak Test requirements were usually finalized later in the product development cycle. Any delays to these test requirements would almost surely delay the Overweld machine design if the operations were combined. This could in turn delay the machine qualification and launch dates, putting the customer at risk.

This was a good example of one of the failure modes that was identified earlier: *penny-wise, pound-foolish*. On paper, combining the two operations seemed to minimize part handling, floor-space, and cost. In reality, it would lead to under-utilized capacity across the entire process and add risk to an already tight launch schedule.

Consequently, the team performed the motion kaizen activity for Operation 110b, splitting off the Leak Test into Operation 110c (Figure 3.30).

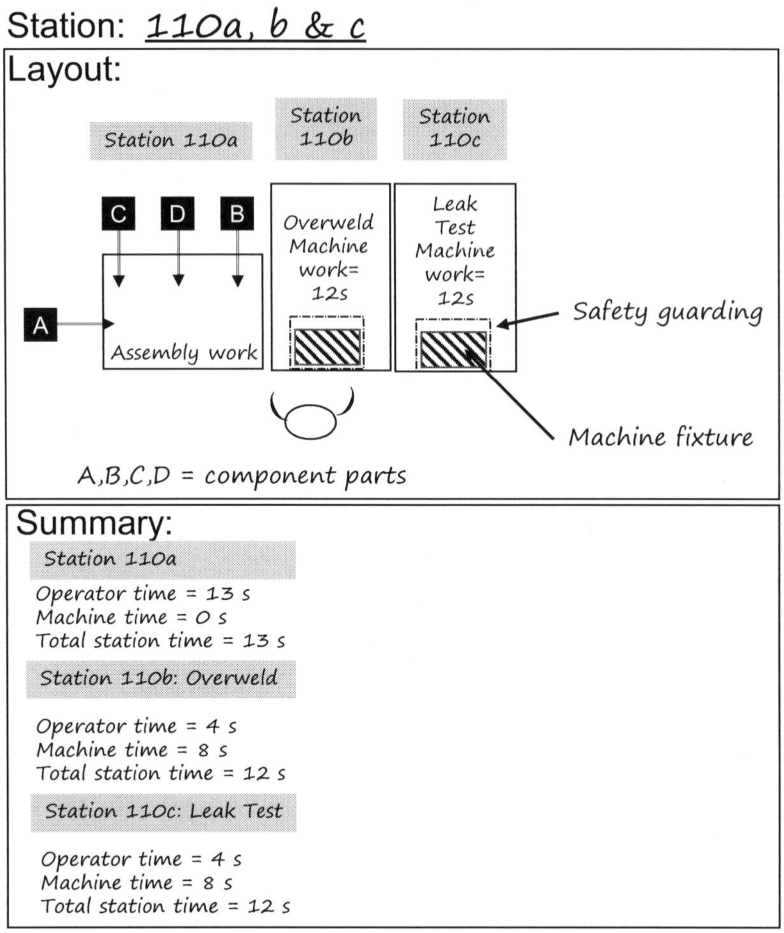

Figure 3.30 Station 110 decoupling.

Based on all the improvements and experiments, the Concept 4 Operator/Machine Balance Matrix was updated (Figure 3.31). Even though the NCT was 15 seconds, the majority of the team felt that a PCT for the process of 30 seconds would be more reasonable. Based on this, the team would still need two of these lines for peak volume.

Operation	Description	Operator Time	Machine Time	Total Operation Time*	Equipment Cost	Notes
10a	Device Sub-Assembly 1	6 sec	0 sec	6 sec	$0	Motion Kaizen (-4 sec)
10b	Press Tab 1	4	6	10	$25,000	
20a	Device Sub-Assembly 2	6	0	6	$0	Motion Kaizen (-2 sec)
20b	Press Tab 2	4	6	10	$25,000	
30	Device Heat Weld	4	7	11	$135,000	
40	Device Label	4	0	4	$0	
50a	Plate Sub-Assembly 1	9	0	9	$0	
50b	Crimp 1	4	4	8	$30,000	
60a	Plate Sub-Assembly 2	7	0	7	$0	
60b	Crimp 2	4	6	10	$30,000	
70	Plate Bolt Driving (4)	14	0	14	$15,000	Inline Feeder (-12 sec)
80	Plate Label Press	4	2	6	$35,000	
90	Switch Assembly	15	0	NCT 15	$0	Motion Kaizen (-5 sec)
100	Switch Bolt Driving (4)	14	0	14	$15,000	Inline Feeder (-12 sec)
110a	Case Assembly	13	0	13	$0	Motion Kaizen (-4 sec)
110b	Overweld	4	8	12	$80,000	Decoupled from Leak Test
110c	Leak Test	4	8	12	$80,000	Decoupled from Overweld
120	Packout	3	0	3	$0	

Total Manual Work per Part = 123 seconds, 18 Stations
Capital Cost = $470,000

Total Operation Time = Operator Time (load, internal prep work, unload) + Machine Processing Time*

Figure 3.31 Operator/machine matrix for concept 4.

In a quiet voice Steph said to Jorge, "They're not quite there on NCT, but we'll come back to that later." Jorge nodded once, slowly, in agreement.

"I have a question," said Melinda, "I like the use of the scorecard to compare options and to drive a discussion, but where is quality represented? Many of these measures relate to productivity" (Figure 3.32).

Concept	Effective Labor Efficiency	Capacity Flexibility (sec / unit)	Lifecycle Cost per Unit	Manual Work per Unit (sec)	Total Lifecycle Labor Investment	Total Lifecycle Capital Investment	Total Lifecycle Operational Cost (Labor + Capital)
1	51%	16	$2.26	120	$6,150,000	$3,600,000	$9,750,000
2	86%	60, 90, 180	$1.88	158	$5,642,857	$2,475,000	$8,117,857
3	86%	30, 45, 60, 90, 180	$1.61	158	$5,642,857	$1,320,000	$6,962,857
4	80%	15, 30, 45, 60, 120	$1.23	123	$4,392,857	$940,000	$5,332,857
					Cost Avoidance:		$4,417,143

Figure 3.32 Scorecard w/concept 4.

Dave Laplace chimed in, "That's been bothering me as well—and I'm the finance guy! I've been noodling on a way to represent that in these very early stages. Can I run it by you, Melinda, and if it makes sense, we'll add it to our thinking?" "Deal!," said Melinda.

"What about delivery?," asked Gary. "You are welcome to join us," said Dave.

After completion of these same table-top mock-ups, the team did a rough mock-up in 3-D using cardboard, flexible piping, and basic work benches. The purpose of this was to get a real image of the proposed flow, as well as to incorporate in the part presentation points, machine footprints, and more.

This was a valuable activity, and the team discovered many opportunities for improving the process. In one example, Ted was able to demonstrate the difficulty in performing the bolt driving operation if the drop-down driver did not move out of the way of the work area when it was not needed. Without doing the 3-D mock-up, this would have been missed. Steph summed it up by stating, "Use the simplest prototype to learn what you need to know."

THE STEERING TEAM—DEPTH, THEN BREADTH

At 8:00 am the following Monday, the Project Franklin steering team meeting drew to a conclusion. The leadership members—Jon Jain, Dave Laplace, Leslie O'Brien, Paul Larsson and Cheryl Henricks—were both impressed and enthusiastic about the fast progress made by the team.

The meeting was held at the obeya using the working boards and mock-ups. No special preparation was required, and Jon loved that. "If we could only clone this throughout the organization, I'd get out of attending these fake dog-and-pony shows people always invite me to," Jon thought. The team shared their progress by reviewing their master schedule, what they had learned, and the results.

In an earlier meeting, Dave Laplace had taken the steering team through the logic behind the Lean scorecard, so everyone understood what the card was telling them. Dave also explained the addition of a process stability measure to the scorecard. It was the product of a quality risk assessment and a delivery risk assessment—a scorecard feeding a scorecard. The team endorsed this process stability measure, as it was difficult to directly measure the quality levels and delivery performance of a concept.

Jon thanked the team for their work. "With an estimated cost avoidance of $4.4 million as compared to our typical approach, why not implement concept 4?," Jon asked with the impatience of a company president.

Cheryl jumped in, "Jon, we need to let the team follow their process. It's been working so far, so let's not allow our penchant for fast results short circuit this."

Jon nodded in agreement. "That's one reason I want HR involved in this process," Jon thought. "Cheryl will intervene and help me to be a better leader."

Later that day in Jon's office, the steering team gathered together again. "Thanks for correcting me, Cheryl," Jon started.

"Just doing my job," she said. Cheryl continued, "If we do this right, we'll not only have a positive impact on the product & process aspects of the business, but I see a lot of potential to impact the people in a very positive way."

"How so?," asked Jon.

Cheryl responded, "Did you see the engagement in the room? People were speaking with both confidence and pride. They were able to readily answer your questions, partly because they were able to show their actual work. The mock-up or the value stream or the timing chart. It wasn't a diluted PowerPoint they were sharing. If we can document this working style and replicate it, even into the back offices, I think it'll be the largest single thing we can do to improve employee engagement."

"That's actually been my experience," said Leslie. "What should we expect next?," asked Jon.

Leslie answered, "As their master schedule showed, they are about to transition from the Concepts stage to the Convergence stage—so they will continue to converge down to a single concept and after that they will do the detailed work of Configuring that concept."

"What are the risks?," asked Jon.

"Losing momentum because of the appearance of our success," said Paul. "Remember, this is all preparation work–knowledge work. We don't have a working system yet. So, everyone, including us, has to stay engaged in the process. I have seen this movie before and if we aren't careful, someone gets pulled to another project, we let other priorities interfere with our steering meetings, and the final result is a rush to implement something before the start of production date."

"We'll make sure that doesn't happen," said Jon.

Must-Do Actions for Concepts

1. Develop a plan to capture emerging learning, with a plan to share, spread, and cascade the knowledge to others for capability building.
2. Understand what natural cycle time (NCT) means for your new process, and what impact it has on the three capacity types (actual, planned, and installed).
3. Use physical mock-ups of the process with real, tangible parts to best understand the flow of value at the fundamental work level.
4. Practice the improvement hierarchy (O^1-S^2-I^3) to develop the muscle memory for *creativity before capital* ideas.

Key Questions for Concepts

- What are the key points of your Operational Declaration? Are they being met? What needs to be adjusted?
- How many different process concepts will you develop before convergence?
- What will be the Lean-style cost model that you plan to use for comparing the value of the different process concepts? How will you measure progress with regard to Safety/Ergonomics, Quality, and Delivery as well?
- What are the fundamental operations that make up the process, including their precedence?
- How will you get a 3-D image of each operation to support fast learning and testing at different fidelity levels?
- How will you quickly capture the motions required for every step in the process concept, as well as data, facts, and opportunities?
- What is your Natural Cycle Time (NCT) target?

Chapter 4

CONverge

Isolation is a blind alley....Nothing on the planet grows except by convergence.

—Pierre Teilhard de Chardin

Purpose: testing/modeling the initial design concepts and narrowing them down to select an optimal design through rapid learning cycles

Section Prologue: *With four early concepts brainstormed and identified, the Lean Process Creation team begins the critical work of Converge. Referencing the 4-2-1 methodology for down-selecting, the team will take these initial four concepts to create a set of two new concepts by incorporating in higher level improvement ideas such as equipment modifications and challenging the product design where appropriate. Finally, the team will then incorporate all the learning and ideas into a final concept that they will propose for the new HVS process.*

4-2-1

The team was gathering in the obeya, or the Franklin Stove, as a new sign on the door called it. The air conditioning was not working quite right, so the room had a tendency to get warm in the afternoon. So, Tavern was out and Stove was in. Although the past week was supposed to be a hiatus from Project Franklin, allowing everyone to get caught up on their other duties, many of the team members found themselves using the obeya as home

DOI: 10.4324/9781003219712-6

base. They had grown to appreciate the usable wall space, the rolling white boards, and the open environment.

And when they needed to shut out distractions, there were a few empty offices along the east wall they could use. Just the day before, Jorge had overheard a conversation between Tom and Jolene where they were saying that work was fun again. Jorge pretended to not notice, but he felt the same way.

As everyone settled in around the main conference table, Stephanie Waterson rolled a white board to the front and began addressing the team, "We are about to begin the Converge phase of our Lean process creation journey. Just so you understand where this is going, in the Concept phase we developed four ideas, or concepts, to overuse the word. I'm stretching the idea of 'we' a bit here. The first two concepts were almost givens. I'm not passing judgement, but the first one was our traditional approach of automating to avoid labor. The second one was essentially a copy of what operations has called their Lean cells – production processes shaped like a letter 'U' and balanced with a chase-style work method."

Steph continued, "Being hyper-aware that we are on a learning journey as well as a process creation journey, Jorge and I deliberately wanted these first two concepts to be explored as they are Acme's current paradigms. The rest of the organization needs to see the benefits in this new way of approaching process design. If we didn't consider Acme's pre-conceived notions, there would be doubt. But by considering these typical ideas and using sound logic to show what better can be, we will move everyone towards this new approach. Does this make sense so far?"

"I see the four," said Gary, "but where is the two and the one?"

Steph continued, "I'm getting to that. I think someone's had a bit too much coffee this morning. Two and one is where Converge comes in to play. Leveraging what we know from concepts one through four, we are going to introduce some additional thinking to generate two more concepts, or converge to two concepts, and then eventually to one concept" (Figure 4.1).

"Is the 7th concept the one that gets implemented?," asked Jolene.

"Not necessarily," said Steph. "When we get to the 7th concept there may be things we need to learn, things that drive experiments. And the outcomes of those experiments may drive us to create additional concepts."

Steph asked, "Is this still making sense?" Heads were nodding around the table, but Alexis had a curious look on her face. "What are you thinking, Alexis?"

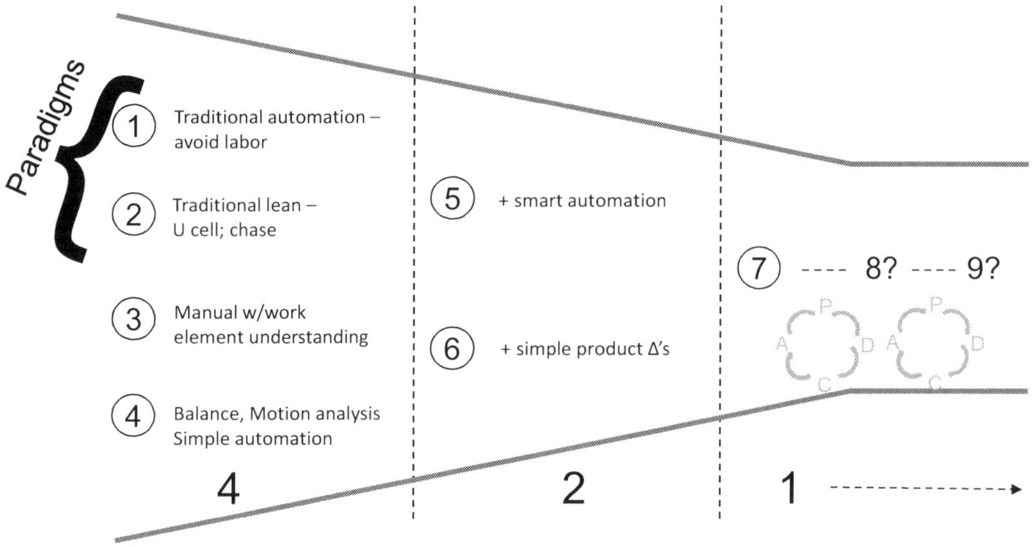

Figure 4.1 4-2-1 convergence.

"I see you've written next to 5 & 6 to add smart automation and to add simple product changes". Alexis asked, "Why not consider both of those together?"

Steph responded, "Remember, we are in a learning mode, we're trying to figure out what a better process creation method can look like. And it is important that we don't get ahead of our learning. So, we are purposely taking it slow. In the end, we will learn about the impact of adding smart automation and then we may build on top of that to come up with concept 6."

"That sounds like we've converged already," said Jolene.

Steph was starting to feel a bit frustrated but did not let it show. "You could argue that. Remember that our Lean process creation experiment isn't perfect. Early on we decided, for timing reasons, that the product design was largely locked down. Ideally, we would be developing the initial four concepts before all of the product decision had been made."

Steph went on, "A good rule of thumb is that one of the four is the simplest manual method and another is automated in nature. Logically the other two are somewhere between, but they can be used to explore the impact of certain product options such as an aluminum housing instead of the typical steel. In that case we would truly be converging four ideas to two and then to one. So, we're stretching the thinking a bit here. But the thinking is the important part. Just like the five-why principle of root cause analysis does not always use five whys, 4-2-1 is not always exactly four, then two, then one. We want multiple ideas at the start, then we want to converge the ideas together as we learn more, eventually reaching that one concept we are going to implement. Does this make sense?"

Steph added, "This is different than set-based convergence, where you keep all of the ideas active until you learn enough to remove an idea. Here we will start with a few concepts, converge them via experimentation, and continue to iterate" (Figure 4.2).

Concept	Effective Labor Efficiency	Capacity Flexibility (sec / unit)	Lifecycle Cost per Unit	Manual Work per Unit (sec)	Total Lifecycle Labor Investment	Total Lifecycle Capital Investment	Total Lifecycle Operational Cost (Labor + Capital)
1	51%	16	$2.26	120	$6,150,000	$3,600,000	$9,750,000
2	86%	60, 90, 180	$1.88	158	$5,642,857	$2,475,000	$8,117,857
3	86%	30, 45, 60, 90, 180	$1.61	158	$5,642,857	$1,320,000	$6,962,857
4	80%	15, 30, 45, 60, 120	$1.23	123	$4,392,857	$940,000	$5,332,857
						Cost Avoidance:	**$4,417,143**

Figure 4.2 Scorecard with Concept 4.

The Lean Process Creation Team was beginning to see how their deep brainstorming and challenging of ideas were paying off in expected performance gains for the new High Voltage Switch process. The amount of manual work to build one part had been reduced from 158 to 123 seconds (22%) from Concept 3 to Concept 4. Capital investment for Concept 4 was almost 75% lower than the initial Concept 1 capital request of $3,600,000 down to $940,000.

Creativity before Capital Revisited

"Who recalls the improvement hierarchy $O^1S^2I^3$?," asked Jorge. Among the nods, Carla spoke up, "It looks like we all do."

Jorge then asked, "Okay, which of the three levels of improvement have we considered so far?"

"Methods and parts presentation?," said Ted.

"I think we went further into machine improvements," said Tom. "Remember the in-line bolt feeding, that cost money."

"Not that the exact answer matters," added Jorge, "but the important part is that we started with low risk, low dollar ideas. Remember—creativity before capital. $O^1S^2I^3$ is another way of thinking. In fact, as Acme applies this thinking more broadly beyond Lean process creation, it's important to understand that you can apply an 80/20 rule to it. Eighty percent of the time you will follow the flow of methods, equipment, then layout. But there will be times when you need to or have to jump ahead. They should just be the exception, not the rule."

"Can you give us an example?," asked Carla.

Jorge continued, "Sure, and we'll get two for the price of one—it won't even be a manufacturing example, because I want everyone to understand that this thinking can apply anywhere. Does anyone here remember the anxiety associated with New Year's Eve on December 31, 1999?" As Jorge glanced at the young faces around the room, he realized that very few of them were aware of the issue at the time.

Jorge continued, "There was a lot of concern that large networks of computer systems would crash because many computer programs that relied on dates were written with a two-digit date field. So, to the software, we were about to take a step back in time going from year 99 to 00. In an effort to avoid issues, thousands of retired computer programmers who knew the early computer language COBOL were contracted to rewrite programs with four-digit date fields. My previous company had six different business units whose information systems were a patchwork of old software in need of replacement."

"At the same time", Jorge explained, "in the years just preceding 1999, we were in the midst of learning a lot about lean by practicing it everywhere. We had made the deliberate decision to learn about lean and develop simple computer tools to support our efforts using low-cost methods. Namely, we were using Excel to do level loading, to calculate kanban card requirements, to print them, and the list goes on. The computer equivalent of the first level of improvement. Rather than buying new software, we were letting the lean improvements inform the Excel tools first."

Jorge explained, "Then as we learned more and improved the tools, cheaply and quickly, we started to create some simple, stand-alone Access databases. That cost us some money to get the licenses and the training to use Access properly. Think level two of improvement. Level three would be to purchase the large-scale ERP software solution. But instead of buying something off the shelf, we let our fast learning cycles and improvements from levels one and two inform what level three should look like. So, now we could specify what we needed to support our process and not let the ERP system dictate what our process should be."

Jorge concluded, "It was a great plan, except for one flaw, our business unit that produced filters. It was the oldest business unit and had the oldest computer software in the company. There weren't enough COBOL programmers in the world to fix that software before 12/31/99. So, the decision was made in that business unit to jump to an off-the-shelf ERP system. In the end there were no issues at our company related to Y2K, but that particular division did have to live with a suboptimal ERP system which continues to haunt them to this day. So, in this case we jumped to the third level of improvement, because the uniqueness of the situation dictated it. If there aren't any questions, let's start looking at the machines and equipment—smartly."

At this point, Steph introduced the team to the degrees of automation. "The degrees don't represent all different combinations of what could be automated, but rather the degrees represent the normal, logical progression of automation for an operation." Steph explained that, in general, there are four actions that may be automated.

- Loading a Machine Operation (Load Machine)
- The Operation's Machine Cycle Itself (Machine Cycle)
- Unloading an Operation (Unload Machine)
- Transfer of the Part to the Next Operation (Transfer Part)

Steph continued, "***Degree I*** of automation is entirely manual. A person loads an operation, the value-add work required is entirely manual, for example pressing a tab. And then a person unloads the operation, and a person transfers the part to a later operation. ***Degree II*** is the same as Degree I, with the exception of automation of some or all of the value-add work required at the operation, like the machine now presses the tab."

"***Degree III***," Steph explained, "builds upon Degree II with the addition of automatic unloading or ejection of the part when the machine cycle is complete. This allows an empty nest to be available to place a part when it is time to run the operation again and eliminates a handling step of unloading the operation. ***Degree IV*** then adds in the automatic loading of the machine."

"And finally," Steph concluded, "***Degree V*** adds in automatically transferring the part to the next operation, typically with a pallet or puck on a conveyance system. This is an important concept. Often, when design engineers work in isolation without an understanding of Lean principles, they may target Degree V as the ideal condition since their mental models focus on minimizing all direct labor and minimizing touching the part. Certain operations in the process may not be able to be fully automated, so the engineers will decide to put in manual work in these trouble spots. What ensues is a mixture of Degree I and Degree V automation on a process that does not flow effectively or efficiently."

> **KEY POINT**
>
> Automation is not inherently good or bad and it is important to select the appropriate degree, based on your unique situation.

Steph summarized, "Looking at our options a little deeper, from an investment standpoint, moving from Degree I to Degree II and from Degree II to Degree III where appropriate, has high return. Once you reach Degree III, the return may not be as great or even positive, depending on the situation. Typically, the capital costs go up an order of magnitude that is not offset by labor or other savings."

"In addition, process reliability," Steph explained, "may be reduced with higher complexity equipment that requires maintenance, changeover, increased indirect costs, and other disruptions. However, safety or quality reasons could force a higher level of automation for a given operation. Looking at our work so far, Concepts 2, 3, and 4 were all at Degree II automation. Our next challenge is to explore incorporating low-cost automation into the process to further add value, approaching Degree III. And what we learn from our mock-up and scorecard will be our guide."

Concept 5

Concept 5 would need to take into account all of the learning from the four concepts, plus the Lean thinking principles that had been taught by the design leaders at key points (Figure 4.3). One observation from all of the manual process concepts was that for each operation that had a machine step, the operation required an initial unloading of the completed part. These operations were candidates for a higher-degree of automation, which would be to safely and effectively auto-eject the part when completed and provide an empty nest for the next part.

The team brainstormed each operation using the full-size rough mock-up. Five operations were identified as candidates for auto-eject: Operations 10b, 20b, 30, 50b, and 60b. The team simulated auto-eject by having Gary and Ted provide the function for the practice build on the mock-up at each candidate station. Gary jokingly muttered, "four years of college and now I'm a

Operation	Description	Operator Time	Machine Time	Total Operation Time*	Equipment Cost	Notes
10a	Device Sub-Assembly 1	6 sec	0 sec	6 sec	$0	Motion Kaizen (-4 sec)
10b	Press Tab 1	2	6	8	$35,000	**Add Auto-Eject (-2 sec)**
20a	Device Sub-Assembly 2	6	0	6	$0	Motion Kaizen (-2 sec)
20b	Press Tab 2	2	6	8	$35,000	**Add Auto-Eject (-2 sec)**
30	Device Heat Weld	2	7	9	$150,000	**Add Auto-Eject (-2 sec)**
40	Device Label	4	0	4	$0	
50a	Plate Sub-Assembly 1	9	0	9	$0	
50b	Crimp 1	2	4	6	$40,000	**Add Auto-Eject (-2 sec)**
60a	Plate Sub-Assembly 2	7	0	7	$0	
60b	Crimp 2	2	6	8	$40,000	**Add Auto-Eject (-2 sec)**
70	Plate Bolt Driving (4)	14	0	14	$15,000	Inline Feeder (-12 sec)
80	Plate Label Press	4	2	6	$35,000	
90	Switch Assembly	15	0	NCT 15	$0	Motion Kaizen (-5 sec)
100	Switch Bolt Driving (4)	14	0	14	$15,000	Inline Feeder (-12 sec)
110a	Case Assembly	13	0	13	$0	Motion Kaizen (-4 sec)
110b	Overweld	4	8	12	$80,000	Decoupled from Leak Test
110c	Leak Test	4	8	12	$80,000	Decoupled from Overweld
120	Packout	3	0	3	$0	

Total Manual Work per Part = 113 seconds, 18 Stations
Capital Cost = $525,000

Total Operation Time = Operator Time (load, internal prep work, unload) + Machine Processing Time*

Figure 4.3 Operator/machine matrix for Concept 5.

part unloading device." Although adding auto-eject to these stations would cost an estimated $55,000, it would reduce the total manual build time for one part by 10 seconds, from 123 to 113 seconds. This, in turn, better balanced the work at the front of the process.

The team was amazed that they continued to "squeeze water from the rock" and gain smoother flow of the work with improved performance. And at the same time, they were beginning to feel worn down by the amount of detailed work and thinking that it took to get to this point. With a planned cycle time of 30 seconds per part and the flexibility to run at different rates, the scorecard was updated for Concept 5 (Figure 4.4). It was time to call it a day.

Concept	Effective Labor Efficiency	Capacity Flexibility (sec / unit)	Lifecycle Cost per Unit	Manual Work per Unit (sec)	Total Lifecycle Labor Investment	Total Lifecycle Capital Investment	Total Lifecycle Operational Cost (Labor + Capital)
1	51%	16	$2.26	120	$6,150,000	$3,600,000	$9,750,000
2	86%	60, 90, 180	$1.88	158	$5,642,857	$2,475,000	$8,117,857
3	86%	30, 45, 60, 90, 180	$1.61	158	$5,642,857	$1,320,000	$6,962,857
4	80%	15, 30, 45, 60, 120	$1.23	123	$4,392,857	$940,000	$5,332,857
5	82%	15, 30, 45, 60, 120	$1.18	113	$4,035,714	$1,050,000	$5,085,714
					Cost Avoidance:		**$4,664,286**

Figure 4.4 Scorecard with Concept 5.

Concept 6

The next morning Steph and Jorge wanted to take the team through a brainstorming session to generate product and process change ideas that could be simulated and evaluated. Steph would lead, but she wanted to avoid jumping to ideas. "Based on the current state of the mock-up and the data like cycle times (Figure 4.5) that we've collected, what are the biggest challenges that are going to require significant effort?," she asked.

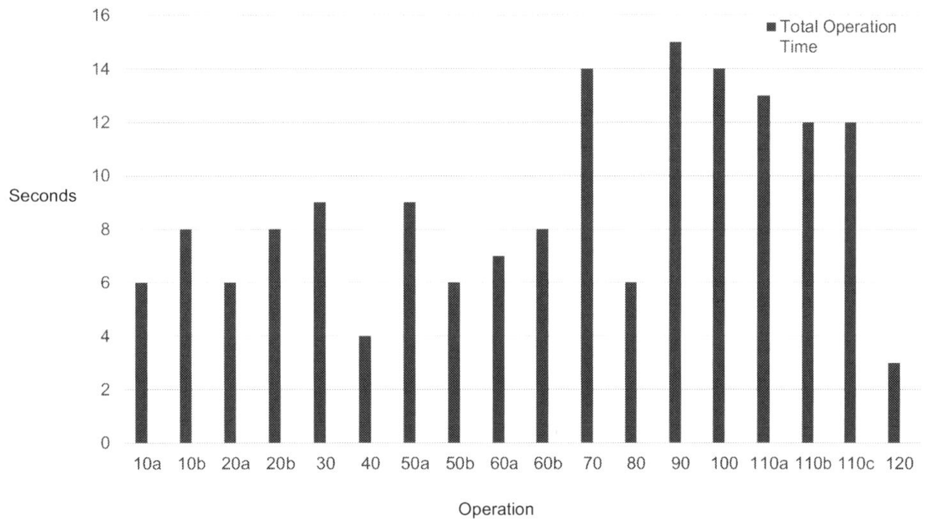

Figure 4.5 Concept 5 imbalance across operations.

There was quick agreement that the process was not balanced across all the stations. The device subprocess area was fast cycle time (about 8–9 seconds), plate subprocess area was a wider range of 9–14 seconds and a mix of manual and machine operations, and final assembly subprocess area was on the higher end of cycle time (about 13–15 seconds) and also had a mix of manual and machine operations (Figure 4.6). In addition, the entire process flow had about half the machine operations with auto-eject, the other half with manual unload. This could potentially be a confusing flow for people, as they experienced during practice builds on the mock-up.

KEY POINT

Even though there are traditionally seven types of waste in operations, one of these types is typically the source of the others, and that waste is overproduction. When a process is initially designed with imbalance, this will naturally lead to overproduction, as well as many of the others wastes.

"Great observations," said Steph. "In general, a process will flow most effectively and efficiently when there is a separation of manual-style operations from machine-style operations. In addition, it will be important later on to balance the work across the necessary number of line members since wait time is very difficult to manage. People naturally want to stay busy. When operations are imbalanced, overproduction and excess inventory will emerge."

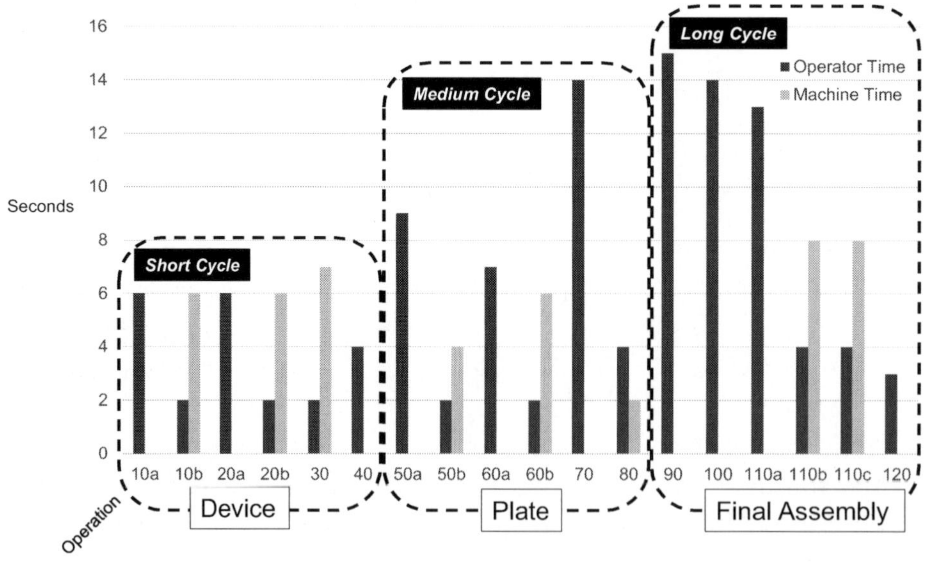

Figure 4.6 Operator/machine balance chart for Concept 5.

Steph continued, "Balance is so critical, but so often overlooked. Too often, process development is satisfied with having enough capacity, regardless of the balance of the work. If we don't identify enough work for one person at a particular operation, or make a person wait for a machine to finish cycling, that specific person may either build ahead or not follow the standard work. Also, from a health and safety perspective, the most reasonable expectation is for us to develop work operations that are meaningful, safe, and balanced."

Steph further explained, "Consider the example (Figure 4.7) where the line planned cycle time is 60 seconds, and five people are all balanced to 50 seconds. There will be a natural tendency to overproduce, as well as it will be difficult to tell abnormal from normal on a cycle-to-cycle basis."

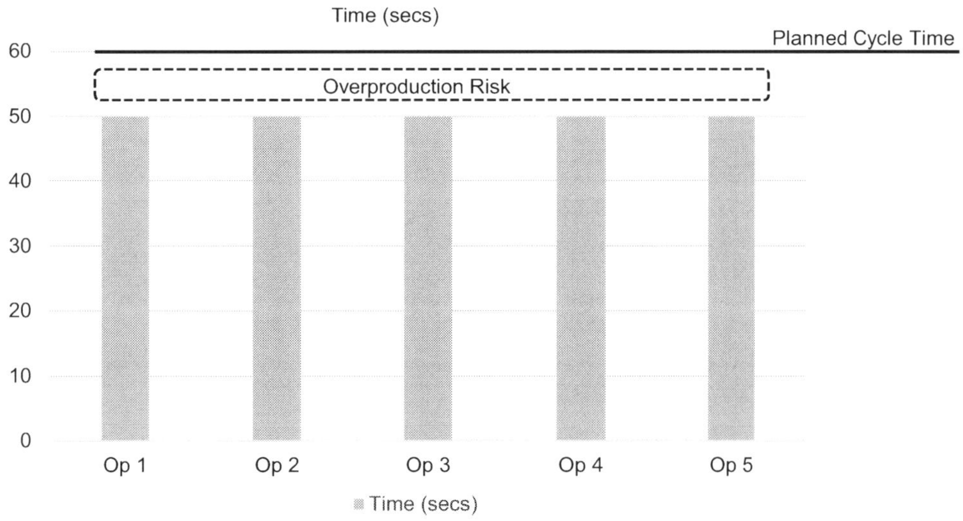

Figure 4.7 Traditional line balancing.

"Can I give you a high-five!?," said Ted. "I've never thought about it this way, but I struggle every day, running operations. Ted, your operator's not following standard work. Ted, why are there extra parts on the line? Ted, where's the lead-off team member? We need to do a change over and she disappeared. Finally, I can see how a poor balance is the root cause of a lot of my operational problems. If the line is balanced and someone doesn't follow the standard work, it will be obvious immediately. And if the line is balanced, I won't have to deal with complaints that this job is too hard, I want that one."

"Great insights, Ted," said Jorge.

Steph closed out this discussion on her example. They could strive to balance their operations and limit overproduction to the planned cycle time of 60 seconds with the previous scenario. In this next scenario (Figure 4.8), four people would be loaded up to 60 seconds, and the fifth person would do remainder of the work that was under the cycle time. This fifth person could help with cycle-to-cycle variability due to product mix or other issues, as well as any noncyclic work that could be isolated at that station from the others, as long as it did not impact the line cycle time.

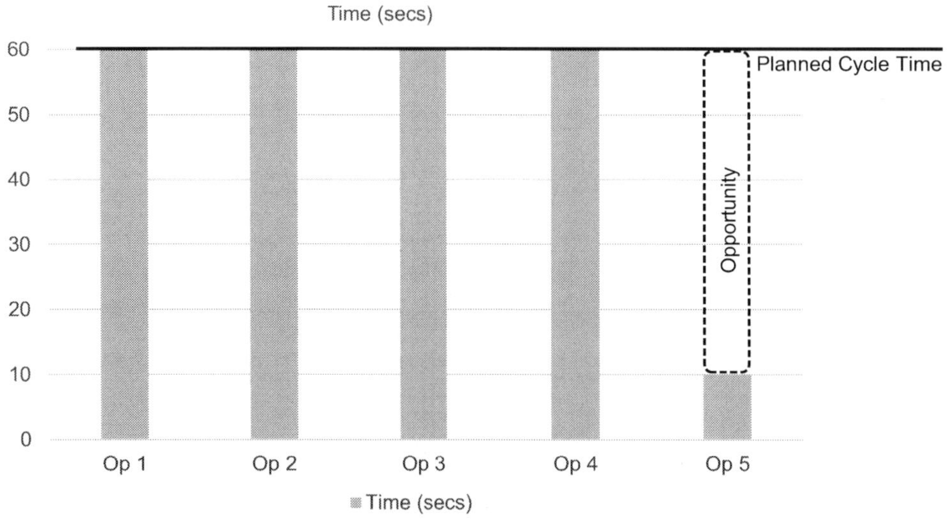

Figure 4.8 Another viewpoint of line balancing.

"Building on that, let's focus on the Plate subprocess area, stations 50a–60b," said Steph. "The challenge will be to develop product- or process-related ideas that will smooth the flow of value-add work through the operation."

A number of ideas were discussed, and one stood out right away—have plates "pre-crimped" by the supplier, or in another area before entering the high-voltage switch (HVS) process. The team felt that crimping was really a fabrication-style process and did not belong in an assembly-style processing area.

Tom and Jolene suggested that one option would be to modify the die design that stamped the plate so that crimping could be done as part of that stamping process. Another option would be for the supplier of the stamped plate to crimp the product for Acme. The current situation in concept 5, with the crimping in-line, would require Acme to invest $80,000 upfront and have manual work done for 4 seconds at the two operations. Additionally, the operations would require about 20 total square feet of space.

Steph asked Tom and Jolene to get an evaluation team of the appropriate stakeholders. Both Tom and Jolene would lead this Crimp Team to figure out how to best bring in pre-crimped plates for this HVS process. The Crimp Team would get 4 hours to brainstorm and come up with 2–3 options to improve safety, quality, and delivery, with the total cost not to exceed $100,000 for any of the options.

To start, the Crimp Team figured out the total lifecycle volume for the High Voltage Switch Product over the estimated 10 years of proposed volumes. The 10-year volume was projected to be 4.32 million units. Every penny of purchased price increase from a supplier would cost $43,200 for Acme over the 10 years. If Acme were to eliminate in-line crimping, it would have to be done for less than 2.3 cents price increase per part, based on the $100,000 cost target.

The options that came out of the brainstorming session focused on two alternatives: re-design the die to enable crimping during the supplier stamping process or have the supplier crimp the plate separate from their stamping area before it was shipped to Acme. The estimated cost to modify the die design with required qualification production test runs was $60,000. The supplier cost estimate to crimp the plate in-house and ship to Acme was a purchase price increase of 11 cents per part, as the supplier would have to pay for the new crimping machines and provide the labor.

Later, the Crimp Team presented the facts they had gathered at the next obeya review along with their recommendation. “Great work,” said Steph. “It looks like modifying the die design to enable in-line crimping is the way to go.”

“I would like to add something,” said Melinda, her mind never far from her quality engineering role. “I have this breakdown of warranty issues and plate edge deformation is the highest occurring defect in regions with extreme temperatures, whether hot or cold. Currently, the components are heat treated then crimped later. With this proposed change the parts will travel through heat treat while crimped, and this will strengthen the edges. This should reduce the specific warranty issue.”

“In other words, you are saying that you support this change too?,” said Steph jokingly. “Absolutely!,” said Melinda.

Jorge stood up, “This reminds me, I want to add a new section to our obeya called ‘Next Time.’ We will begin capturing ideas we have about improving our process creation activities next time. And I think we should start with brainstorming ideas to address our current warranty issues in the new product and process design."

"That would really help us proactively address warranty issues," said Melinda.

Jorge continued, "I want to encourage anyone with a 'Next Time' idea to just simply write it on a post-it and add it to the board (Figure 4.9). These will be part of our reflection after launch."

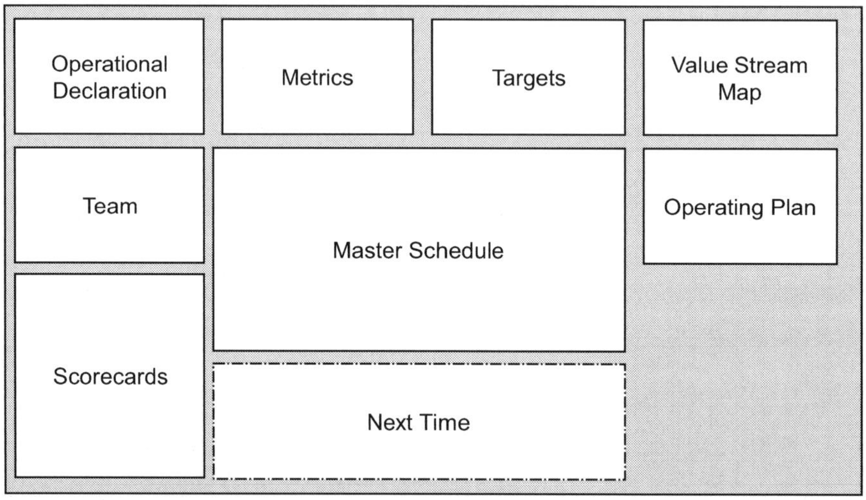

Figure 4.9 Updated obeya.

The pre-crimped part change would be a huge impact if the team could engineer the idea. Based on process knowledge and experience, Tom and Jolene knew that this was highly feasible. With the crimping operations, stations 50b and 60b, now being literally *engineered-out* of the process, the team was also able to do further motion kaizen for the remaining operations of 50a and 60a. The team was going to include the $60,000 die re-design with their scorecard matrix (Figure 4.10) as a cost, but both Steph and Jorge wanted to capture these costs on a separate worksheet since this was what they considered new product and process design *touzen*,[1] or rework.

[1] For further study see, *From Staff Conducting Programs to Line Managers Solving Problems*, Gemba Walks 2nd Edition, p. 71, Jim Womack, Lean Enterprise Institute, 2013.

Operation	Description	Operator Time	Machine Time	Total Operation Time*	Equipment Cost	Notes
10a	Device Sub-Assembly 1	6 sec	0 sec	6 sec	$0	Motion Kaizen (-4 sec)
10b	Press Tab 1	2	6	8	$35,000	Add Auto-Eject (-2 sec)
20a	Device Sub-Assembly 2	6	0	6	$0	Motion Kaizen (-2 sec)
20b	Press Tab 2	2	6	8	$35,000	Add Auto-Eject (-2 sec)
30	Device Heat Weld	2	7	9	$150,000	Add Auto-Eject (-2 sec)
40	Device Label	4	0	4	$0	
50a	Plate Sub-Assembly 1	7	0	7	$0	**Motion Kaizen (-2 sec)**
~~50b~~	**~~Crimp 1~~**	~~2~~	4	~~6~~	**~~$40,000~~**	**Pre-crimpled by Supplier**
60a	Plate Sub-Assembly 2	6	0	6	$0	**Motion Kaizen (-1 sec)**
~~60b~~	**~~Crimp 2~~**	~~2~~	~~6~~	~~8~~	**~~$40,000~~**	**Pre-crimpled by Supplier**
70	Plate Bolt Driving (4)	14	0	14	$15,000	Inline Feeder (-12 sec)
80	Plate Label Press	4	2	6	$35,000	
90	Switch Assembly	15	0	NCT 15	$0	Motion Kaizen (-5 sec)
100	Switch Bolt Driving (4)	14	0	14	$15,000	Inline Feeder (-12 sec)
110a	Case Assembly	13	0	13	$0	Motion Kaizen (-4 sec)
110b	Overweld	4	8	12	$80,000	Decoupled from Leak Test
110c	Leak Test	4	8	12	$80,000	Decoupled from Overweld
120	Packout	3	0	3	$0	

Total Manual Work per Part = 106 seconds, 16 Stations
Capital Cost = $445,000

Total Operation Time = Operator Time (load, internal prep work, unload) + Machine Processing Time*

Figure 4.10 Operator/machine matrix for Concept 6.

The resulting process was reduced to 16 operations and 106 seconds of work per unit (Figure 4.11). Stations 50a and 60a could arguably be combined to one operation since it was similar manual work, but that was a decision that could wait until later.

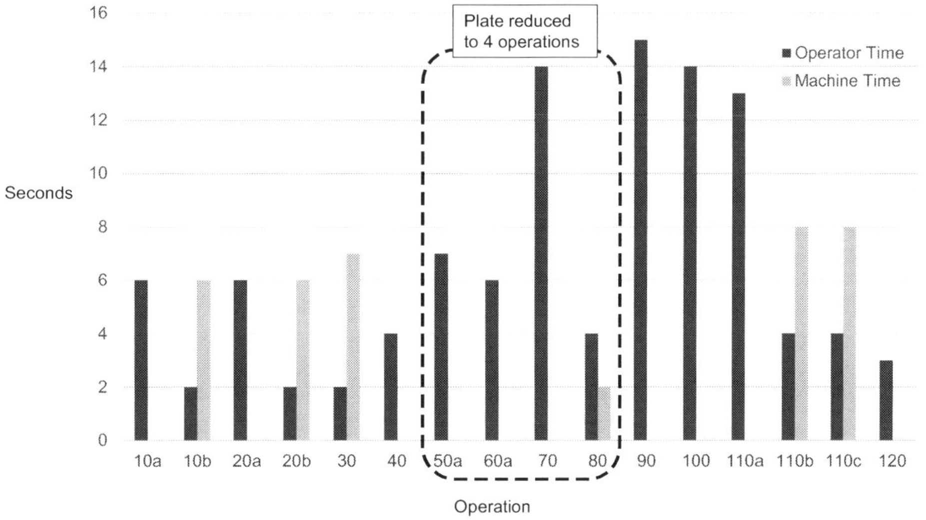

Figure 4.11 Operator/machine balance chart for Concept 6.

More importantly, the team aligned around the fact that the Natural Cycle Time (NCT) of 15 seconds could reasonably match a Planned Cycle Time of 15 seconds at peak volume with workstation designs that exceeded health, safety, and ergonomics targets. With this agreement, there would only be one line necessary to meet peak demand at current forecasts (Figure 4.12).

Concept	Effective Labor Efficiency	Capacity Flexibility (sec / unit)	Lifecycle Cost per Unit	Manual Work per Unit (sec)	Total Lifecycle Labor Investment	Total Lifecycle Capital Investment	Total Lifecycle Operational Cost (Labor + Capital)
1	51%	16	$2.26	120	$6,150,000	$3,600,000	$9,750,000
2	86%	60, 90, 180	$1.88	158	$5,642,857	$2,475,000	$8,117,857
3	86%	30, 45, 60, 90, 180	$1.61	158	$5,642,857	$1,320,000	$6,962,857
4	80%	15, 30, 45, 60, 120	$1.23	123	$4,392,857	$940,000	$5,332,857
5	82%	15, 30, 45, 60, 120	$1.18	113	$4,035,714	$1,050,000	$5,085,714
6	87%	15, 30, 45, 60, 120	$0.98	106	$3,785,714	$445,000	$4,230,714
					Cost Avoidance:		**$5,519,286**

Figure 4.12 Scorecard with Concept 6.

Concept 7

At this point, the Lean Process Creation Team was near the end of narrowing down concepts from experimenting and learning. From an individual operation standpoint, each station was simple and efficient. But from an overall flow perspective across the stations, the part movement and work were not balanced or smooth. Operations 70 and 90–110c were almost double the cycle time of the other operations. In addition, stations 110b and 110c were the only manual/machine mix stations that did not have auto-eject. For Concept 7, the team decided to add the auto-eject for these two stations (Figure 4.13) to reduce the overall work time by 4 more seconds (Figure 4.14).

Operation	Description	Operator Time	Machine Time	Total Operation Time*	Equipment Cost	Notes
10a	Device Sub-Assembly 1	6 sec	0 sec	6 sec	$0	Motion Kaizen (-4 sec)
10b	Press Tab 1	2	6	8	$35,000	Add Auto-Eject (-2 sec)
20a	Device Sub-Assembly 2	6	0	6	$0	Motion Kaizen (-2 sec)
20b	Press Tab 2	2	6	8	$35,000	Add Auto-Eject (-2 sec)
30	Device Heat Weld	2	7	9	$150,000	Add Auto-Eject (-2 sec)
40	Device Label	4	0	4	$0	**Future Challenge**
50a	Plate Sub-Assembly 1	7	0	7	$0	Motion Kaizen (-2 sec)
60a	Plate Sub-Assembly 2	6	0	6	$0	Motion Kaizen (-1 sec)
70	Plate Bolt Driving (4)	14	0	14	$15,000	Inline Feeder (-12 sec)
80	Plate Label Press	4	2	6	$35,000	**Future Challenge**
90	Switch Assembly	15	0	NCT 15	$0	Motion Kaizen (-5 sec)
100	Switch Bolt Driving (4)	14	0	14	$15,000	Inline Feeder (-12 sec)
110a	Case Assembly	13	0	13	$0	Motion Kaizen (-4 sec)
110b	Overweld	2	8	10	$90,000	**Add Auto-Eject (-2 sec)**
110c	Leak Test	2	8	10	$90,000	**Add Auto-Eject (-2 sec)**
120	Packout	3	0	3	$0	

Total Manual Work per Part = 102 seconds, 16 Stations
Capital Cost = $465,000

Total Operation Time = Operator Time (load, internal prep work, unload) + Machine Processing Time*

Figure 4.13 Operator/machine matrix for Concept 7.

KEY POINT

Balance and optimization of the overall process are the priority over individual workstation optimization. Imbalance leads to overproduction, delays, queues, and inventories, all of which erode value to the customer and the process.

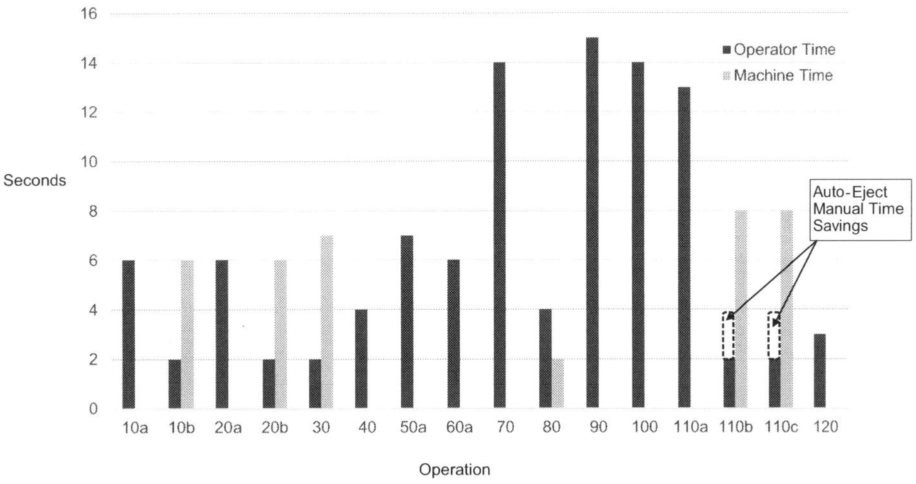

Figure 4.14 Operator/machine balanace chart for Concept 7.

Even though the capital investment from Concept 6 to Concept 7 would go up by $20,000 (Figure 4.15), this more than offset by the fact that each of the 4.32 million units built for the next 10 years would require 4 less seconds of manual time per part, as long as the remaining work could be balanced evenly across the process.

Concept	Effective Labor Efficiency	Capacity Flexibility (sec / unit)	Lifecycle Cost per Unit	Manual Work per Unit (sec)	Total Lifecycle Labor Investment	Total Lifecycle Capital Investment	Total Lifecycle Operational Cost (Labor + Capital)
1	51%	16	$2.26	120	$6,150,000	$3,600,000	$9,750,000
2	86%	60, 90, 180	$1.88	158	$5,642,857	$2,475,000	$8,117,857
3	86%	30, 45, 60, 90, 180	$1.61	158	$5,642,857	$1,320,000	$6,962,857
4	80%	15, 30, 45, 60, 120	$1.23	123	$4,392,857	$940,000	$5,332,857
5	82%	15, 30, 45, 60, 120	$1.18	113	$4,035,714	$1,050,000	$5,085,714
6	87%	15, 30, 45, 60, 120	$0.98	106	$3,785,714	$445,000	$4,230,714
7	84%	15, 30, 45, 60, 120	$0.95	102	$3,642,857	$465,000	$4,107,857
					Cost Avoidance:		$5,642,143

Figure 4.15 Scorecard with Concept 7.

Concept 8

With the practice builds complete for the mock-up of Concept 7, Jorge rolled a portable white board into position, line-side. Steph, armed with markers in hand, started asking the team questions. "What did you observe as we worked the mock-up?"

"Up through plate sub-assembly, I think its station 60a, the work flowed pretty well," said Ted. "But beyond that station the work moves in fits and starts because of differing cycle times."

Station 80 was the Plate Label Press. In the past, the customer-required plate label was always attached to the bottom of the plate once the subassembly was complete. In Concept 7, this Station 80 was an outlier—surrounded by all-manual stations that would be difficult to balance with the label work.

"What if we move the plate label press after the leak test," asked Melinda. "This could actually serve an error-proofing purpose as well as help the balance. We would only label the bottom of the plate if the part passed the Leak Test. If an HVS did not get labeled, the part would be deemed not having passed the test station. And parts that did not pass leak test could be put into a quality hold bin near the station for review as part of the team leader standard work" (Figure 4.16).

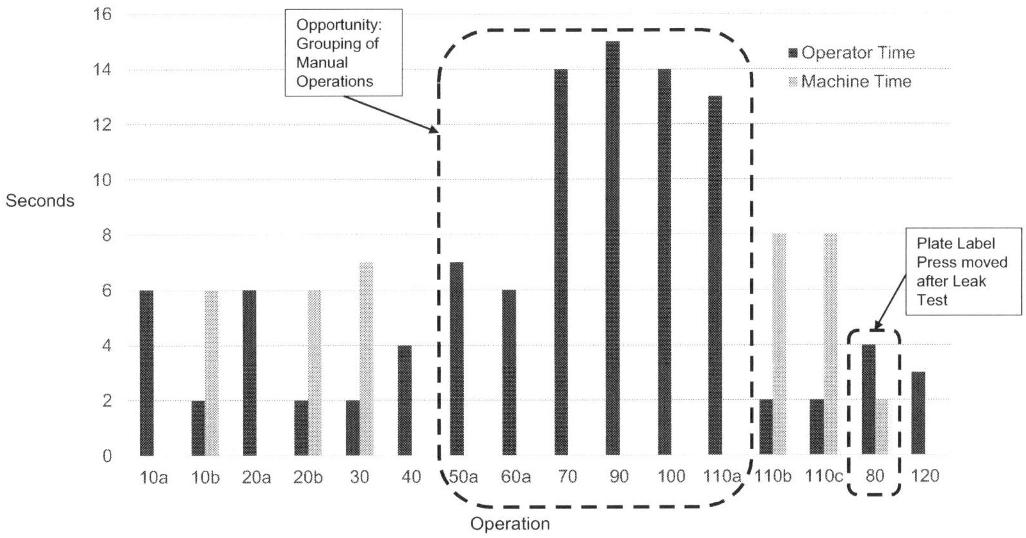

Figure 4.16 Operator/machine balance chart for Concept 8.

"Love your thinking!," said Steph. "Too often people think that quality and productivity are mutually exclusive concepts. If productivity goes up, quality must suffer and vice versa. But if we are creative and tenacious, we can have it all."

"One thing we haven't addressed, and it gets missed in the balance chart, is the issue with station 70," said Ted.

"Can you elaborate?," asked Steph.

Ted said, "Sure, changeover. The plate bolt driving station still has a 10-minute changeover time and we have three different plate options to handle there."

"Ted, Tom and I have been looking at that," said Jolene. "We have a design for a common plate fixture that can easily accommodate all three plate types. We just weren't sure when to share that with the group."

"Now is a great time," said Ted smugly. Jolene shared the concept with Ted and the team. The general consensus was that the idea was fundamentally sound, and they would make a prototype fixture to test the suggestion while observing any consequences to the overall process.

"I'm still wondering, do we really need three different plates?," asked Alexis.

Jorge replied, "Capture that thought on a post-it in the 'Next Time' section of our obeya. We should at least have a conversation about part proliferation and the impact that has on changeover. There might be a common part solution, or perhaps there isn't, so we have to think about creative changeover methods. But in either case, it would be best to have these discussions even earlier, before the product design is settled."

The flow of the HVS process was much more even but would still need to be improved in the Configure phase (Figure 4.17). The longer manual workstations were all co-located, but the process still was imbalanced overall—the first half was much faster than the latter half. From an operational standpoint, this process was highly capable and the next phase of Lean process creation work would develop countermeasures to balance the flow even better.

Operation	Description	Operator Time	Machine Time	Total Operation Time*	Equipment Cost	Notes
10a	Device Sub-Assembly 1	6 sec	0 sec	6 sec	$0	Motion Kaizen (-4 sec)
10b	Press Tab 1	2	6	8	$35,000	Add Auto-Eject (-2 sec)
20a	Device Sub-Assembly 2	6	0	6	$0	Motion Kaizen (-2 sec)
20b	Press Tab 2	2	6	8	$35,000	Add Auto-Eject (-2 sec)
30	Device Heat Weld	2	7	9	$150,000	Add Auto-Eject (-2 sec)
40	Device Label	4	0	4	$0	Future Challenge
50a	Plate Sub-Assembly 1	7	0	7	$0	Motion Kaizen (-2 sec)
60a	Plate Sub-Assembly 2	6	0	6	$0	Motion Kaizen (-1 sec)
70	Plate Bolt Driving (4)	14	0	14	$15,000	Inline Feeder (-12 sec)
90	Switch Assembly	15	0	NCT 15	$0	Motion Kaizen (-5 sec)
100	Switch Bolt Driving (4)	14	0	14	$15,000	Inline Feeder (-12 sec)
110a	Case Assembly	13	0	13	$0	Motion Kaizen (-4 sec)
110b	Overweld	2	8	10	$90,000	Add Auto-Eject (-2 sec)
110c	Leak Test	2	8	10	$90,000	Add Auto-Eject (-2 sec)
80	Plate Label Press	4	2	6	$35,000	**Product Re-design**
120	Packout	3	0	3	$0	

Total Manual Work per Part = 102 seconds, 16 Stations
Capital Cost = $465,000

Total Operation Time = Operator Time (load, internal prep work, unload) + Machine Processing Time*

Figure 4.17 Operator/machine matrix for Concept 8.

From a timing perspective, the team needed to begin configuring the selected concept in order to meet start of production (SOP) targets. In addition, the team needed to continue capturing the knowledge that was gained going through the HVS process creation cycle, in order to feedback the learning for the next generation of concurrent product and process development (Figure 4.18).

Concept	Effective Labor Efficiency	Capacity Flexibility (sec / unit)	Lifecycle Cost per Unit	Manual Work per Unit (sec)	Total Lifecycle Labor Investment	Total Lifecycle Capital Investment	Total Lifecycle Operational Cost (Labor + Capital)
1	51%	16	$2.26	120	$6,150,000	$3,600,000	$9,750,000
2	86%	60, 90, 180	$1.88	158	$5,642,857	$2,475,000	$8,117,857
3	86%	30, 45, 60, 90, 180	$1.61	158	$5,642,857	$1,320,000	$6,962,857
4	80%	15, 30, 45, 60, 120	$1.23	123	$4,392,857	$940,000	$5,332,857
5	82%	15, 30, 45, 60, 120	$1.18	113	$4,035,714	$1,050,000	$5,085,714
6	87%	15, 30, 45, 60, 120	$0.98	106	$3,785,714	$445,000	$4,230,714
7	84%	15, 30, 45, 60, 120	$0.95	102	$3,642,857	$465,000	$4,107,857
8	84%	15, 30, 45, 60, 120	$0.95	102	$3,642,857	$465,000	$4,107,857
					Cost Avoidance:		$5,642,143

Figure 4.18 Scorecard with Concept 8.

THE STEERING TEAM—PLANNING FOR BREADTH

The obeya meeting the prior day went very well. The steering team was impressed with the progress made to date. Even though the steering team was regularly meeting with the Lean Process Creation team in the obeya, Jon Jain had chosen to keep the smaller steering team meeting functioning as well. "Just my small band of thieves," he thought. He liked the idea of the steering team having time to discuss strategic issues without an audience present.

"It scares me to think that our status-quo would have launched with concept 1," said Jon.

"Yes, and spent an extra $5,000,000 without even knowing it," said Dave.

Jon continued, "We have smart, well-intentioned employees—how could things be so wrong?"

"It really comes down to a few things", said Leslie. "As you said, we have the people. How engaged they are is another question. We can tell them we want their input. We can launch engagement initiatives with detailed surveys, but until the work they do enables engagement, it's just words. It is kind of like the difference of wanting to be healthier and just making New Year's resolutions versus actually changing your behavior and exercising. The new style of working has to be more than words, it has to be part of a process."

"Speaking of process, although it may be obvious to you and to the Lean Process Creation team, I'm not seeing a lot of the process being documented," said Cheryl. "I'm thinking about how we spread this to other employees. I do not, I repeat, I do not want a typical training rollout. I think we can do better with some sort of on-the-job approach. But that will be hard to design if this better process is just the collective experiences of the chosen few. Can we get them to begin writing this down without overburdening the team?"

"Great points, Cheryl. I think we just have to make the ask," said Jon.

"I was thinking the same thing during our last obeya meeting," said Paul. "The obeya is losing a bit of its program clarity. Although I love the idea of the 'Next Time' section, it really doesn't help with this program. I was going to suggest to Steph that the team creates a second obeya focused on the overarching process. Ask them to start documenting their steps, things they'd do differently, rework they've done—just to name a few items. And put them all on this second obeya. It would help to clean up the Project Franklin obeya and help us to see the new process."

"And help us to think about how to broadly deploy what we are learning," added Leslie.

Must-Do Actions for Converge

1. Agree on the plan to "thin the herd" of options (4-2-1, 7-4-2-1, etc.).
2. Determine the target-level of automation to aim for with the process.
3. Balance across your process (and understand the consequences of poor balance).

Key Questions for Converge

- What were the key points of your Operational Declaration? Are they being met? What needs to be adjusted?
- What is the proper degree of automation for your process?
- Where are the opportunities to use low-cost automation to support the people doing the work?
- What process design challenges would help to improve the value?
- What product design challenges would help to improve the value?
- How will you quantify the new concepts that emerge during this phase?
- How balanced is the flow of the product through the operations in your process?

Chapter 5

CONfigure

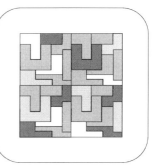

There's no magic in magic, it's all in the details.

—Walt Disney

Purpose: Refining the selected process concept to maximize value-added activities supported by a robust material and information flow system and an appropriate management system (MS).

Section Prologue: *With the best-known concept selected, the team begins the work of Configure. To meet the goals of Configure, the team will need to look at the detailed work in each station, the station as it relates to others, the integration of all materials in and out, and the resulting production system's connection into the value stream and the Adrian plant footprint.*

Engaging the Remaining Enterprise

"Although we've accomplished a lot in just a few weeks, as they say, the devil is in the details," said Steph, who was unusually bright and chipper for such an early hour. "Concept 8 is essentially a schematic work flow with accompanying rough mock-ups. Not bad, but we have much more to learn and do. We need to continue to reach out beyond our team and engage more and more stakeholders."

"This team seems large already," observed Carla.

Steph replied, "Yes, it is—but the truth is there are a lot of stakeholders that make a good process come together. And if we exclude someone in the name of keeping the team artificially small, we'll miss something. I'm not

DOI: 10.4324/9781003219712-7

saying we need dedicated resources from every function that touches Project Franklin, but we do need to figure out whom to engage and how to do it most effectively."

"So, whom else do we need?," asked Melinda.

"I'd like to get a team member involved," said Alexis. "Their input on the workplace design would be invaluable. They have to do this work over and over and they'll notice things none of us will see."

"I can make that happen," said Ted. As the operations representative, he had already made up his mind to engage the team members. But it was even better if someone else on the team brought up the idea. Ted continued, "The team members have a list of issues with the current workplace designs and it would be a big win, and create a lot of buy-in, if they could be part of eliminating those issues. In fact, I've got another item for our 'Next Time' board—engage team members in the concepts phase and do a current issues review."

"Add it to the board," said Jorge.

"I'd feel more comfortable if we engaged key machine vendors, especially for our more complicated or specialized equipment," said Jolene.

"Yes, device heat weld, overweld and leak test at a minimum," added Tom. Steph captured the comments on a whiteboard. "Anyone else?," she asked.

"Yes," said Gary, "we need to involve our suppliers as well. Material is often an afterthought and we end up shoe-horning racks around the cell at the last minute and no one is happy."

"Sounds like we have all of the angles covered," said Steph, "People, machines, and materials. Gary, I'm going to ask you to lead the work on materials. I know you have some deep experience to add. Alexis, please take the lead on the people aspects. And Tom, it's only natural you have machines. Pull on the core team members as you need their help and reach out beyond the core team as well. Melinda, I'm going to ask that you rotate between all three groups, as quality impacts all of them."

Steph continued, "We'll start each morning with a debrief of accomplishments from the previous day, next steps, and help needed. This will keep us all aligned. And at any time, if one of you needs to get everyone together, just pull the andon with Jorge and me and we'll round up everyone else. As we integrate the team member, machines, and materials, there will be trade-offs. And when making trade-offs, a good question to ask is, what is best for the team member?"

Materials

Gary had gathered representatives from purchasing, safety, and transportation into a make-shift conference room in the northwest corner of the obeya room. Separated from the rest of the room by a few rolling white boards, Gary had prepared to review a bit of a history of material flow improvements at Acme, just to be sure everyone was on the same page. Alexis and Tom also joined–partly to work through decisions that might affect their sub-teams, and partly to support Gary.

Gary began, "A key target for all the Project Franklin components is to keep team member motions in the 'green zone' for safe and efficient movement (Figure 5.1). This means that the components need to be delivered as close to the point of use as possible."

Figure 5.1 Target zone.

Drawing a quick sketch on one of the boards, Gary continued, "This is what our workplaces used to look like. A team member surrounded by large containers of component parts, which resulted in long reaches and twisting motions. The materials were actually in the way of their own flow."

"Is this why we've been shifting to smaller containers of parts from our vendors?," asked one of the purchasing agents. Gary responded, "Yes, but you will see the impact of those smaller containers goes far beyond the workplace to our internal transportation systems, to our supermarket designs, and to our inventory turns themselves. I'm digressing a bit, but learning to present the materials to the team member in smaller containers was a critical first step."

Gary continued, "Once we have smaller containers, we still need to get them to and from the team members without getting in their way. And this means placing as much material as possible right in front of the team member. Of course, this is impossible if we purchase equipment that has a control panel mounted in the way. So, we learned to locate control panels out of the way of the material flow as well, typically keeping them low to the ground. In fact, we developed a five-step method to design a work station with the engineers." Gary listed out the five-step method on a white board.

1. Place the necessary tooling in the optimal work envelope or zone
2. Present all component parts perfectly and closely within the field of vision ("green zone")
3. Determine the container removal and replenishment method
4. Mount the hardware and control enclosures (e.g., back-side of machine)
5. Attach the appropriate and reasonable safety guarding

"At the Adrian operation, we've experimented with many different component delivery techniques over the past five years. Early on, the material movement strategy was to put all the components on pull, which used min/max levels and physical cards to signal replenishment. The pull system seemed rather simple, but had its limits. This worked well where a component had limited variety. Where there was high variety, work stations tended to be over-sized to fit all the components for presentation, which led to drawn-out visual searches and long, inconsistent reaches."

Gary quickly sketched another image of a frustrated team member surrounded by smaller containers, but lots of different varieties. It was as though someone replicated the stockroom right in their workplace, just a bit smaller.

Gary continued, "About three years ago, the Adrian plant started sequentially delivering all the components at a set time, based on observations from benchmarking visits to automotive and aerospace companies. Components would be kitted in a separate area and delivered to the point of use on the assembly line. This worked well to minimize the amount of line-side inventory for high variety components that accumulated due to changeovers, but it also had its limitations. If there was rework or scrap on a part, the entire production line could stop while waiting for delivery of the replacement components. Safety stock near the line helped with these types of issues, but component rotation needed to be practiced and it was also a time-consuming process."

Lastly, Gary added, "In addition, kitting is an expensive activity since it was essentially re-packing of supplied parts. For some parts, the process of kitting seemed illogical since every finished product needed the same item, so little value came from counting out low-cost bolts or plastic end caps, for example."

"Thanks for that history, Gary," said Tom. "But I'm a bit confused, neither approach seems to work that great—so, which is best for Project Franklin?"

"Does it have to be an either-or situation?," asked Alexis.

"I think you are on to something," said Gary excitedly. "I've been thinking that we have two types of parts. Those that are used on most or all of our final assemblies and those that we need to swap out at change over. Why not use different techniques with the different parts?"

Common and Unique Parts

Gary continued, "I've been leveraging my participation with this team to proactively create a part plan database, commonly called the Plan for Every Part (PFEP). I've started simple (Figure 5.2). It includes the part numbers, storage locations, where used, packaging size, box quantity, part weight, order frequency, supplier, supplier location, transport method and more. The beauty is that we can add fields as we discover new needs. This

Acme Devices, High Voltage Switch	
External Plan for Every Part (PFEP)	
Assembly Numbers:	FA-1 to FA-22 (22 final part numbers)
Assembly Name:	High Voltage Switch, Generation 3.0

Total Daily Usage =	3200 parts
Shifts per Day =	2 shifts
Usage per Shift =	1600 parts
Average Usage per Hour =	200 parts
Planned Cycle Time (PCT) =	15 seconds per part
100% Usage per Hour =	240 parts

	Part Number	Description	Average Daily Usage	Usage Location	Market Storage Location	Order Frequency	Minimum Order Quantity	Supplier Name	Supplier City	Supplier State	Supplier Country	Expendable or Returnable Tote	Total Container Weight (lbs)	Part Weight (lbs)
	DB1	Device Base	3200	10a	AA-A-1	Daily	4000	ABC	Fort Wayne	IN	USA	Expendable	25	0.10
20 types	CB1	Circuit Board	3200	10a	AD-B-3	Weekly	360	Board-Com	Phoenix	AZ	USA	Expendable	3	0.05
3 types	PL1	Aluminum Plate	1248	50a	AF-C-1	Daily	2400	Stamp City	Grand Rapids	MI	USA	Returnable	12.5	0.25
	PL2	Aluminum Plate	1728	50a	AF-C-2	Daily	2400	Stamp City	Grand Rapids	MI	USA	Returnable	12.5	0.25
	PL3	Aluminum Plate	224	50a	AF-C-3	Weekly	2400	Stamp City	Grand Rapids	MI	USA	Returnable	12.5	0.25
	BS1	Battery Snap	6400	50a							USA			
5 types	MBB1	MicroBattery Backup, Type1	2400	60a	AN-B-1	Daily	1000	Battery Mart	Buena Park	CA	USA	Expendable	20	0.02
	MBB2	MicroBattery Backup, Type2	600	60a	AN-B-2	Daily	1000	Battery Mart	Buena Park	CA	USA	Expendable	20	0.02
	MBB3	MicroBattery Backup, Type3	100	60a	AN-B-3	Bi-Weekly	1000	Battery Mart	Buena Park	CA	USA	Expendable	20	0.02
	MBB4	MicroBattery Backup, Type4	50	60a	AN-A-1	Monthly	1000	Battery Mart	Buena Park	CA	USA	Expendable	20	0.02
	MBB5	MicroBattery Backup, Type5	50	60a	AN-A-2	Monthly	1000	Battery Mart	Buena Park	CA	USA	Expendable	20	0.02

Figure 5.2 Plan for Every Part (PFEP) database.

simple database helps us to plan out our entire material movement system. We often collect this data at the last minute or even after start of production, but I felt, to do this right, we needed to capture the data as early as possible."

"Using this database," said Gary, "I was able to construct this simple final product/component matrix–and it is quite revealing (Figure 5.3). Down the left you see all of the final assembly part numbers and across the top you see all of the component families, as well as their corresponding part numbers. In the body of the matrix, I have places 'X' marks in cells to indicate that a particular final assembly uses a particular part number. Following me so far?" Heads were nodding around the room which just energized Gary a bit more. "For our discussion, let's focus on FA-1 through 5, they represent 70% of the volume and can demonstrate the use of this matrix. What do you notice?"

	Component Type											
	Control Boards				Plates				Bolts			
Final Assembly	CB1	CB2	CB3	CB4	PL1	PL2	PL3	PL4	BT1	BT2	BT3	BT4
FA-1	X				X					X		
FA-2			X		X					X		
FA-3		X			X					X		
FA-4				X	X					X		
FA-5				X		X				X		

Figure 5.3 Product/component matrix.

A purchasing agent sitting near the door said, "It looks like we only need one bolt for everything."

Gary responded, "Yes, it does seem that way. The other bolts get used on very low volume models, but for most of the time, BT2 is the one we need. We're going to call this a *common part.* What else do you see?"

"If the bolts are common, the control boards are just the opposite. They seem to be different for every final assembly," said Tom.

"Exactly!," said Gary. "We are going to call this a *unique* part."

"And what about the plates?," asked Alexis. "Let's come back to those in a minute," answered Gary.

For the new high-voltage switch (HVS), there were two primary types of components—common and unique. This was an important categorization since common components will have a different signaling method for delivery than a unique component will have.

"Envision this," said Gary, "common parts are delivered via a two-card kanban system. They are simply replenished as they are consumed. But the unique parts are kitted, except the kit is created real time, order by order."

"I'm kind of following you," said Alexis, "keep going."

"See if this helps," said Gary, and he quickly drew a sketch on the board (Figure 5.4).

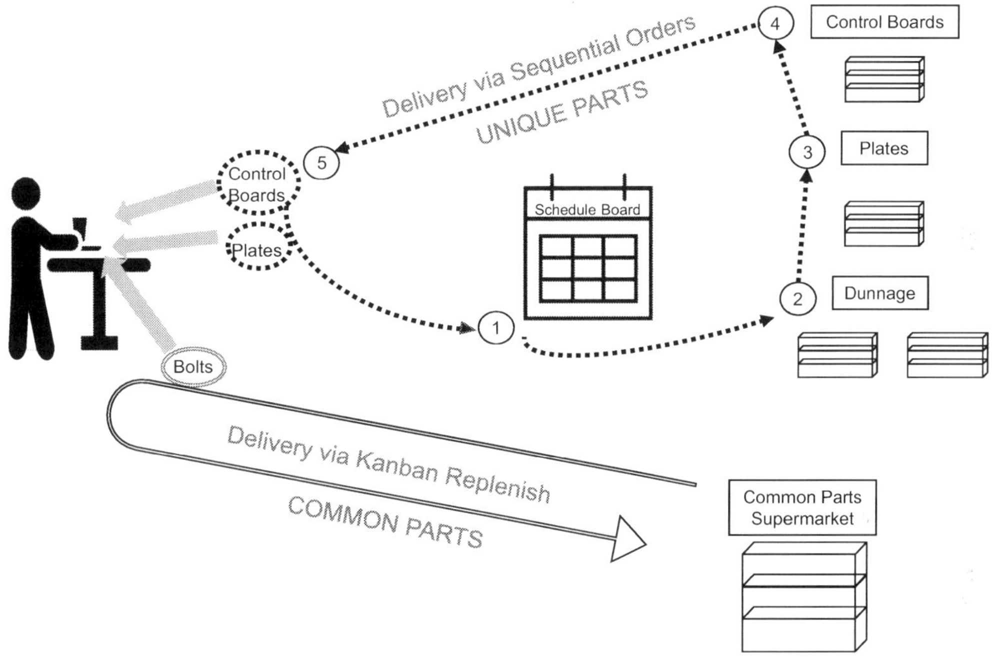

Figure 5.4 Common/unique routes.

Gary continued, "First, you see how the bolts, or common parts, are on a different material delivery route than the unique parts? They need to be simply replenished. On the other hand, the unique parts need to be introduced in just the right quantity, right when the line is changing over. This is almost impossible if there are multiple sources of scheduling information, but if we leverage a single scheduling board—somewhere near shipping and where we store our empty dunnage—the arrival of the sequential parts can be the schedule (Figure 5.5). In this case, the materials person will grab the next order from the scheduling board, select the appropriate dunnage in the quantity needed, and then proceed to the plate and control board areas and do the same. In essence, they are building the 'kit' for the order using the order itself."

Alexis interjected, "If I am following you, all operations does is build what they receive in the sequence it is received?"

"Yes," said Carla.

Alexis continued, "This can be huge—operations focusing on building quality parts and not worrying about schedule or component availability! Melinda will be geeked."

Gary responded, "Yes, that's part of the logic of having the schedule board near shipping. If production control does their job, operations shouldn't really care about the schedule. They know that they are going to receive their next order in so many minutes. Meanwhile, production control in shipping does need to know the status of all of the orders. So, the schedule board can be laid out like so."

Gary added, "Anyone walking by this board can see the instant health of the entire plant in a single glance."

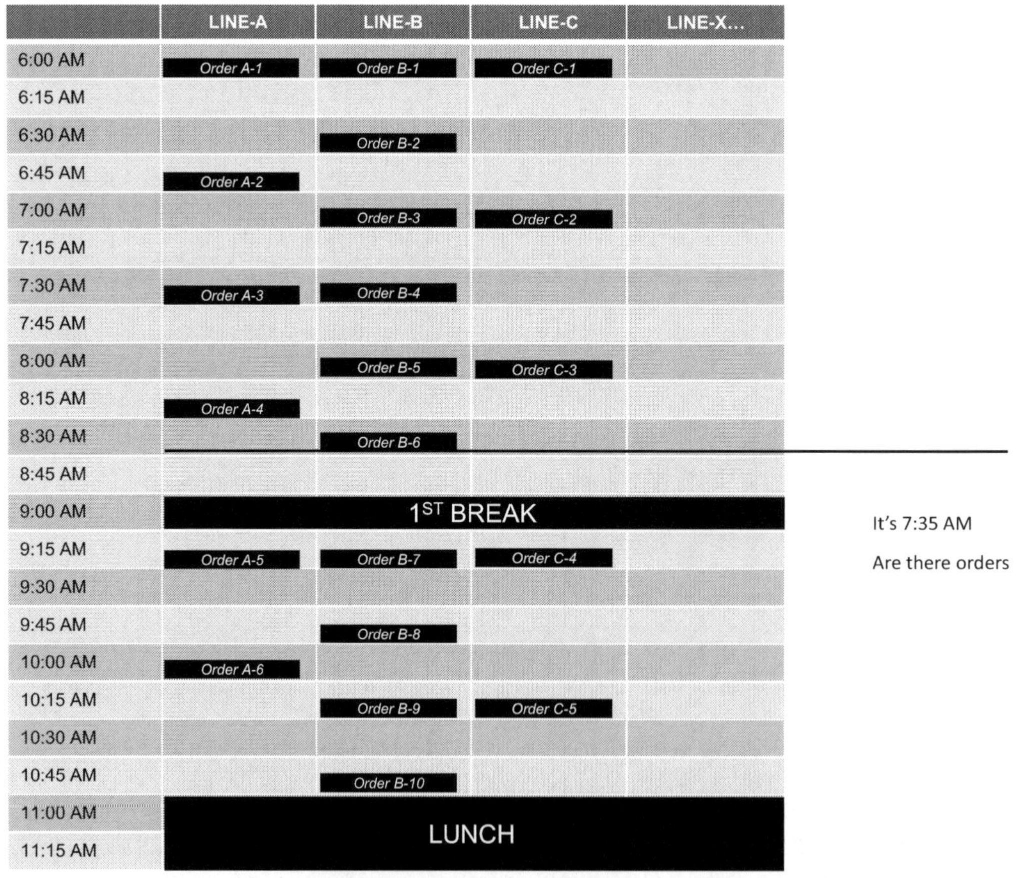

LINE-A
LINE-B
LINE-C
LINE-X...
6:00 AM
6:15 AM
6:30 AM
6:45 AM
7:00 AM
7:15 AM
7:30 AM
7:45 AM
8:00 AM
8:15 AM
8:30 AM
8:45 AM
9:00 AM
9:15 AM
9:30 AM
9:45 AM
10:00 AM
10:15 AM
10:30 AM
10:45 AM
11:00 AM
11:15 AM
Order A-1
Order B-1
Order C-1
Order B-2
Order A-2
Order B-3
Order C-2
Order A-3
Order B-4
Order B-5
Order C-3
Order A-4
Order B-6
1ST BREAK
Order A-5
Order B-7
Order C-4
Order B-8
Order A-6
Order B-9
Order C-5
Order B-10
LUNCH
It's 7:35 AM
Are there orders

Figure 5.5 Example of a schedule board layout.

"How so?," asked the transportation manager.

Gary answered, "If it is 7:35, there should not be any orders remaining on the board at 7:30 and earlier. In this case, if order B4 is still on the board, I need to see what is going on at line-B. And that person can be the shipping supervisor, it can be the plant manager, or it can be anyone else" (Figure 5.6).

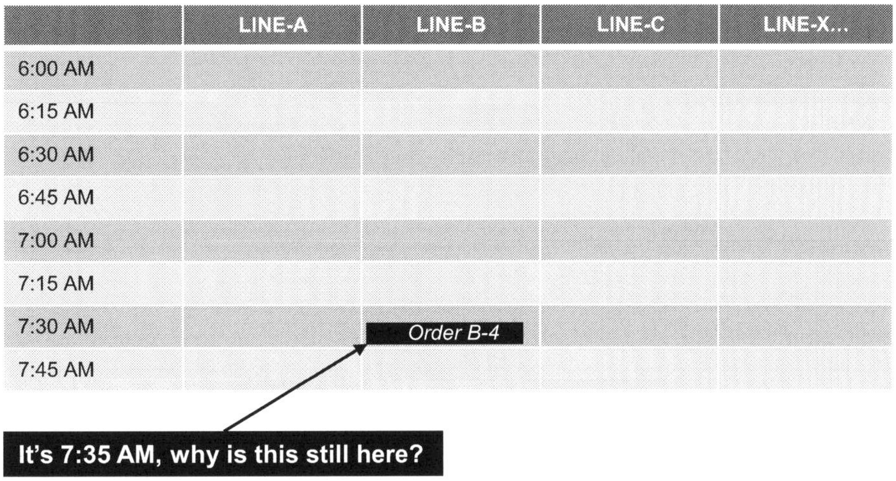

Figure 5.6 Schedule board abnormality.

"But isn't this all in the computer?," asked a buyer.

"Maybe," answered Gary. "It's in the computer if someone puts it in there or if we add technology to make people put it there—but now we have strayed from doing value-added work to feeding the beast. On the other hand, parts don't lie. If the order is still on the board, I can quickly walk to the line and see what is happening. If they are idle and waiting for incoming parts, then we have a material delivery issue. If they have parts but are behind, we can see what is going on and get them the help they need. Simple–nothing to update, except when we actually ship the order, then the computer is critical. But we're keeping the computer work away from the value-added work at the line."

The buyer seemed satisfied with that answer.

"I'm still thinking about the plates," said Alexis. "A replenishment system certainly appears to be simpler—it doesn't rely on the ballet-like timing of connecting materials delivery to change over. Is it possible to treat them like a common part and have both, or even all four, available on the line?" (Figure 5.7)

	Component Type											
	Control Boards				Plates				Bolts			
Final Assembly	CB1	CB2	CB3	CB4	PL1	PL2	PL3	PL4	BT1	BT2	BT3	BT4
FA-1	X				X					X		
FA-2			X		X					X		
FA-3		X			X					X		
FA-4				X	X					X		
FA-5				X		X				X		
	Unique				Common Candidate?				Common			

Figure 5.7 Updated product/component matrix.

"Great question," said Gary. "Our first hurdle is the cost of a plate. If they are relatively inexpensive parts, then they might be a candidate for replenishment. The next hurdle is understanding if they will fit. And if yes, the final hurdle is not as obvious, but it is how to present them such that they can be easily reached, but error-proof their presentation so the wrong one can't be accidently selected."

"I think we have yes on both one and two," said Alexis, "but I'm not sure about three. The error-proofing specifically."

"Let me share a simple idea—just as a thought starter," said Gary. As Gary sketched another diagram, Alexis thought, "No wonder he's been so quiet up until now—his guy needs a pen in hand to talk." This made her smile a bit.

Gary continued, "Think about creating a part presentation device that holds all the types of plates (Figure 5.8), three in this case, but only the plate currently being used is accessible—the other two are blocked off in some manner. I've seen this done with simple inserts or doors placed in the way during set-up, and I've seen gates that are physically integrated into the part rack itself. And for our plates, I'm sure there are other options too."

"Cool," said Alexis, with a smile on her face that revealed she did have another idea.

As the meeting adjourned there was a buzz around the room. Buyers and purchasing managers now had a better understanding of why smaller packaging was so critical. Transportation could see how a schedule board managed by production control, but kept in the shipping area, was critical to the overall flow of the plant. And Tom and Alexis had enough of an

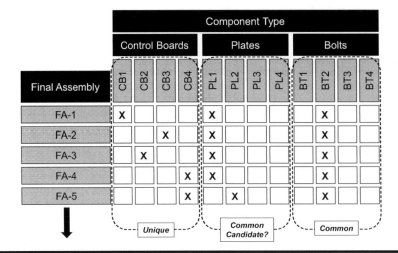

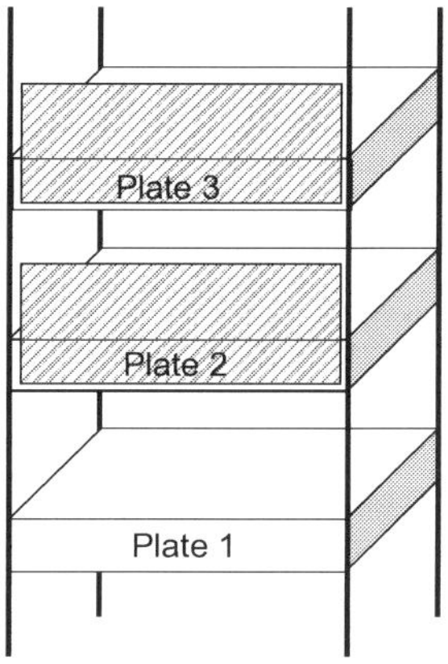

Figure 5.8 Example error-proofed material rack.

understanding of the materials vision that they were confident in moving forward with their sub-teams.

Workplace Design Details

Foundational to the Acme Production System were the two pillars of its house: Quantity Control and Quality Control. Quantity Control was well under way with Gary's leadership in Production Control and Logistics. It was now time for Alexis and her sub-team to tackle Operation's primary role of Quality Control. Alexis asked Melinda to be part of her sub-team for workplace design. Ted and Jolene asked to participate as well. Alexis also asked Ted to bring production team members to their meeting–something they should have done much earlier. "Well, next time," she thought.

> **KEY POINT**
>
> When we think of "QC," we have a tendency to think "quality control." Another key "QC" term is "quantity control." With Lean process creation, the goal is to have QC and QC—*quantity control and quality control.*

As the team filed into the room, they noticed a handwritten agenda on the board (Figure 5.9).

Alexis began, "Today we're going to leverage the mock-up in this room to refine each of the workstations. On the board, I have written four steps we will go through for each workstation. But I want to call your attention to what I have written at the bottom of the board, it's a progression of standard work capability of sorts, complete with a true north. It starts with a system

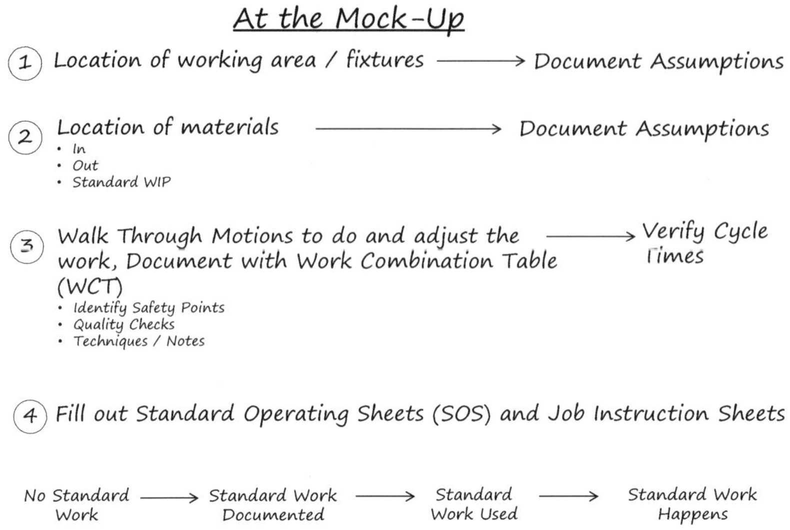

Figure 5.9 Mock-up agenda.

in which there is no standard work. Many organizations say they understand the need, then document the standard work and stop there. It is as though the purpose was to write it down."

Alexis added, "We need to be thinking about developing standard work that will actually be used and become the basis for improvement. And better yet, we should be thinking about designing the workplaces such that standard work just happens—the layout of the workplace suggests the standard work, it is almost intuitive. In other words, we make it easier to do the work correctly than to do it wrong. I realize that isn't possible everywhere, but it is a good ideal to reach for. But that's enough about true north, let's take a look at Operation 10a, Device Sub-assembly 1."

The team pretended to build parts at the station for 10a, paying particular attention to the location of the fixture, the activation switch, incoming materials, and outgoing materials. With a focus on simplifying the work and minimizing the motions, they made adjustments to the location of the incoming materials. The team member had noticed that the circuit boards, which require precise handling, were at the 3:00 position, while the tabs, which are easy to handle and orient were at the 12:00 position (Figure 5.10).

Alexis asked, "Can we swap these part locations? That way any team member can grab the circuit board at 12:00 with their dominant hand."

"I've never thought about placing the difficult to manipulate parts at 12:00, but it sure makes sense," said Ted.

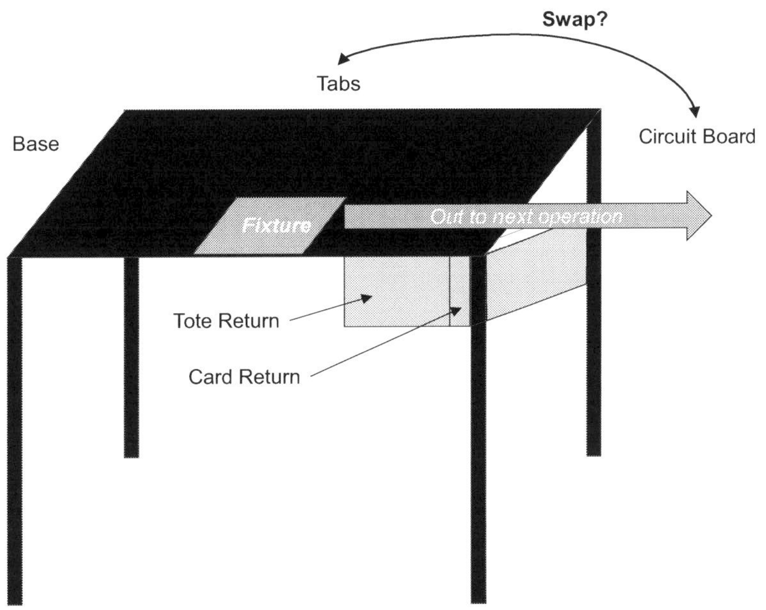

Figure 5.10 Station 10a workstation detail.

The team also had a discussion about the location of the return flow rack for empty totes. They decided to locate the rack under the workstation, as placing the rack between operation 10a and 10b would make the cell larger, adding walking or reaches.

"I've watched the material handlers on our current cells struggle to search for kanban cards to replenish," said Jolene. "Can we standardize the card chutes, and maybe even paint them a bright color, to simplify the searching?"

"Let's give it a try on the mock-up, and then we can bring a material handler by to get their reaction," said Alexis.

The team decided to finalize each operation's layout before documenting the work in a work combination table (WCT), standard operating sheet (SOS), and job instruction sheet (JIS), just in case the layout decisions made in one operation impacted the location of materials in another. As each WCT, SOS, and JIS was completed, a copy was taped up on the corresponding set of stations. Eventually the entire mock-up had been documented (Figure 5.11).

Standing back and observing the mock-up, Tom spoke, "I appreciate all the detailed work we've done, right down to the second. But I feel like the elephant in the room are the minutes and hours we often lose to downtime and set-ups."

Job Instruction Sheet	Part Number: FA-1	Required Quantity: 1600 per shift at peak demand	Dept: Assembly Shop	Team Leader: J.Morgan
Stations: 110b, 110c, 80, and 120	Part Name: High Voltage Switch	Date: December 12, 2020	Prepared by: MZ /EE	Supervisor: J.Shook

#	Step	QC Sampling	QC Tool	Notes	Manual Time
1	Get Part from Case Assembly WIP and Load Overweld Fixture			*Overweld Machine CT of 8 seconds*	2
2	Load auto-ejected part from Overweld to Leak Test Fixture			*Leak Test Machine CT of 8 seconds*	2
3	Check appearance of welded area	100%	Visual	Simultaneously check while moving part to next step	
4	Load auto-ejected part from Leak Test to Plate Label Press				4
5	Wait 2 seconds for Plate Label Press Machine Cycle and unload Part				2
6	Check appearance of Label	100%	Visual	Simultaneously check while moving part to next step	
7	Packout Finished Part				3
				Total Manual Work	***13***

TT: 16 seconds | **PCT: 15 seconds** | **Std WIP: 3 parts** | **Quality ◇ Safety Std WIP**

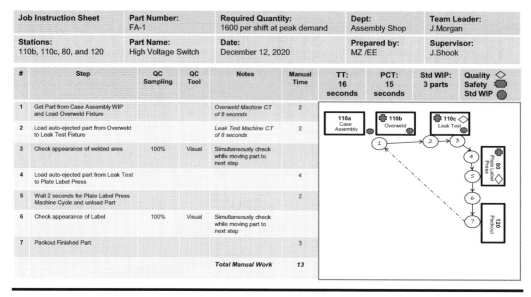

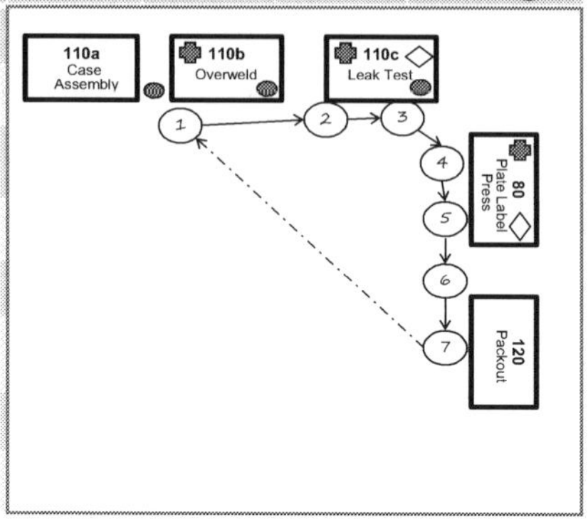

Figure 5.11 Job instruction sheet example.

"No argument from me," said Alexis. "So, let's talk about our approach to preventive maintenance (PM) and set-up reduction. The Adrian plant already has a PM program that we should link up with. A key input is our assessment of which stations have the greatest need for PM based on potential impact to safety, quality, delivery, and cost. They have an analysis matrix template available, but for such a simple production system, I think we can skip that step. Historically, which stations or machines have the greatest impact on our ability to safely make good parts, on schedule?"

"Not to pick on process engineering," started Melinda, "but anywhere we have a machine."

"Well, let's pick on a machine then, how about Leak Test?," asked Alexis.

"As good a place to start as any," said Tom.

The team reviewed the maintenance calls and the PM standard work for leak test equipment elsewhere in the plant. "Rough and dirty, we'd like to see only 20% of the maintenance time attributed to fixing breakdowns and 80% of the maintenance time attributed to preventive work," said Ted. "But right now, for leak testing equipment, it's running about 50/50."

One thing the team noticed was that the PM activities defined work to be done by skilled trades, but there was no mention of the team member's role.

"Let's borrow the standard work for the skilled trades, but expand it to include cleaning and simple maintenance items for the team member, at least at the beginning of each shift, more often if necessary," said Jolene.

Everyone agreed on this approach and they shifted their attention to another station. By the end of the day, they had a complete PM plan for the new production system.

The next morning, Jorge and Alexis met on the long walk in from the parking lot. "How's the cell configuration going?" asked Jorge.

"Well...I think...," said Alexis. They paused at an aisle intersection as a materials tugger drove by.

"Why the pause?," asked Jorge.

"I struggle when we break the team into subgroups. The decisions we are all making are so interdependent," said Alexis.

Jorge responded, "Don't worry, that's why we start each morning with a quick status meeting. Although we have a team focused on Project Franklin, we need to learn to divide and conquer, yet stay aligned. I wish I could give you a linear checklist, but it doesn't work that way. Just like the Concepts and Converge phases, Configure has lots of PDCA cycles within it and the conversations are much more detailed than before."

"Maybe that's what's bothering me," said Alexis, "I'm concerned that we are spending a lot of time on details that could be wrong."

"Could be?," said Jorge with a smile, "Some are! But now is the time to figure that out, before we spend the money. The obeya, the mock-up, the maps—all of these help us to communicate our thinking and highlight issues. Now is the time to make the big mistakes."

Alexis's face broke into a relaxed smile. "He's right," she thought.

Quality Control

The cell configuration sub-team re-assembled in the obeya in a make-shift conference area. Melinda Jones was ready at the whiteboard, with marker in hand. "Today is the day to make a preemptive shift in how we plan for quality," she thought. She had a flashback to the day she heard about Project Franklin, the formation of this team, and how she decided to insert herself into the process while working up the courage to ask Leslie O'Brien if she could be involved. And how quickly Leslie had said yes. Melinda recalled Leslie strolling away with a happy smirk on her face.

Once everyone was seated with caffeine in-hand, Melinda began with the speech she had practiced in her head while getting ready for work that morning, "Although Acme is known for the quality of the products shipped to our customers, we achieve that at a cost. Since a recurring theme in

Project Franklin is to be proactive and deliberate in the process design—whether it is the workplace we are considering, the material delivery, even how we maintain the equipment—I think this is the perfect opportunity to plan for built-in quality during the design of the process."

As Melinda glanced around the room everyone seemed to be agreeing. "What's not to like," she thought, "I haven't asked them to do any work yet." She continued, "We need to consider what we know about defects and then to create countermeasures that we incorporate right into the process design, that will eliminate the defects and minimize the need for inspecting in quality."

Jolene spoke up, "Melinda, do you have any thoughts on where we should focus? Everyone wants perfect quality, but there is a big difference in wanting it and getting the organization to agree on how to get there. I sit in on our weekly quality meetings for the Adrian plant and it feels like an exercise in finger-pointing. We look at charts that show the number of a certain defect, but where the defect originated is anyone's guess since we are not good at catching and recording the defects at the source."

"Thanks for the set-up Jolene, I owe you a lunch," said Melinda. Melinda was noticing that this new working arrangement, with short but frequent interactions, was actually changing the culture of the organization. People were less confrontational and more empathetic towards each other. In years past, if she had started a meeting like this, the reaction would have been one of "quality is trying to give me more work," certainly not the reaction from Jolene, which was more of "help us focus and get there."

Melinda continued, "I hear you on the data trust issue. We are good at counting defects, but we're very inconsistent in documenting where they come from. I want us to spend this morning constructing a process-defect opportunity matrix. Although the idea is rather simple, it can be difficult for people to wrap their heads around because it's almost too simple to start."

Melinda began writing defect descriptions on the whiteboard, down the left side. "We're going to start with "known" defects—these are defects what we see today in our current product and, without a deliberate design or process change, we'd expect to see in Project Franklin. These are coming directly off our current quality report, along with the weekly frequency we are currently seeing in the process." The initial defect matrix began to take form (Figure 5.12a).

Types of Defects	Reference	# of Defects	Type
ESD Damage	Frequency of occurrence on similar processes (weekly)	410	Known
Missing Plate Bolts		235	Known
Missing Case Bolts		190	Known
Case bolts wrong torque		160	Known
Warped circuit board		95	Known

Figure 5.12a Initial defect matrix.

Melinda added, "Along the top of the matrix, I am going to add our process steps in sequence—right from our current mock-up."

Once those columns were added, Jolene asked, "At this point, what would we typically try to do with the matrix?"

"I know that one, we'd argue about how many of the 410 ESD (electrostatic discharge) damaged parts came from which station," began Ted, "and then we'd run out of time and jump to some half-baked solution."

"Always appreciate your candor, Ted," said Melinda with a bit of surprise in her voice. Smirking she continued, "I want to suggest we skip that step. Try to follow me on this, let's simply put an 'X' under each station that could cause each defect. Let's not worry about assigning blame—that's a no-win situation. So, considering ESD damage–at which stations could that occur? Just think to ask yourself that question, station by station." Soon the team had created what they now called their initial Quality Diagnostic, or QD, matrix (Figure 5.12b).

"This is very, very interesting," said Tom thoughtfully, "I could see using this on our existing lines. It's pretty clear that we need to do something about ESD at device sub-assembly and at final."

"Agree completely," said Melinda, "this is a simple tool for helping a team decide where to shine their spot-light in the name of quality improvement. But let's keeping going, it gets better, we're dealing with a new product, and we have some other sources of quality data to add. We have defect data from our mock-up. We've run about 112 assemblies so far and

X = Opportunity to Generate the Defect

Operations

				Device						Plate			Final Assembly						
				Device Sub-Assembly 1	Press Tab1	Device Sub-Assembly 2	Press Tab2	Device Heat Weld	Device Label	Plate Sub-Assembly 1	Plate Sub-Assembly 2	Plate Bolt Driving (4)	Switch Assembly	Switch Bolt Driving (4)	Case Assembly	Overweld	Functional Leak Test	Plate Label Press	Packout
Types of Defects	**Reference**	**# of Defects**	**Type**	10a	10b	20a	20b	30	40	50a	60a	70	90	100	110a	110b	110c	80	120
ESD Damage	Frequency of occurrence on similar processes (weekly)	410	Known	X	X	X	X	X	X				X						
Missing Plate Bolts		235	Known									X							
Missing Case Bolts		190	Known											X					
Case bolts wrong torque		160	Known											X					
Warped circuit board		95	Known	X	X		X	X											

Figure 5.12b Initial Quality Diagnostic (QD) matrix.

recorded the defects that were generated. Let's add those to the bottom of our matrix. We'll call these 'emerging' defects as they don't occur or register in our current processes, but they have been observed in our new process" (Figure 5.12c).

X = Opportunity to Generate the Defect

Operations

				Device						Plate			Final Assembly						
				Device Sub-Assembly 1	Press Tab1	Device Sub-Assembly 2	Press Tab2	Device Heat Weld	Device Label	Plate Sub-Assembly 1	Plate Sub-Assembly 2	Plate Bolt Driving (4)	Switch Assembly	Switch Bolt Driving (4)	Case Assembly	Overweld	Functional Leak Test	Plate Label Press	Packout
Types of Defects	**Reference**	**# of Defects**	**Type**	10a	10b	20a	20b	30	40	50a	60a	70	90	100	110a	110b	110c	80	120
ESD Damage	Frequency of occurrence on similar processes (weekly)	410	Known	X	X	X	X	X	X				X						
Missing Plate Bolts		235	Known									X							
Missing Case Bolts		190	Known											X					
Case bolts wrong torque		160	Known											X					
Warped circuit board		95	Known	X	X		X	X											
Battery snap upside down	Frequency observed on mock-up (after running 112 mock-up cycles)	12	Emerging							X									
Wrong micro-battery		8	Emerging								X								
Wrong circuit board		7	Emerging	X															
Wrong plate		6	Emerging							X									
Bulb does not light		4	Emerging										X						

Figure 5.12c Partial Quality Diagnostic (QD) matrix.

"We should call Station 10a an emerging pain in the butt," said Ted.

"Yes!," said Melinda, "Those are the types of patterns I want us to see. I'm not ready to draw conclusions yet since there is one more category to add, but when you see a vertical column of 'X' forming, you want to pay particular attention to that process and, at a minimum, focus on that process first. The final level of defect that I want to add is leveraging the Process Failure Modes and Effect Analysis (PFMEA) data that we generated. If we add those projected failures and their RPNs, what do we end up with?" (Figure 5.12d).

X = Opportunity to Generate the Defect

				Operations															
				Device						Plate			Final Assembly						
				Device Sub-Assembly 1	Press Tab1	Device Sub-Assembly 2	Press Tab2	Device Heat Weld	Device Label	Plate Sub-Assembly 1	Plate Sub-Assembly 2	Plate Bolt Driving (4)	Switch Assembly	Switch Bolt Driving (4)	Case Assembly	Overweld	Functional Leak Test	Plate Label Press	Packout
Types of Defects	**Reference**	**# of Defects**	**Type**	**10a**	**10b**	**20a**	**20b**	**30**	**40**	**50a**	**60a**	**70**	**90**	**100**	**110a**	**110b**	**110c**	**80**	**120**
ESD Damage	Frequency of occurrence on similar processes (weekly)	410	Known	X	X	X	X	X	X				X						
Missing Plate Bolts		235	Known									X							
Missing Case Bolts		190	Known											X					
Case bolts wrong torque		160	Known											X					
Warped circuit board		95	Known	X	X		X	X											
Battery snap upside down	Frequency observed on mock-up (after running 112 mock-up cycles)	12	Emerging							X									
Wrong micro-battery		8	Emerging								X								
Wrong circuit board		7	Emerging	X															
Wrong plate		6	Emerging							X									
Bulb does not light		4	Emerging										X						
Battery insertion wrong	PFMEA score (Severity x Occurrence x Detection; using 1,3, 5, 9)	405	Projected								X								
Functional failure		225	Projected	X	X	X	X	X		X	X		X				X		
Cracks in device base		125	Projected	X	X		X												
Wrong bar code device label		75	Projected						X										
Leak Test failure		75	Projected												X	X	X		
Scratched Case		75	Projected												X	X	X		X

Figure 5.12d Quality Diagnostic (QD) matrix completed.

Melinda added, "This is the basic quality diagnostic matrix. Any thoughts on how to interpret what we are seeing?"

"When I see a series of Xs across a row, I think this is a global issue–something we need to countermeasure everywhere," said Alexis. "So, we should be considering how to ESD protect the device sub-assembly process and the first station at final assembly. No need to ESD protect the plate assembly."

"Great observation, and how should we interpret a vertical line of Xs?," asked Melinda.

"We sort of touched on this," started Ted, "stations 10a, 10b and 20a are critical to quality. There might be something we do differently in the standard work, or in team member certification perhaps?"

"You are on the right path—but let's not worry about specific countermeasures yet," said Melinda, "I want to initially focus on general interpretation. Here's another thing to look for that isn't as obvious. Notice how there is a lone 'X' for the functional failure defect under functional & leak test—station 110c? That X exists since there is the possibility that the functional test could make an error. The preceding X is under station 90, Switch Assembly. The processes between station 90 and station 110c actually do not affect product functionality, they are related to assembling and sealing the high voltage switch. In a case like this, we can consider moving a process, in this case the functional test, upstream to switch assembly and do the testing there."

Melinda continued, "Once we pass switch assembly, product functionality is guaranteed. None of the other processes can introduce a functional error. So, why not catch the issue earlier, and in the process, simplify the test at station 110c, making it into a leak test only? This is a concept we call a quality gate. It's a good practice to have a gate at the end of each subassembly, as you want to ensure you do not pass bad parts to the next process, but there may be other opportunities to create gates as well within a line or cell. Here are the highlights of what we have covered thus far." Melinda listed out the following points:

- Across=Global solution
- Vertical=Critical process step
- Isolated=Re-sequence; quality gate opportunity

Melinda continued, "Let's talk about how we can enhance the matrix. First, where one exists, replace an X with a description of the current quality control techniques or countermeasures. Here is a slide I have that provides a list of the various techniques, and their relative costs and risks" (Figure 5.13).

TECHNIQUE	DESCRIPTION	RELATIVE QUALITY RISK	RELATIVE IMPLEMENTATION COST FOR EXISTING DESIGNS
Error proofing	Defect is designed out of the product	Very Low	Very High
Mistake proofing	Process does not allow the defect to occur	Low	High
Alarm limits	Physical parts represent the SPC limits	Medium	Medium
Statistical Process Control (SPC) & Audits	Statistically determined limits calculated and parts monitored	Medium	Medium
In-process Inspection	Work is designed to create "overlap zones" where the standard work of the subsequent operation naturally checks the quality of the previous operation	Medium	Medium
Successive Inspection	Each operation inspects the quality of the previous operation before performing additional work	High	Low
Self Verification	Each operation inspects their own quality before passing work to the next operation	Very High	Low

Figure 5.13 Quality control techniques.

Melinda further shared, "Once you've completed this step, for any remaining X, show your vulnerability. Also, the more you are relying on self-verification and successive inspection, the more at risk you are. This can help to set further priorities for countermeasures. But wait, there is more!" Melinda paused. The team needed a break. "Let's take 15 minutes and I will finish the story."

When the team returned to the obeya, they found the following sketch (Figure 5.14) on the board with the title, Add Your System Requirements:

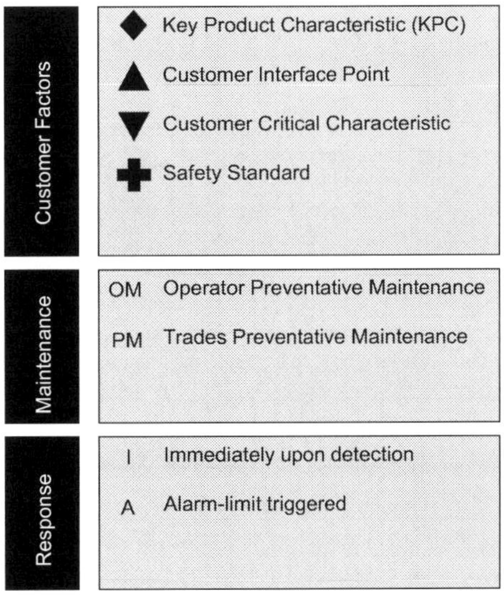

Figure 5.14 Examples of quality system requirements.

Melinda started, "Recall that we started our conversation this morning about how to prioritize, where to focus. Each successive addition to this matrix provides another set of criteria which can be used to have an objective discussion about where to focus our built-in quality efforts. With that in mind, 'adding your system requirements' means adding additional columns where you might flag customer factors. Or you could flag the response method for a defect or maintenance expectations. These could be flagged in a column or indicated at a particular process/defect intersection point."

KEY POINT

Design overlap inspection of critical quality control points into the normal standard work routine of the value-adding workers on the line. Each person can "build-in quality" without additional time being added.

The team worked on completing the matrix, followed by a healthy discussion on how to most effectively address defects. Others working in the obeya could hear Ted's voice rise, saying, "I'm not NASA here building satellites, I can't afford to have four people check for the presence and torque of a bolt. We need a simpler solution!"

"There is an elegant solution to this," said Alexis. "It's called in-process inspection, but it is less of an inspection and more of an overlap of work elements. We have four bolts to be inserted and tightened to a specific torque. Typically, we have the team member who installs the bolt also adjust the torque level. In-process inspection would separate the job of installation and torqueing. This simple overlap in the work creates a natural inspection for the presence of the bolts. If you go to torque a bolt and it is missing, you will see it."

"What if the person responsible for torquing skips their work?," asked Jolene.

Alexis answered, "That's where we can add focused mistake proofing. We can add intelligence to the torque wrench to look for four acceptable torque readings before releasing the part from the fixture. But instead of adding this cost to every station, it is now at one station."

Alexis shared, "This idea of overlapping work as a natural inspection can be carried over to a lot of different applications. Never let the same team member install something and then add a cover over it, since it's possible to add the cover without installing the item being covered. On the other hand, if one person does the installation and another person adds the cover, they will naturally look at the location of the item to be covered—and if it's missing, they'll notice it." The team continued looking through the QD matrix, discussing each X and replacing it with a deliberate countermeasure.

About this time, Jorge walked into the room to observe the team at work. He and Steph were happy with the technical progress the team had made, but equally impressed with how they were actually working together.

Supporting the Team Members

Ted spoke up to the entire group, "We are putting all this effort towards fine tuning each operation, but when we encounter a defect, the balance and standard work in process inventory will go out the window. What is going to be the plan to deal with all these interruptions throughout each and every day?"

"On our most recent installation in Adrian, we used the concept of Zone Control for this very issue," said Jolene. Internally, Melinda felt a sense of accomplishment and pride. Now the process people were tuned in to what they could do to improve quality and maintain process throughput. It was no longer an either/or choice!

Jolene added, "It's basically a signaling system for a team member to say that they've found a defect and need help to get to the root cause, modeled after Toyota's andon system. If the team leader, with support, can't determine the cause and countermeasure immediately, the issue will be documented and escalated to the problem-solving portion of our daily stand-up meeting."

Jorge interjected at this point, "A natural next step would be to determine who is going to support the response to all of the line or sections of the line. I'd like to suggest holding that step until you consider the actual shape of the line. And for that discussion, I'd like to get the whole team back together tomorrow morning."

KEY POINT

There are periodic work elements that may happen during the shift, but not part of every normal work cycle for a part. This may include work such as handling containers every ten parts, changing consumable tooling every 4 hours, and more. It is important to identify these periodic work elements and have a plan for doing the necessary periodic work without interrupting the normal work for every part. These periodic work elements may be done by the team leader or other person that is not doing 100% value-added work in the process.

THE STEERING TEAM—NORMAL VS. ABNORMAL

It was dinner time for most people, but Jon Jain had asked that his steering team gather in the obeya at 6:00 pm. Although very supportive of the Lean process creation activities which were underway, Jon was still figuring out his role. "How do I supply the right support at the right time and not interfere with progress?," he would constantly ask himself. So hence the evening meeting—to get an update and a bit of coaching, without interfering with the process.

Along with the core steering team, Jorge and Steph were asked to attend as well. "So, what's the latest?," asked Jon.

Steph started, "We're in the configuration phase—so we have a general understanding of the process concept we are going to pursue, and now we are in the messy details of understanding every work motion, every piece of material movement, and how to make everything happen with perfect quality, on time, and at the targeted cost."

Paul asked, "What's left to do in the configuration phase?"

Steph continued, "We are probably 70% complete. Tomorrow we are going to determine the shape of the line, after which we can revisit the connection system, the supporting management system, and finally how to engage all of our suppliers, equipment, and materials to make the launch successful."

"Line shape?," said Jon, "I thought lean lines or cells were all in the shape of the letter U?"

"And that's why I'm glad we are talking as a leadership team," said Leslie, "That's a misconception that I have seen lead to a lot of wasted time, resources, and capital–both the money kind and political. My mentor taught me that there are a lot of letters in the alphabet, and U is only one of them. So, tomorrow the team will consider the work to be done, how that work interacts with the equipment and materials, and derive the best shape for the process."

"Sounds like I've touched a nerve," said Jon.

"Yes," retorted Leslie sternly.

"What happens after the process is configured?," asked Cheryl.

Jorge answered this question, "We'll begin the process that we call Confirm—it's the evolution of the obeya plus some additional tools and processes to ensure a successful launch."

"And we defined the attributes of a successful launch a few weeks ago—if you look right here on the obeya," said Dave Laplace. Dave was particularly excited about this aspect of his involvement. As a finance professional he had often felt as though his contribution to new program success was a bit disconnected and mostly was a reaction to things that already happened. This process, he thought, would be more proactive and flag issues early.

"Although the obeya is impressive, and it is obviously working for the team, it's not immediately obvious to me how the team is progressing, where they have gaps, and where they need help," said Jon.

"Agreed," said Steph, "We'll work on that for our own good, not just for you. And yes, it has been very helpful to the team—but it could be better."

The steering team continued to study the obeya. The Operational Declaration caught Jon's eye and he asked, "this document makes a lot of sense—shouldn't we adopt this across all of our plants?"

"In time," said Leslie, "I want to create evidence on the production floor that it's actually better. When Adrian begins to outperform all of the other plants, that'll get everyone's attention, and then we'll spread the declaration to the other new programs and facilities."

Jon responded, "I'm okay with that, but are there some early lessons learned that we could begin to share with others? I understand wanting to have some results to back up this new way of thinking and doing, but I also have a whole business to run and if we learned some things, I'd like us to figure out how to share them in an effective way. I don't need an answer right now, but think about it."

Cell Shape

The next morning came quickly for Steph and Jorge. They did not leave the plant until 7:30 pm the previous night and then both slept poorly as they pondered Jon's request on what to share and when. After grabbing coffees from the tool room, they went into the obeya. Over the next 30 minutes the entire team wandered in one-by-one. Actually, Alexis was there before everyone else sketching layouts in her notebook.

"Let's get to work," began Steph. "We've made great progress on each operation and its design. That said, it is time to consider the actual layout or shape of the line. My mentor constantly reminded us that even children know there are many letters in the alphabet. Use the one that makes sense. A U-shaped cell is a specific tool and we have to be careful to not confuse tools with goals."

"So, for our specific situation, one challenge we have is that the first six stations which build the device subassembly are much faster than the rest of the line," Steph said gesturing to the current machine balance chart on the obeya (Figure 5.15).

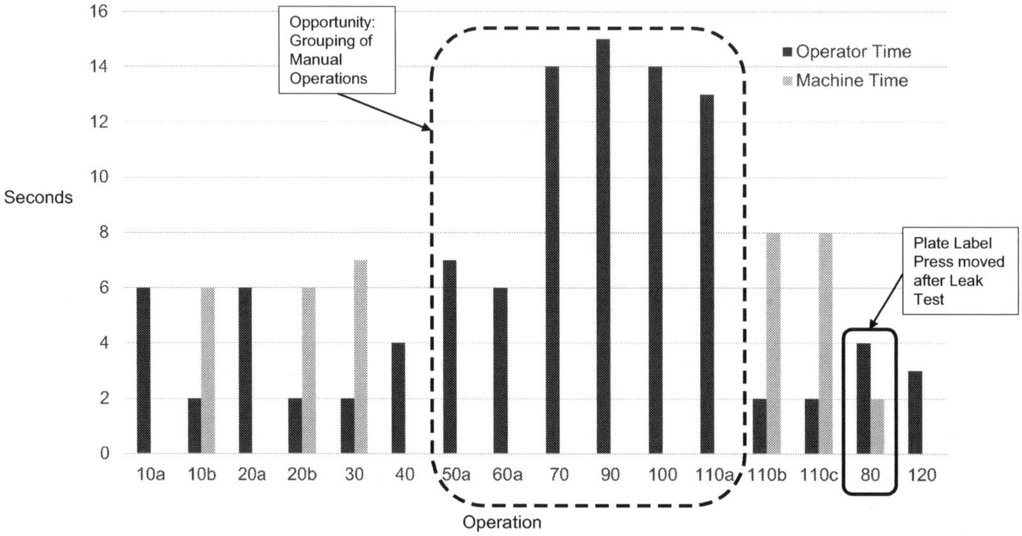

Figure 5.15 Operator/machine balance chart for Concept 8.

Steph added, "And another thing my mentor used to say to us was, 'wait time is hard to manage'—people naturally want to stay busy, and when they have idle time, they make up things to do, things they think are helpful but often are not."

"Like building extra WIP?," said Ted.

"Yes," said Steph. "So, achieving balance between these connected stations, as closely as possible, is critical. And respect for people means providing them with a reasonable work routine. One that doesn't naturally lead to the worst type of waste—overproduction—because we couldn't figure out how to balance the overall process. Does this make sense to everyone?"

KEY POINT

It is disrespectful to design work for people that requires them to wait every cycle. The challenge is to minimize the amount of wait time across the people's work at each operation.

Around the table heads nodded as Jorge started to speak, "Another challenge becomes evident if we look at the updated precedence diagram" (Figure 5.16).

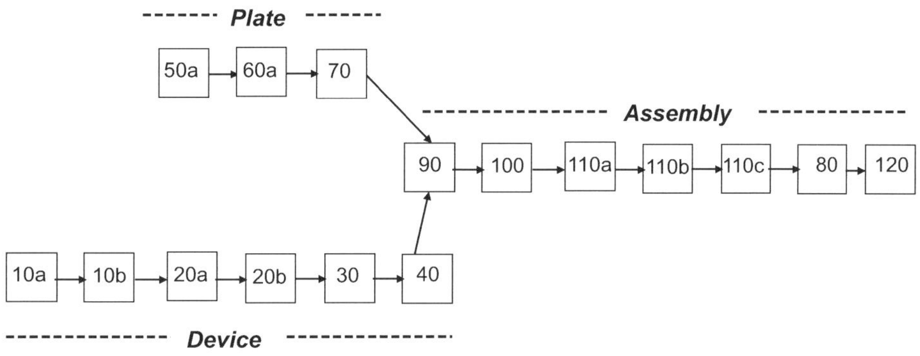

Figure 5.16 HVS updated precedence breakdown.

Jorge continued, "Parts from station 40 are supposed to, somehow, get to station 90, where they are needed next. If we could change the product architecture, we might be able to easily build in a straight sequence, but that's not the case right now."

As Jorge finished this sentence, Carla, ever thinking about her product engineering role, created a post-it that said, "Consider product architecture's impact on build sequence" and added it to the parking lot of improvements to move upstream next time. Jorge continued, "I asked Lex to bring paper cut-outs of the various stations so we can all participate in layout development. See if we can come up with seven different layouts in the next hour. Focus on stations 50a through 120, as we saw they could flow pretty smoothly when we ran the mock-up."

Although this exercise seemed like a step backward to some of the more computer-savvy engineers, they could not argue with the level of engagement among the team members. Rather than one person "driving" the computer and everyone watching on screen, anyone could make a quick suggestion by just moving the cut-outs around. As though Steph's speech about the line shape never happened, each option ended up in some sort of wraparound shape, such as the letters U or J.

Jorge smiled as he saw this. "Can't really blame them, as that is what most of the cells in this plant look like," he thought. The first six stations of this configuration were manual-only operations and three of the last four were a mix of manual and machine work.

"I think these last four operations should definitely be 'load and go' style operations," said Lex. "This would free the value-adding person to work more than one of these stations at the end of the line."

Ted jokingly added, "If only we didn't have 10a through 40 to consider, this would be a piece of cake."

Steph, now a believer in divine intervention, interjected, "I know this wasn't your intent Ted, but think about a layout option for *decoupling* the Device subassembly from the line" (Figure 5.17).

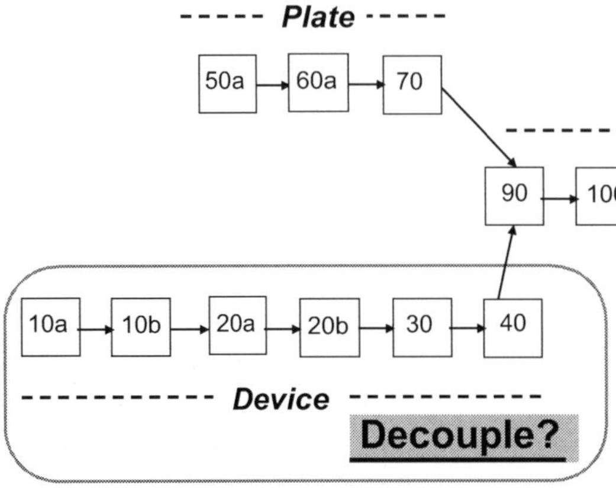

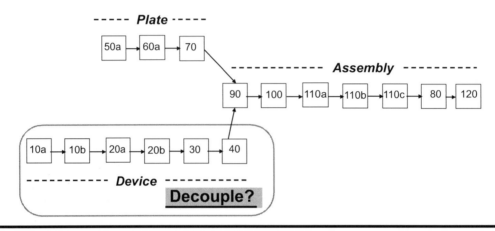

Figure 5.17 HVS device decoupling.

This idea met with resistance immediately, as the mental model for the team was that one-piece flow with no inventory was the ideal. The perception was that this would violate the ideal goal and risk increasing overproduction, inventory, and other wastes.

Steph continued, "Let's pause a minute—I've obviously touched on something here. I was in your shoes once. We learned about single-piece flow, the waste of material movement, all of the typical Lean stuff. We evolved our assembly cells to be attached directly to our injection molding presses. After all, that was the natural evolution of this line of thinking—keep connecting it all together. But like any idea, when taken to extremes it can have unintended consequences. Again, our mentor intervened and explained that when to couple or decouple processes is actually not a simple question."

Writing on a white board, Steph added, "For example, here are some conditions that frequently exist and would be a reason to decouple processes."

- Significant cycle time differences
- Capital investment differences

- Change over time differences
- Reliability issues and differences

Steph explained, "Decoupling is not the purpose, but rather an option to handle variation in the operational value stream. The real purpose is to eliminate the root-cause problem for why you needed to decouple in the first place."

With the HVS, the device subassembly portion dictated 90% of the final HVS part configuration, since the control circuit board component was the differentiating factor in most cases. Another key factor to consider was that with all the components of the HVS, the one that was most susceptible to technological change was the device subassembly.

The plate subassembly and final assembly portions were forecasted to be able to handle technology improvements quite easily, since the components and operations were simple and flexible. The device technology was the core competitive advantage for Acme Devices. With the device subassembly coupled to the overall flow, any technology change would impact all 16 stations.

KEY POINT

Decoupling is one countermeasure to handle cycle time variability, capital investment differences, changeover disruptions, reliability concerns, product design volatility and other issues that will impact the flow and value for the customer. The purpose is to get to the root-cause of each issue and then to couple the operations back into the main process.

"You know, just thinking ahead, because of increased software requirements, in twelve months we may need to add a burn-in step to Device sub assembly," said Tom. "If it were decoupled, we would avoid impacting a lot of the operations."

The team continued to refine and improve the various layout options over the next few days. Additional information came to the team that Acme Devices was currently in discussions with a potential strategic overseas partner to sell four of the device subassemblies as products on their own in an emerging market, separate from the already forecasted volumes for the HVS product line.

Based on this information and current operational data, the Process Creation Team decided to formally decouple the Device subassembly portion of the process. The team narrowed the options down to three layouts for the plate subassembly through final assembly portion with 10 stations (Figure 5.18).

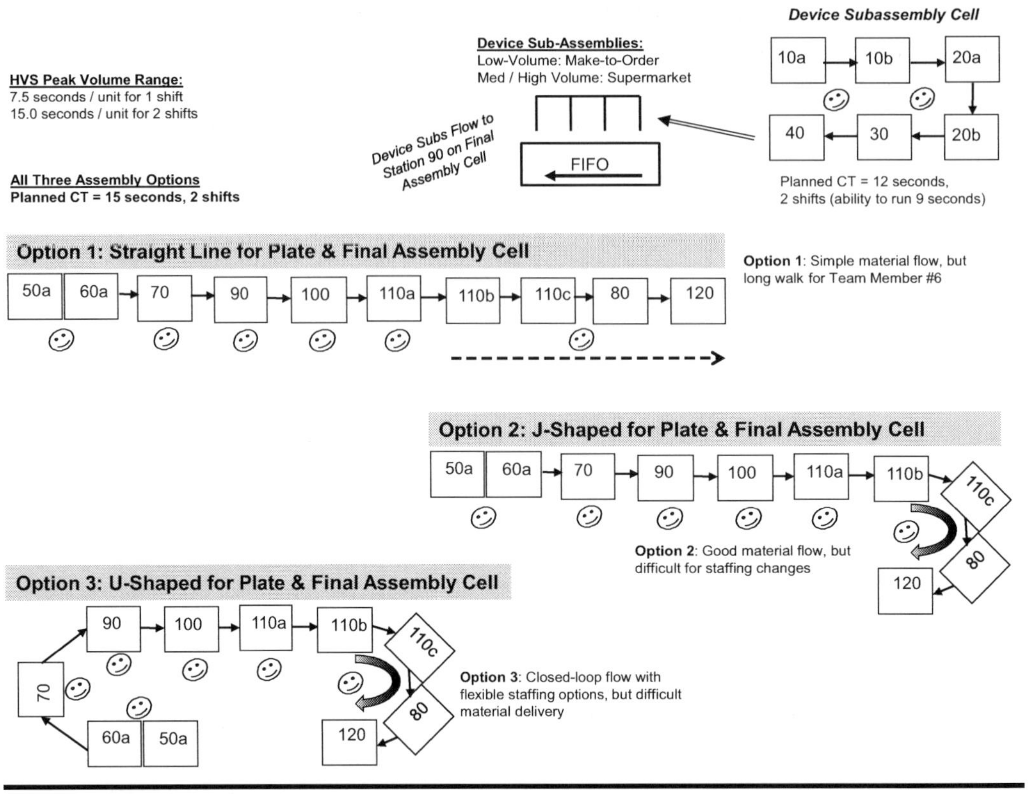

Figure 5.18 HVS assembly options.

The three layout alternatives based on peak volume and six team member resources on the line were:

- **Option 1**: Straight Line
- **Option 2**: J-Shaped
- **Option 3**: U-Shaped

Each of the options had pros and cons. ***Option 1*** was better for material flow and delivery, but not optimal for the beginning and end of line where people would have excess travel back to the start of their work. In addition, at lower volumes and higher takt times, there would be increased walking without work.

Option 2 was better for minimizing wasted motion and movement for the last team member in the process, but made it more difficult for material delivery and potentially would waste more layout area. At lower volumes and higher takt times, there would still be excess walking with fewer staffing.

Option 3 reduced the wasted motion and allowed for multiple staffing options without much loss of efficiency. The drawback was that it would require more time and effort to deliver material to the point of use.

Jorge encouraged the team to think about the product lifecycle and choosing the layout that best fit each moment in time. But this did not mean choosing a layout shape and keeping it the same for the entire product lifecycle of 10 years. The team would need to understand the different lifecycle periods, such as ramp-up, harvest, and ramp-down, and adjust the line layout to that period.

For ramp-up, the U-shape would be the best layout as team members would be in the learning curve phase and could help each other out more easily. For the harvest period, the straight-line or J-shape would be better since volumes would be high with little need to have wide-ranging staffing levels. Plus, the process would be rather stable at that point. For the ramp-down period or aftermarket, the U-shape would once again be the best layout as demand was slowing and there would be a need for multi-station work for each person.

"I think we have a great set of layouts," said Jorge, "but we need to engage our facilities team. To make this reconfiguration possible, we will need to install these cells as flexibly as possible. Everything on wheels, flexible power drops, electricity as the only utility—you folks know the drill. Question everything."

The next days were spent with the team reconfiguring the mock-up to first match the U-shape design with device subassembly decoupled. This allowed further refinement of the part presentation, work in-process inventory levels, and motions required to perform the work. Although the decoupled processes now flowed smoothly within themselves, angst was building in the team on how to manage the connection between the decoupled device subassembly and the main line. Steph and Jorge saw this as the opportunity to move the team on to a key idea of the configuration phase which is often overlooked this early in the process creation—how to connect everything together.

Connections

It had already been a long morning for Jorge. He had finally silenced his phone the previous evening at 10:00 pm as he was copied on an email string related to a production problem on one of the existing control board fabrication lines at Adrian. He knew he was being copied as a courtesy, but it was enough information to keep him from sleeping well. At 4:30 am, he decided he might as well get up and go into work. Upon arrival, the good news was the production issue was under control, but the bad news was the toolroom coffee area was out of coffee—so he had to rely on the machine stuff just to make it this far.

Compounding the issue was a meeting notice related to last night's production problem. It was to be an update and reflection meeting. It would be good to attend, but Jorge was determined to maintain the integrity of the Lean process creation pilot. If he delayed or canceled meetings with the team every time there was a crisis, they would have never progressed so far.

Jorge had decided he would designate someone to attend the update/reflection meeting and spend the morning with the Lean process creation team. This activity was just too important. Suddenly, as though a divine glow encompassed the room, Steph entered with two Starbucks cups in her hands. The day was saved.

Through the early morning, team members made their way into the obeya and started working on open issues. Tom and Jolene had brought a team member to the mock-up to further refine one of the auto-eject concepts they were working on, which if successful, would bring two stations that much closer to being exactly balanced. Alexis and Ted were continuing to refine the part presentations on each station, making them easily accessible to both the team member and the material delivery person.

And there were Gary and Melinda working on a system for removing and sequestering defects from the line to maintain flow, but still ensure quality and support root-cause problem-solving.

"This level of cross-functional engagement is exactly what we need to establish as a norm at Acme," said Steph to Jorge.

Jorge responded, "Agree. What's so great is that they are actually working together versus arguing about impressions of a problem in a conference room. Have you ever seen production control and quality engage like this before?"

Steph rolled her eyes a bit. "Yes, this was better," she thought.

9:00 am was supposed to be the start of the deep dive on connection. Steph could see that if she did not remind everyone, they would keep working on their current tasks right through the meeting. "Fifteen minutes warning!," she yelled to the room. "Please get to a good stopping point and make your way over to the conference table!"

"Earlier in the week we identified a gap in our design—how do we have the subassembly effectively feed the main line?," began Steph.

"Aren't we just going to use pull signals and have our material handlers move the materials on their regular routes?," asked Gary. To Gary, this was a nonissue, and his area of expertise as production control and logistics manager for the Adrian plant. They had functioning material delivery routes, and this was just another stop along the way. In fact, he and his sub-team had worked out the conceptual details early in the configuration section.

"That's where we want to end up," said Jorge, "but remember, we are charged with delivering a profitable value stream—so we should look at the impact of this idea, and what we know about our evolving cell, on the value stream and other value streams as well."

"Now that I think about it," started Gary, "we usually wait until the start of production, add the additional stop to the delivery route, see what happens, and make adjustments to all of the routes in the ensuing weeks. It would be kind of nice to figure this out before we have to ship to the customers."

Jorge said, "Well, let's look at the updated, high-level value stream map (Figure 5.19) with the decoupled sub-assembly. What is it telling us?"

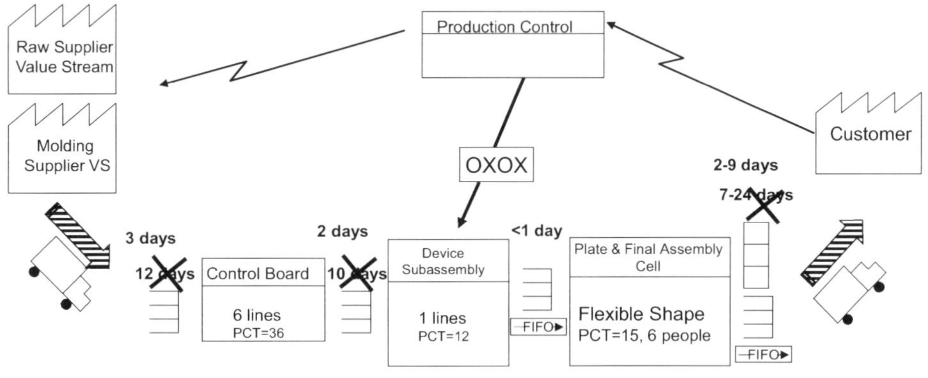

- **Original HVS Value Stream Lead Time = 29-46 days**
- **Target HVS Value Stream Lead Time = 7-14 days**

(72% value stream lead time reduction)

Figure 5.19 HVS high-level updated value stream map.

The room was silent for a bit. It looked similar to the initial map, with one additional box. "To be honest, this isn't helping me that much," said Alexis. "There is one more box, the decoupled device subassembly, connected by a market like Gary suggested. But it's not helping me understand the impact to the material routes."

"Or even thinking bigger, the material routes have an impact on the flow of the information on the map, so anything impacting the routes could actually impact the schedules throughout the plant," said Gary.

"Yeah, it is as though the value stream map has been helpful at a macro level to this point, but we need more detail if we are going to create a plan proactively," said Alexis.

"Good lead-in," said Jorge, "I'd buy you a coffee Alexis, but we only have the machine stuff today." Jorge's Starbucks cup did not go unnoticed to Alexis's eyes.

Jorge added, "Continuing in our approach of training-on-demand, Steph and I want to show you another tool, a connection map (Figure 5.20), that can help us think through this next step. Think of the value stream map as a higher-level tool that helps us understand material and information flow, while the connection map, looking very similar, provides another level of detail when it's called for. Take a look at this training example of a connection map. What do you notice that is similar to a value stream map?"[1]

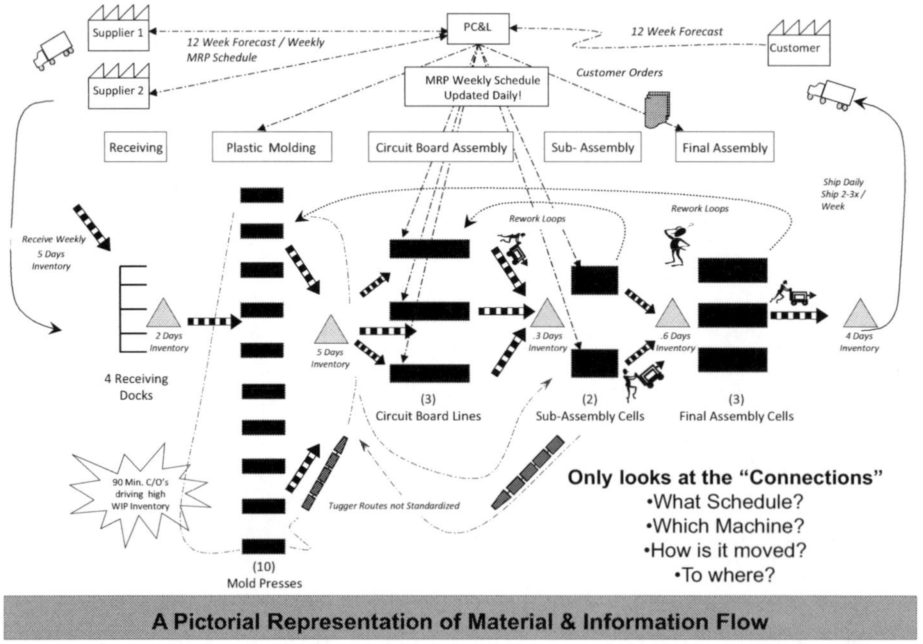

Figure 5.20 Example connection map.[1]

[1] Figure contributed by Deb Smith.

Jolene started, "The icons look similar, for the most part. I see process boxes, inventory triangles, markets, and material movement methods."

"And speaking of process, it shows the processes, in sequence, from left to right," added Ted.

"Building off of that, it shows the overall process flow from left to right along the bottom and the overall information flow from right to left, across the top, which drives the process flow," said Alexis.

"What about differences?," asked Steph.

Alexis continued, "I can see more detail about the individual machines. If we were to apply this approach to our target value stream map, I think instead of showing a single process box for the control board with a label stating there are six lines, we would actually show the six individual lines."

"And there is less detail for each process step, such as no cycle time data or set-up times," added Jolene.

"All correct," said Steph. "Going back to Alexis's point about showing the individual machines, what could this do for us?" The room was silent as everyone stared at the map. "Let me restate that, what can we see with this connection map representation that we can't see with our value stream map?"

Slowly, Carla started to speak, "The unique material and information flows that may exist between process steps?"

"Or that we may need to design," added Stephanie. "Connection maps and value stream maps are closely related, and each have their strengths. And the purpose of introducing the connection map right now isn't to suggest there is something wrong with using the value stream map. But right now, we are trying to understand the detailed impact of this control board subassembly line on the overall scheduling and material movement system for the plant—so using a tool focused on that is appropriate. The connection map captures the

KEY POINT

Connection Maps are a key tool to use for more detailed design of the material and information flows to interlink the processes and equipment in the value stream. Four questions will help guide in creating connection maps:

- What are the main process flows and how are the flows operated?
- For the process flow, how many machines or lines are available and how many are used?
- For the material flow, how do components and parts move between process flows and the specific machines or lines?
- For the information flow, how does each process know what, where, and when to make products?

specific schedule points, schedule methods, materials flows, inventory levels, and lead time at each process resource step."

Steph and Jorge walked the team through the creation of a connection map for Project Franklin. The first step was to start with the value stream map to understand the overall process flow vision. Problem points in most value streams occur when there is a break in continuous flow. Therefore, the connection points between decoupled processes are usually the weakest part of a value stream for overproduction and other wastes to creep into place.

This resulted in the connection map for Project Franklin (Figure 5.21).

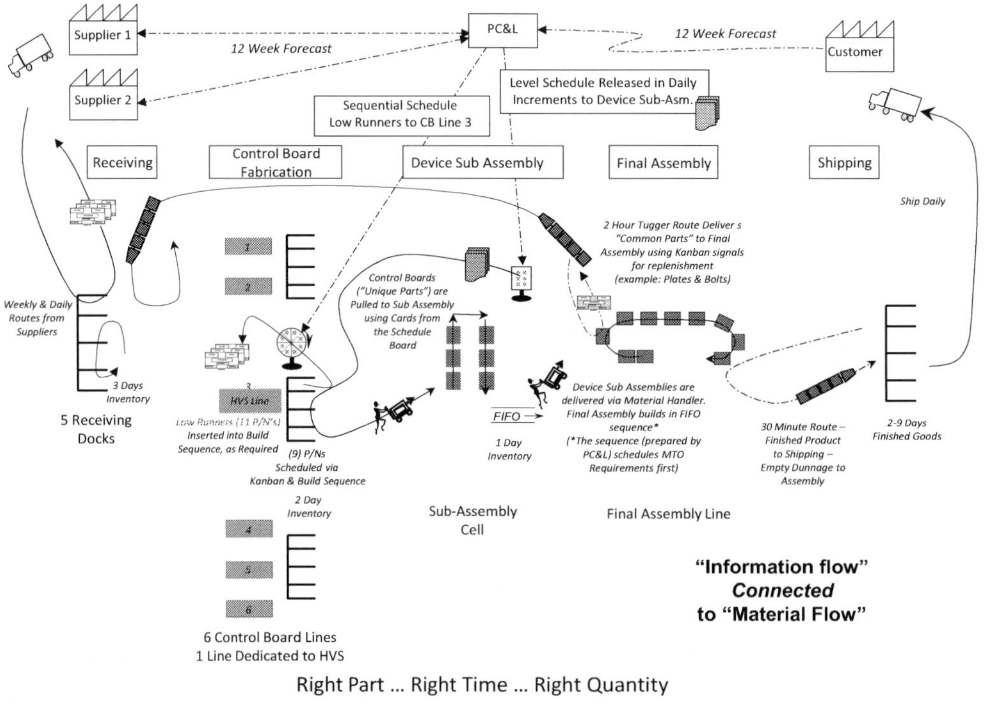

Figure 5.21 HVS connection map.[2]

Key discoveries and decisions made were:

1. Since the market for control board fabrication would hold up to 20 unique part numbers, it was feasible for a material handler to feed the device subassembly process on a manual route, hourly.
2. A combination of first-in/first-out (FIFO) and pull scheduling would be used for two categories of materials for circuit boards. Eleven of the part numbers constituted 2% of the volume. They would be built in a

[2] Figure contributed by Deb Smith.

FIFO manner. The remaining 98% of the volume, nine types, would be built using a two-card pull system. Both of these methods would be managed using a wheel to set priorities.
3. Device subassemblies would be sequenced into the final assembly process based on the production control and logistics schedule.
4. A 2-hour tugger route would deliver the final assembly line common parts, including bolts and plates, based on Kanban signals.

"Thoughts? Reactions?," asked Jorge.

"I can see how this approach will make managing this area simpler and more floor oriented," said Ted. "Instead of talking about inventory levels on a report, you should now be able to walk past the markets and lines and have a good sense of normal versus abnormal, with visual management on the floor as a key enabler. As we know, parts don't lie. They are either there or they aren't. But I do have a question. If we aren't careful, I can see a bunch of over-exuberant managers walking by at different times and all trying to help in different ways. How do we manage our management? When I need help, I need help."

Supporting the Team Members—Take 2

"I guess that I owe you a machine coffee too," said Jorge. "After lunch, let's talk about normal versus abnormal and the response process. But something tells me you already know the answer–Adrian has been working in this space for a while now."

As the team broke up for lunch, members trickling out of the room, Ted walked up to Jorge and asked, "Can I present Adrian's management system history after lunch? We've put a lot of thought and sweat-equity into this and I want to use Project Franklin to improve our thinking, and certainly, not take a step backwards."

"I was hoping you would offer this up. I'll give you a few extra minutes to prepare–I'll send a group text letting everyone know we are restarting at 2:00 pm," said Jorge.

At 2:00 pm promptly, Ted started talking to the entire team. He shared Adrian's work on their management system (MS). Ted started by writing this equation on a white board:

$$OS \times LB = MS$$

Referencing the model proposed in *Designing the Future*,[3] Ted explained that the MS was the product of two components. The first, the operating system (OS), was largely the focus of discussion up to this point. It included the visual management countermeasures integrated into the process design, plus the cadence of support meetings that aligned with the personnel structure. In the current Adrian operations, the plant had moved toward a team leader structure based on learning from the automotive industry.

KEY POINT

The management model to support the value-add workers in the process is just as critical as the design of the actual physical process. Variability will destroy any well-designed system, and the team leader structure is a first-line of defense to deal with abnormalities and variability before they amplify into bigger problems.

Previous to this model, the plant had the traditional operator/supervisor structure. Ted happened to be part of the new plant leadership structure as a group leader. This new structure enabled basic problem solving to occur when a problem was detected.

In the traditional plant model, there was a plant manager (one plant manager) with four superintendents (four superintendents total). Each superintendent had three supervisors (12 supervisors total). There were no team leaders on a line and each supervisor had 50 direct operators across the multiple process areas to manage (600 operators total). When a problem occurred, there was no investigation or problem-solving process.

Since there was no formal way to substitute another capable person, when an associate needed to be away for a short time period for a meeting or discussion, it just was not allowed. There were customer orders to be filled. When a new person started, there was no assigned mentor to develop the person's capability and ultimately, there were limited development pathways. You only had a one in fifty chance of moving to a supervisory position at the next level. Ted stated that perhaps the biggest weakness with this model was not utilizing the associate skills and abilities to respond to real problems as they occurred.

In the emerging Adrian plant OS structure (Figure 5.22), there remained a plant manager (one plant manager). Instead of superintendents, there were area managers (four area managers total). Each area manager had five group leaders, which were not part of the traditional model (20 group leaders

[3] *Designing the Future*, p. 204, James M. Morgan and Jeffrey K. Liker, McGraw Hill & Lean Enterprise Institute, 2018.

Traditional Adrian Management Model		Emerging Adrian Management Model	
Role	Number of People	Role	Number of People
Plant Manager	1	Plant Leader	1
Superintendent	4	Area Leader	4
General Supervisor	12	Group Leader	20
Line Leads	0	Team Leader	100
Direct Operators	600	Team Member	450
Total People	617	Total People	575
Total Output	1.00X	Total Output	1.25X

Figure 5.22 Adrian plant management models.

total). Each group leader managed a set of five team leaders (100 team leaders total). These team leaders were each covering a specific process area to manage and support. Each team leader managed a set of 4–5 team members on average (450 team members total).

In this system, when an abnormal condition occurs, the team member alerts the team leader and a formal problem-solving process starts. Typically, problems will get resolved within 1 minute or less. The issues are tracked for frequency and root cause.

For deep issues, the team members meet with their team leader on a weekly basis for 1 hour after their normal shift time to use the A3 problem solving process. Each team member has their own A3 that they are responsible for owning through alignment with the team. The team leader has an important mentoring and development responsibility at this level. In addition, similar interaction occurs between the group leader and the team leaders, the area leader with the group leaders, and the plant leader with the area leaders.

Over the course of many years of transitioning to this model, the performance results in the emerging system were far better than the traditional model. Quality defects as measured by PPM were cut in half, delivery performance to customers was improved above 95%, plant output increased 25%, and productivity was 30% higher than the traditional model.

Ted cited the second component of a MS to be the leadership behaviors (LB). Referring back to the mentoring and development responsibilities, Ted explained that when a team member signals for help, his or her manager needs to respond in a way that actually feels like help. If the behavior of the manager is negative, then team members will quickly learn that it is best to let their problems and struggles remain hidden. And the whole system falls apart.

Configuration was ready to turn a corner. Steph spoke, "As a team you should really be proud of yourselves. Although we started this phase with a great plan, through experimentation and creativity we've come up with a much better plan. I think it is time to put our theory into practice, and along the way we will continue to use PDCA to verify our system will hit its targets. We're moving into the Confirm phase."

Must-Do Actions for Configure

1. Define QC as both Quality Control and Quantity Control and use overlap inspection of critical areas for free quality control between team members
2. Respect the team members by respecting their valuable time: avoid wait times for the people within work cycles
3. Separate out periodic work from normal, cyclic work for smoother flow
4. Support the team members with a management model that quickly senses abnormal conditions and provides the right, timely help
5. Challenge the team to understand the options and consequences with coupled versus decoupled operations

Key Questions for Configure

- What were the key points of your Operational Declaration? Are they being met? What needs to be adjusted?
- What degree of mock-up is required for which stations?
  - Table-top
  - Rough
  - Detailed
- What is your quantity control plan at each station? (WCT, SOS, JIS, Set-up Reduction, PM)
- What is your quality control plan at each station? (Quality Diagnostic Matrix, Error proofing)
- How will you signal for and replenish materials with minimal delay? (PFEP, Common and Unique Parts, Connection Map)
- What is the design for Lean zone control?
- What layout shapes will best support the customer demand? How will you enable stations to be rearranged easily?
- What is the decouple strategy?
- What is the updated Material and Information flow for the Value Stream Map?
- What is the management system to detect abnormal from normal, as well as the response mechanism?

Chapter 6

CONfirm

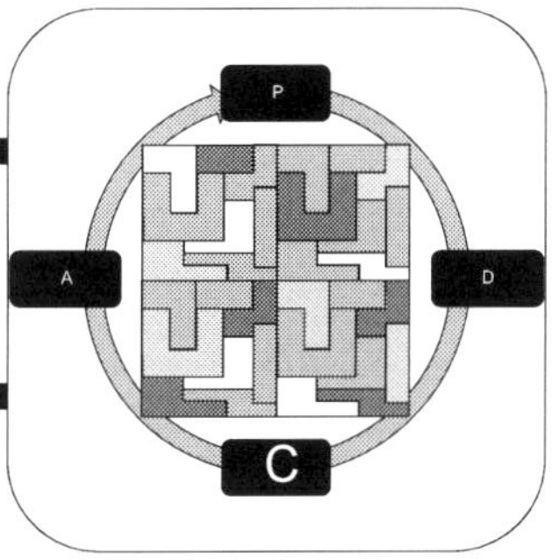

> Data is, of course, important...but I place the greatest emphasis on facts.
>
> **—Taiichi Ohno, Founder of the Toyota Production System**

Purpose: leveraging a robust launch readiness approach to finalize the process while ensuring it meets the targets set in the business plan

Section Prologue: *The team is reaching the point where equipment is being built and will soon arrive in the plant, but to make the transition to production successful they need to do more than drop the machines on the dock. They need to define what success looks like, as well as early process indicators of success. Some team members will be skeptical of doing anything different—or will have trouble seeing how this new approach is actually better. Some will view this as a bunch of extra work that they do not have time for and a waste of expensive parts. But ultimately the team, by entering a series of PDCA loops, will slowly grow their capability in this phase, be able to claim success, and develop a list of ideas to make this process better on the next development cycle.*

Value Stream Readiness

The weeks since the process configuration was finalized were incredibly busy. It was the work that the team was accustomed to:

- Building of the equipment and tools

- Working with suppliers to ensure readiness
- Preparing the manufacturing floor space to accept the new process

But they also felt a different level of certainty, as though they were well prepared. Nevertheless, Jorge and Steph continued to pull the team together at the obeya daily. It was typically a short, 30-minute meeting focused on status. So, when they requested everyone set aside 2 hours for that day's meeting, everyone wondered what was on their minds.

Once everyone settled into the chairs scattered about the obeya, Jorge began. "For past process designs the team's role was to spec the system, buy and debug the equipment, and then perform a 'run at rate' to prove to manufacturing and the customer that the equipment would perform as specified. Once operations signed off and production began, the team would move on to their next project. Unfortunately, once full rate production began, operations would discover a whole host of problems, some under their control, but many not. System quality would not be at the level needed. On-time delivery would be at risk. Costs would be higher than expected as additional resources were required to compensate for the problems with the system. This would eat into the plant's budget performance as well as distract them from basic continuous improvement."

Jorge glanced around the room reading the expressions. It was a mix of heads nodding in agreement and looks of concern with frowns. Alexis interrupted, "With all of the up-front work we did, don't you think this time will be different?"

"We can't make that assumption," said Jorge. "Don't get me wrong—what we have done so far should be significantly better, but we need to continue to manage this process all the way through completion. And this means we need to hit our business goals. What's frustrating is our past launches were the output of a rigorous approach of what we thought were clear milestones. Milestones requiring proof of quality capability, proof of documentation, and proof of production rate capability. So, why did the organization experience a nightmare time and again? We're going to have to do something different."

Steph took over, "This next phase we call Confirm. We want to confirm that the process, the entire value stream, is going to hit the success targets we defined earlier. We are going to do this by *stressing* the value stream, measuring the performance, identifying gaps, and then making improvements.

Steph continued, "Our first time trying this method will be messy. Don't be afraid to experiment. Ultimately, our goal is to have a system ready to run at its expected performance levels on day #1, and to define the best way we know to make this happen. Questions?"

KEY POINT

The only way to Confirm that the value stream will be effective and profitable is to test and measure the entire value stream.

"So, do you both have an idea of what to do?," asked Ted. "I was probably the biggest skeptic when we started this process, and now I've become a proponent. If we can figure out how to launch at target, I'll be a true believer!"

"Why do you say that?," asked Steph.

Ted answered, "Jorge explained it rather well at the start of this meeting. That's my life on the factory floor. The new, 'better' system gets installed and I spend the next three months trying to make production and fix the system at the same time. And I end up begging and arm-twisting most of you in this room, while we all get further behind on our other work."

"Can we start by agreeing on what success looks like?," asked Dave Laplace. "Back in the Context phase we created an Operational Declaration, and from that we derived criteria for comparing the various process designs we considered. Can we start with that?"

"Another coffee for my practically-minded financial friend!," said Steph. "Yes, we should start there, but then we have to think of leading indicators of reaching those performance levels. Let's hold this thought and go back to Ted's question—do we have an idea?"

Grinning, Jorge said, "The short answer is yes, we have an idea. Think of it as a starting point which we will collectively make better. We are going to start with reorganizing the obeya to group the most important launch-related information together and supplement it with some other additional information. Let me sketch it out for you" (Figure 6.1).

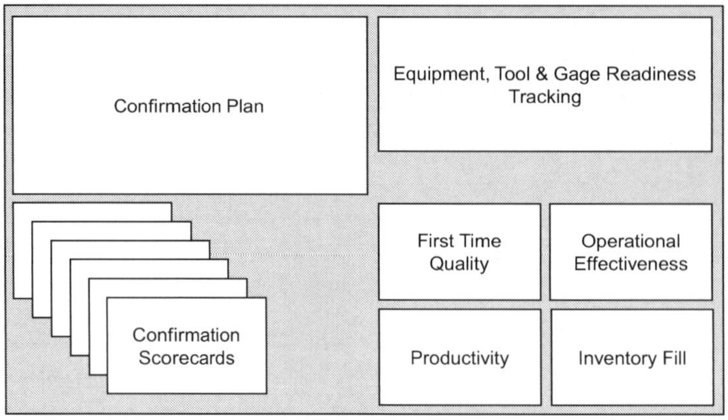

Figure 6.1 Confirmation status board.

Jorge proceeded to explain the following. "To our ever-changing obeya,[1] we are going to add a Confirmation Status board (Figure 6.2). Core elements to this board are the confirmation plan and confirmation scorecard. Remember Dave's question a few minutes ago about defining success? The scorecard is an objective way of measuring those leading indicators of success. Here is an example Steph and I created borrowing from our experiences, good and bad."

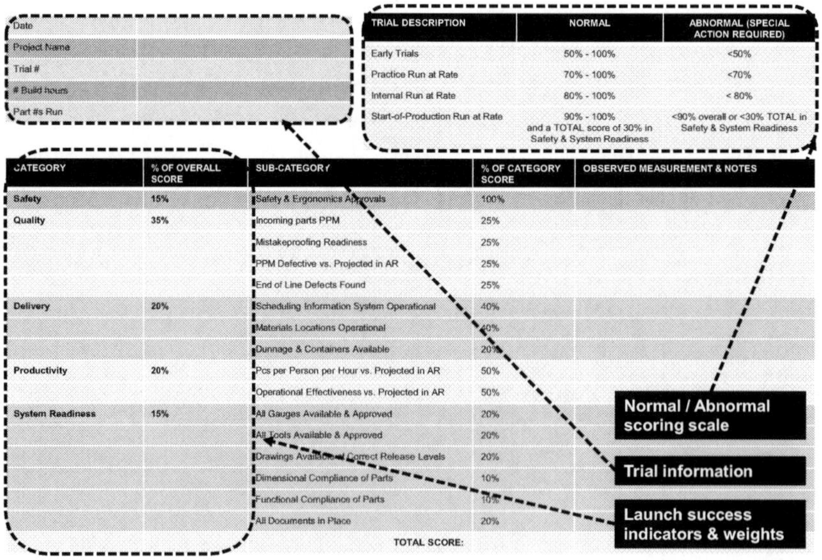

Figure 6.2 Confirmation scorecard.

[1] For further study see, *Developing Your Obeya Stage by Stage*, Dr. John Drogosz, PhD, Lean Enterprise Institute website: https://www.lean.org/LeanPost/Posting.cfm?LeanPostId=765

The team took a few minutes to stare at the sheet. It was a lot to absorb at once. Jorge continued, "Let's use this as a starting point. If we learn something along the way, we can modify it. The point is to have the critical few predictors of launching a successful value stream. Quality, Delivery, and Productivity assumptions are part of the business case and appropriation request (AR) for Project Franklin. Safety is a must, yet there are a few 'system readiness' items we want to track as the launch matures. If these are not ready, perfection in manufacturing will not save the launch."

"Where do we get the data to fill this out?," asked Alexis.

"Another good question," said Steph. "That's where the launch plan comes in." It took a few minutes for Steph to sketch out a high-level confirmation plan (Figure 6.3). She was being careful to include enough detail to make it meaningful to the team, but not so much that she was being overly prescriptive.

"It shouldn't be a surprise that the confirmation plan is a timeline with milestones and activities," said Steph. "Along the bottom are the phases that correspond with the scorecard phases: Early Trials, Practice Run at Rate, Internal Run at Rate, and Start of Production Run at Rate."

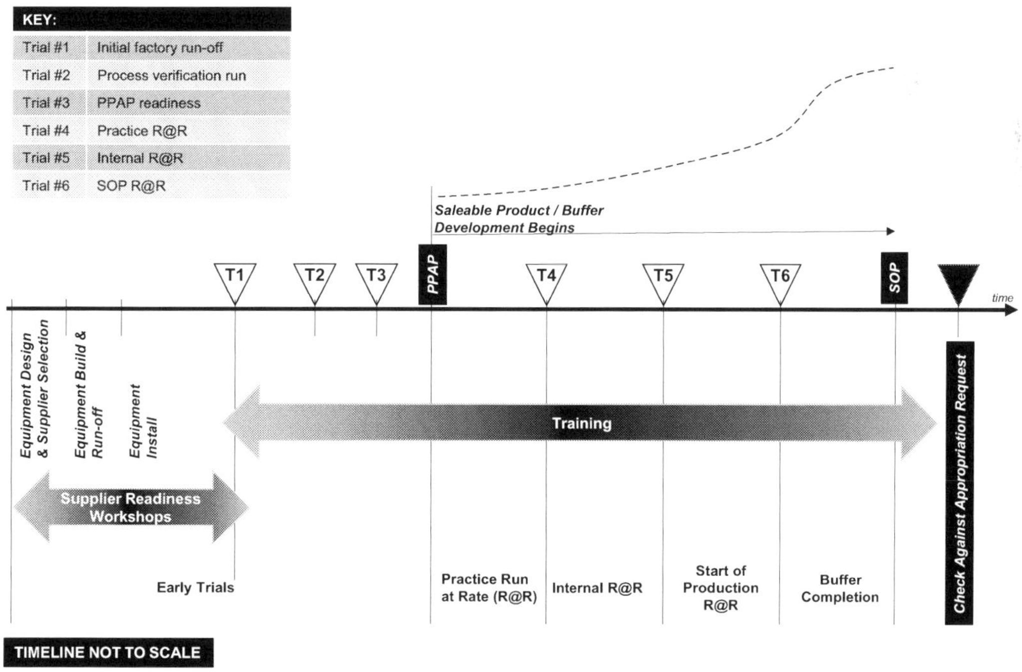

Figure 6.3 Macro confirmation plan.

Gesturing to the left side of the timeline, Steph continued, "We are right here at the end of Configuration and the beginning of Confirmation. Equipment is being designed, suppliers are being selected, and some equipment is even being built. Soon machines will be run-off at the suppliers and arrive here for installation. Once we have equipment installed and run-off internally, we want to begin our trial runs. The number of runs is not fixed, but we need to do a minimum of six."

Steph added, "The first three will prepare us for our pre-production approval process (PPAP) and the last three will finalize the preparation for full rate production. Think of each trial as a 'pilot' of the entire value stream. We will be sending a build signal to the line, the material system will trigger delivery of components, parts will be produced, packed, labeled, and moved to a ship location. Again, we are confirming that the whole value stream works as intended, not just the final assembly line. Thoughts?"

"It could be expensive, building all of these parts," said Jolene.

Jorge spoke, "Great thought. A couple of points to remember. First, we may have to get creative on how we perform the builds to learn what we need to learn, depending on the system's level of maturity. Before PPAP we may do smaller runs. After PPAP, everything produced, if good, is saleable. Those parts will be held in our initial inventory buffer and eventually sold. My second point is, if we think this is expensive, we should not lose sight of how expensive it is trying to problem solve quality, schedule, and productivity issues while running production."

Ted and Jolene both let out abrupt laughs in agreement. Jorge continued, "And it's going to be our responsibility to immediately countermeasure any issues we find. If we find a quality issue, our countermeasures will minimize the parts wasted going forward."

Steph said, "In between the Confirmation Plan and the Scorecard results, we will need some sort of task tracking. This is to track tasks related to the preparation for the next trial run. And by next run, I mean it could be a pre-planned run like those shown on this timeline, or it could be an additional run we had to perform because the scorecard was rated red for a particular trial. If we are red, we have to analyze why, test countermeasures, and re-run the trial before we hit our next trial milestone."

"What about the right side of the board, what's that about?," asked Alexis.

Steph answered, "That's where we will track our actual progress towards our quality, delivery, and productivity goals in the appropriation request. Let me elaborate." Steph drew a quick sketch on the board (Figure 6.4).

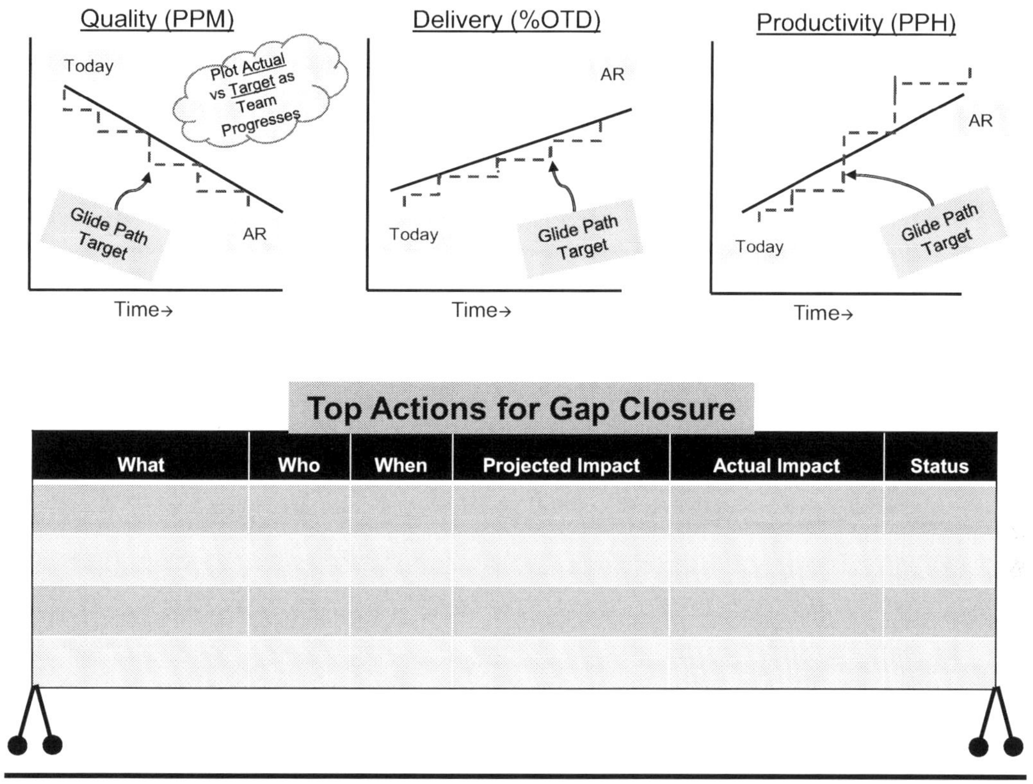

Figure 6.4 Key metric glide paths.

Steph continued, "For each of these metrics, we are at a current level of capability and we need to get to the actual target in the business case for Project Franklin."

"Sorry to interrupt, but isn't this redundant to the scorecard?," asked Carla.

Steph replied, "Not really, at least until SOP. The scorecard is tracking early indicators of items that will affect these metrics as well as the general health of the value stream. Early on, it is possible to be green on the scorecard but still have a quality PPM gap to our ultimate goal. These charts will keep this in front of us. A common mistake in driving improvements towards a goal is to assume linear progress across time."

Gesturing to the red writing on the diagram, Steph continued, "Today we are here and we will hit our target at AR. We want to establish glide paths. In confirmation, these are the predicted improvements against the metric which step up or down based on the impact and timing of the specific countermeasures we plan on implementing. A glide path should look more like a series of steps. And when we plot the actual performance, we observe against the glide path whether we are ahead or behind."

Jorge interjected, "Another item we have found useful to track is general equipment and tool readiness against some key attributes, similar to a checklist. Actions such as technical spec written, out for quotes, funding available, etc. That is what you see on the top right of the board. Speaking of boards, other than the existing obeya, does this board remind you of anything you've seen before?"

"With the quality, delivery, and productivity tracking added, it looks similar to the boards that are used to manage the production areas," said Alexis. Jolene and Ted concurred with Alexis.

"That's the answer I was looking for," said Jorge. "Ideally, we'd like this confirmation board to morph into the production status and management board. They both have a high amount of information in common. In fact, we can use the confirmation phase to not only test the value stream and improve it, but also test and improve the management of the value stream. This is a perfect opportunity for the production team and support staff to learn how to use this board together. But the first step is creating the board, so let's get started."

It took a couple of days to get the confirmation board created and positioned in the plant adjacent to where Project Franklin was going to be installed. Concurrently, the team decided to move the actual cell mock-ups from the obeya to the production floor. The mock-ups would be used to refine and socialize the new process. As pieces of equipment were delivered and installed, they would replace their mocked-up versions serving as a visual of what was ready and what was yet to come.

Trial #1—Poor Planning

In the following month, all of the equipment had arrived, was installed, and the team was ready for their first trial run—the initial factory run-off. This first key trial was now upon them. Leading up to the trial, Ted took a leadership role in getting organized. He coordinated with production to make the team members available. And working through Gary, they readied production control. Special care would have to be taken to keep the program-specific component and finished parts for Project Franklin separated from the other materials in the plant.

Gary and Carla had also worked with purchasing to get two high-risk suppliers to participate in the trial build. The suppliers were asked to observe their parts as they flowed through the process and note any issues they saw in their use and handling. Gary's ulterior motive with the suppliers is that he wanted them to see how dependent the new process was on receiving quality parts, on time, in the specific quantities and pack sizes requested.

It was show time. Everyone was gathered around the line; materials began arriving and then it was discovered that the line was not set up for the correct part number. After a flurry of activity to changeover the line to the correct part number, a limited production run began. It was only after the run was completed when the team discovered that they did not capture all of the information needed to properly fill out the scorecard. This inspired Ted to create a scorecard data collection sheet (Figure 6.5). He worked backward from the scorecard calculation detail and determined exactly what was needed. They would use it tomorrow, when they would re-run the first trial.

The second attempt of the first trial was much more successful. The team learned about the deficiencies of the production system as well as how to do

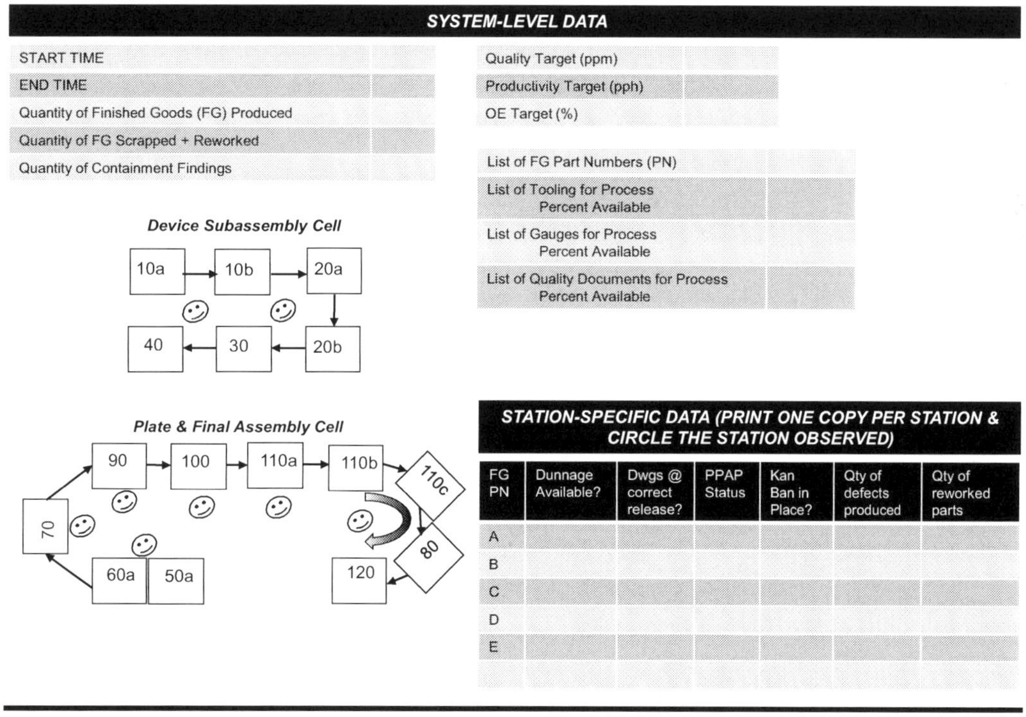

Figure 6.5 Scorecard data collection sheet.

trial runs more effectively. Some of the data collection, such as the lists and statuses of tooling and gauges, could be performed right before the actual run, likewise, with the status of each station. Doing this allowed the team to focus more on observation during the actual trial. Additionally, Ted added a place for names next to each piece of data—so it was clear who was responsible for collecting what.

Once the trial was complete and the parts unique to Project Franklin sequestered, the team met back in the war room to step through the scorecard calculation (Figure 6.6). Ted facilitated the discussion while Alexis ran the computer. All eyes were on the screen looking to see the results of the calculations while Steph and Jorge watched over the room.

As all the data were entered, the score on the screen calculated to be 61%. Steph asked, "How do you interpret a score of 61%?"

"Sounds like a low number to me," said Melinda, influenced by her quality background.

"And if you look category by category, some of the numbers are pretty low. Our operational effectiveness (OE) is only 25% of what it needs to be at the start of production," said Tom.

Date	July 18
Project Name	Franklin
Trial #	1
# Build hours	1
Part #s Run	FA-1

TRIAL DESCRIPTION	NORMAL	ABNORMAL (SPECIAL ACTION REQUIRED)
Early Trials	50% - 100%	<50%
Practice Run at Rate	70% - 100%	<70%
Internal Run at Rate	80% - 100%	< 80%
Start-of-Production Run at Rate	90% - 100% and a TOTAL score of 30% in Safety & System Readiness	<90% overall or <30% TOTAL in Safety & System Readiness

CATEGORY	% OF OVERALL SCORE	SUB CATEGORY	% OF CATEGORY SCORE	OBSERVED MEASUREMENT & NOTES
Safety	15%	Safety & Ergonomics Approvals	100%	100%
Quality	35%	Incoming parts PPM	25%	99%
		Mistakeproofing Readiness	25%	0%
		PPM Defective vs. Projected in AR	25%	100%
		End of Line Defects Found	25%	0%
Delivery	20%	Scheduling Information System Operational	40%	75%
		aterials Locations Operational	40%	60%
		unnage & Containers Available	20%	60%
Productivity		s per Person per Hour vs. Projected in AR	50%	60%
		Operational Effectiveness vs. Projected in AR	50%	60%
System Readiness	15%	All Gauges Available & Approved	20%	60%
		All Tools Available & Approved	20%	50%
		Drawings Available at Correct Release Levels	20%	0%
		Dimensional Compliance of Parts	10%	0%
		Functional Compliance of Parts	10%	100%
		All Documents in Place	20%	0%
		TOTAL SCORE:		61%

"Normal" Total Score: NO Special Action Required

Figure 6.6 Trial #1 scorecard.

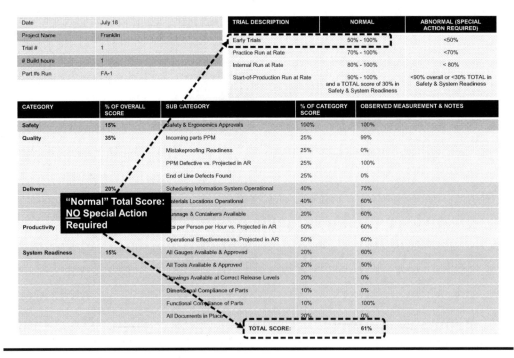

> **KEY POINT**
>
> Launches are fraught with problems, but at what point are the problems actually endangering the success of the launch? Progressive scoring allows the team to make better decisions about when to pull the andon and ask for help.

"All true," said Steph, "but do we need to signal for help?"

"No," said Alexis, "not according to the andon scale at the bottom of the worksheet. For an early trial run, a score above 50% is acceptable."

"That's correct" said Jorge. "This system is designed to help us see normal from abnormal. Since we are still early in the system debug, the scoring is more lenient. The bar continuously raises as we get closer to start of regular production. If we were below 50%, then we would need to create a plan to achieve green before the next milestone, and include any help we may need as part of that plan."

"What do you mean by help?," asked Gary.

"Assistance we need on items we believe are beyond our direct control," said Jorge. "At my last company, we were in the red due to delivery. There were commercial issues with two of our key suppliers, and that was affecting our ability to get dunnage in place, material locations defined, and the scheduling system operational. We needed help beyond the process creation team to get that addressed."

"Any other questions or thoughts about this process?," asked Steph.

Ted answered, "I wanted to say that I got as much from the act of filling out the scorecard as I did from the result. Just the conversation of talking about specific performance attributes, like how many total part numbers will need to be scheduled? How many are already in the system? How many scrapped or reworked units did we have? I feel like we are having the right conversations at the right time."

"That's a big part of the process," said Jorge. "After all, to impact the result of the scorecard, we have to understand and improve the inputs. We can't 'wish' our first time quality (FTQ) to be higher. We have to impact the numerator and denominator of the equation."

Jorge asked, "Jolene, you've been quiet all morning, but I think I see your wheels turning–is there something you would like to add?"

Jolene responded, "Yes—this might be a change of subject, but building on Ted's comment, I can now see what Steph was saying the other day about glide paths for our key metrics of FTQ, OE, and productivity. This first trial has given us a baseline to build from."

"You are absolutely on track with your thinking," said Jorge. "Can you rough out graphs for productivity, OE, and FTQ based on this first trial? We can begin to look at the issues, run experiments, and create A3s, if necessary, to populate the countermeasures sections."

"Sure thing," said Jolene.

"Any other thoughts or questions?," asked Steph. "I'll take the silence as a no, so time for this meeting to end. We have work to do, but tomorrow morning I'd like to start us off by providing a bit more context for future trial runs."

The Next Day

As everyone meandered into the project room, Steph and Jorge had a single large printout affixed to the wall (Figure 6.7). "If you would all gather over here, we want to show you another dimension of rigor that is part of a robust Confirmation process," said Steph.

"Yesterday we discussed how the scrutiny of the trial run scoring escalates as we get closer to SOP. Well, that's not all that changes. The trials

STAFFING	*Initial Factory Trial (Run-off)*	*Process Verification Trial*	*PPAP Trial*	*Practice Run at Rate Trial*	*Internal Run at Rate Trial*	*SOP Run at Rate Trial*
Operations	Limited	Limited / Production intent	Production intent			
Engineering	Present at trail				On standard call	
Maintenance	Present at trail			On standard call		
SYSTEM ATTRIBUTES						
Run Time	Limited			2 hours	4 – 8 hours	Shift schedule
Mistakeproofing	Evaluate status		Test stations with known defects			
Changeover			Evaluate status	Evaluate method; change during trial	Multiple changes during trial	
Parts Variation			Focus on key interfaces; use parts at both ends of tolerances			
Job Instructions	Evaluate status	Evaluate status & update				
Training	Limited		Production intent	Post training matrix	Evaluate training matrix progress	
Spare Tooling			Evaluate suggested inventory	Verify inventory & ability to order		

Figure 6.7 Increasing scorecard robustness.

themselves become more rigorous, morphing to better reflect an actual day in production. This matrix illustrates how each subsequent run introduces additional variables to further test the system."

"So, the bar to be green is actually raising faster than the raw numbers indicate?," said Alexis.

Steph answered, "Yes, take a look. We just completed our first trial but by the third trial, the PPAP trial run, we need to staff the line with our production intent employees. We will also introduce some known-bad parts into the system to see if the error-proofing catches them. We will also include forced part variations—pre-measuring the dimensions of critical parts and attempting to assemble parts on the low-end of the tolerances with those on the high-end. By the fourth trial, we will begin introducing changeovers and longer run durations. Our point is that both the scoring gets tougher as well as the runs themselves."

There was a bit of a murmur among the group. "Questions?," asked Jorge.

"I say we give it a try," said Ted. "After all, we are the pilot for Lean process creation—we can reflect on each run and develop ways to make things better the next time around." With that the team nodded and began planning for the second trial, which was the Process Verification run.

THE STEERING TEAM—WAITING FOR A SIGNAL

The meeting had been preplanned between Steph, Jorge, Leslie, and Paul. It was 6:00 pm in the evening and the executive staff gathered at the Confirmation Status Board. It was the first time the staff observed the board, and it was best that they saw it with a bit of coaching.

"So, you are telling me a score of 61% is okay?," said Jon with a bit of concerned doubt in his voice.

"Yes," said Leslie, "and your outward concern is exactly why we wanted to initially review this board without the whole team present."

Jon continued, "But look at everything that's wrong. I feel like I should be doing something."

Cheryl interrupted, "Jon, I keep telling you that if you always run in and give the answer, then you will own every problem. The organization will sit back and wait for Jon to make the decision. Do you want that?"

"No. And thanks for keeping me honest. So, what is my role?," said Jon.

Leslie continued, "First, we need to provide a forum in your staff meetings for issues to escalate to. These would only be issues that the team is unable to address on their own. As you said, there are many problems, but the team has a handle on them for now."

Paul added, "Fundamentally, we are creating a process in which normal and abnormal look different. In this case, the scorecard with the input of the trial run data provides a sense if things are on track *enough*, given how close we are to SOP. If a trial run produces data that causes the scorecard to turn red, or abnormal, and the team is unable to develop a plan to get to green before the next trial run, then they will signal for help. That signal needs to go somewhere, and real help needs to be provided."

"What do you mean by real?," asked Jon.

Paul answered, "Sometimes when a team is behind or experiencing issues, we make them come to our staff meeting and report out more often, even daily. That's not real help. Real help will come in the form of us, as a staff, making the resources available to overcome the issue."

Jon thought about what Paul said, "Okay, this makes sense, but I have two questions. Am I allowed to come see this board? And should we be changing how issues throughout the organization get escalated?"

Leslie spoke up, "Yes, you can come see the board any time, but you need to think about how you react to what you see. You might want to bring Cheryl along initially, so she can give you feedback later."

"That's my second career," said Cheryl with a tired laugh.

Leslie continued, "In fact, I encourage you to review the board, and the team will appreciate the interest and it will help to continue to motivate them. If you are afraid that you might say something wrong, err towards asking questions versus telling."

"I'll take the second question regarding escalation," said Cheryl. "The answer is Yes! Our employee engagement scores could use improvement, especially in the areas of leadership support and openness to problems. And what I am hearing from Tom and Leslie makes absolute sense to me. But I suggest we let this pilot guide us. We just may need to be prepared to look at the cadence of all of our meetings and how they feed each other."

Jon nodded slowly in agreement with a partial grin. He would listen to Cheryl's recommendation to let this activity be the pilot, but he was rather sure that she was also correct—all of the management meetings would need to be questioned.

Trial #2—Back on Track

A few weeks had passed. The Project Franklin team had sailed through Trial #2 rather easily. More issues were found, but nothing they could not handle, and there was no need to ask leadership for help. A majority of the production team members who participated in Trial #2 were also slated to remain working on this line once full-rate production started. Although it did not directly affect the Trial's score, the team members provided several new ideas to further improve the workplace designs.

Trial #3—Quality Strikes!

The third trial was a different story. As the scorecard was calculated (Figure 6.8), the team was dumbstruck that they only scored a 47%—which changed the program status to red. They needed a recovery plan, but first they needed to know what happened. Again, with Ted facilitating and Alexis "driving" the computer, the team looked at the screen.

Date	August 2nd
Project Name	Franklin
Trial #	3
# Build hours	2
Part #s Run	FA-2

TRIAL DESCRIPTION	NORMAL	ABNORMAL (SPECIAL ACTION REQUIRED)
Early Trials	50% - 100%	<50%
Practice Run at Rate	70% - 100%	<70%
Internal Run at Rate	80% - 100%	< 80%
Start-of-Production Run at Rate	90% - 100% and a TOTAL score of 30% in Safety & System Readiness	<90% overall or <30% TOTAL in Safety & System Readiness

CATEGORY	% OF OVERALL SCORE	SUB CATEGORY	% OF CATEGORY SCORE	OBSERVED MEASUREMENT & NOTES
Safety	15%	Safety & Ergonomics Approvals	100%	100%
Quality	35%	Incoming parts PPM	25%	93%
		Mistakeproofing Readiness	25%	0%
		PPM Defective vs. Projected in AR	25%	20%
		End of Line Defects Found	25%	0%
Delivery	20%	Scheduling Information System Operational	40%	75%
		aterials Locations Operational	40%	60%
		unnage & Containers Available	20%	60%
Productivity		s per Person per Hour vs. Projected in AR	50%	22%
		Operational Effectiveness vs. Projected in AR	50%	28%
System Readiness	15%	All Gauges Available & Approved	20%	60%
		All Tools Available & Approved	20%	50%
		Drawings Available at Correct Release Levels	20%	0%
		Dimensional Compliance of Parts	10%	0%
		Functional Compliance of Parts	10%	100%
		All Documents in Place	20%	0%
		TOTAL SCORE:		47%

"Abnormal" Total Score: Special Action Required

Mistakeproofing failure

Forced dimensional variation affected ability to assemble; Untrained team member

Figure 6.8 Trial #3 scorecard.

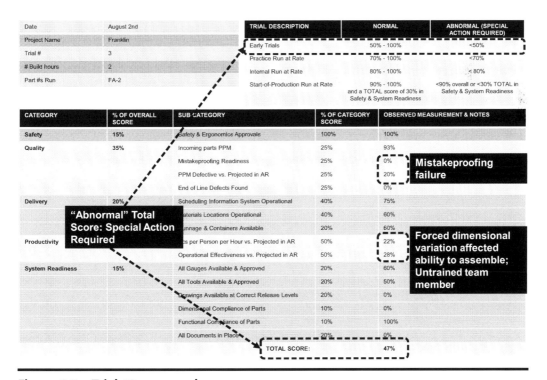

"Productivity and Quality took big hits this time around," said Ted.

"I'm both happy and sad about it," said Melinda. "Sad, because of the poor quality-performance, but happy because we've discovered issues with our system so early on!"

"What did you see?," asked Ted. Melinda continued, "First, we discovered the mistake-proofing on two stations actually allowed us to build known bad parts into assemblies. One station can be easily fixed. I think Tom already has a solution, but the other station could be a problem."

"What do you mean?," asked Ted. Tom jumped in, "Melinda is right—the fix for the first station is underway, but the other station located off a tab feature on the product, and the latest revision level eliminated the tab without telling us. If we can't get the tab back, I'll have to design a completely different approach and that will take time."

Ted asked, "Melinda, can you call a separate meeting between you, Tom, Carla, and anyone else from product to look at our options?"

"Will do," Melinda said, "and let's talk about the other issue—the impact of part variation. When we tried to assemble circuit boards that were dimensionally on the large end of the tolerance range into switch cases on the small end of the tolerance range, the team members had trouble. They ultimately assembled the parts together, but it took a large amount of effort which doubled the cycle time for the station."

"Yes, I saw that happening as well," said Alexis, "and it made me cringe as an industrial engineer. But as you said, the good news is that we now know. Not at SOP, in fact, even before PPAP in front of the customer."

"Melinda, could you add this as a second topic to your meeting with Tool and Product Engineering. We might want to bring in purchasing as well. Just in case we need to change the specs," Ted continued, "And I can speak to the other productivity gap. The intent was to staff the line with the team members who will actually run production postlaunch. Well, one was sick today and happened to be the only person trained on the switch assembly operation. We had to put another team member at that station and it slowed the whole line down. But this is something we can readily countermeasure. I have asked my supervisor to post a training matrix in the area, with critical processes highlighted and to get at least two people trained on each process, starting with the critical ones."

THE STEERING TEAM—HELPFUL HELP: RESPONDING TO THE SIGNAL

Jon's staff meeting had guests on this day. Specifically, Tom was sitting in a chair along the wall and Jorge was by his side for support. As Jon walked into the conference room, he glanced at Tom and Jorge and said, "Get yourselves up to the table, no need to be sitting back there."

"Let's get started," said Jon. "I understand our first Project Franklin issue requiring escalation is the first item on our agenda this morning. Let me start by saying this is great! Not the issue itself, but the opportunity to get better earlier. This new process makes problems visible—problems that would have been hidden with our old ways. Now that we have a problem, how can we help?"

Tom re-capped trial #3, the error-proofing failure, and the missing tab. "That tab helped us differentiate between parts and without it, we need a completely different way to error-proof, which could delay the program. But engineering is reluctant to add the tabs back as there would be a cost with the supplier and their hard-tooling."

"What other options have been considered," asked Paul.

Tom answered, "We've considered a simple barcode reader, but that would require the addition of a barcode to the parts."

"Which option best future-proofs us?," asked Leslie.

"What do you mean?," asked Tom.

Leslie elaborated, "I think we are capable enough to make either approach work, but things change in the future—more part variants are introduced, old ones go away—does one of these approaches offer better flexibility?"

Tom thought a bit and answered slowly, "The barcode would, but we still need our supplier to get the right barcode on the right part."

"What do you need to get the barcode working and keep to our program timing?," asked Jon.

"Just an estimate. We need someone to work with the supplier to error-proof the barcoding on their end and someone to work the commercial aspects, which means someone from quality and someone from purchasing for about a week."

"You got it," said Jon. Turning to Leslie, he asked, "Could you talk to your purchasing and quality managers and ask them to provide someone to help Tom and the team?"

"I will let them know once we finish this meeting," Leslie answered.

After Tom and Jorge left the room, Jon asked, "How do you think that went? Did we help?"

Cheryl was the first to answer, "I think that remains to be seen. We all behaved, and that's a first step. I'm not the technical person here, but I feel like we made a decision based on incomplete information."

"What do you mean?," asked Paul.

Cheryl continued, "Well, we asked Tom a few questions, and he offered up two options—the original one and one alternative. Last time that I checked, the universe is rather infinite in how things can play out. Were other alternatives considered by the team? I don't want to make this bureaucratic, but I would like to know a bit more about the thinking process of the team."

"Cheryl, I agree," said Leslie. "I think we need a bit of standard work associated with escalating issues to this meeting. A simple A3 summarizing the thinking surrounding the issue would be a great pre-read for us. Then we would be better informed, and our questions will be more focused."

"I like that idea, and if practical, we should go and see the issue for ourselves as part of the discussion, or at least individually before the meeting," said Jon. "How do we communicate that expectation?"

"I'll talk to Steph and Jorge," said Leslie.

KEY POINT

Referring back to the Taiichi Ohno quote at the beginning of this chapter, "Data is, of course, important....but I place the greatest emphasis on facts." Facts are best found where the work happens. So whenever possible, Go and See first-hand to gain a deeper understanding."

As Tom and Jorge drove back to the plant, Jorge asked Tom, "So how do you think that went?"

Tom responded, "It was a bit clunky. I didn't like answering those questions on the spot in front of that crowd. They tried to make us feel at home, but they will always be the big bosses to me."

Jorge asked, "What would you change?"

Tom answered, "Well, it's kind of funny, but our error-proofing sub-team did an A3 to analyze our options—and it was the knowledge of that A3 that allowed me to answer the questions. It would have been better if that A3 was shared at the meeting."

KEY POINT

Use the A3 process to have succinct and productive discussions with all stakeholders and at all levels of the organization.

Leslie's upcoming conversation with Jorge and Steph was going to be an easy one.

Trial #4—Back on Track Again

By Trial #4, the team was developing a rhythm for the Confirm-related work. Everyone knew their roles, and Ted knew his role was to verify everything.

Per the plan, the maintenance staff was not present. If a problem arose, this was the time to test the response system. Maintenance was never called, as no equipment issues occurred, even during the single end-to-end changeover that was introduced into the system. One side task the maintenance department did have was to provide an inventory of the spare tooling, verifying both availability and the ability to order additional inventories if necessary.

Ted also added a training matrix to the Confirmation Status board. Along the left side was a list of all of the team members assigned to the Project Franklin production area and across the top was a list of each workstation. The body of the matrix contained an assessment of the skill level that each team member had achieved for each workstation. Ted found the exercise of creating the matrix very valuable. It had already revealed key initial cross-training gaps.

In the end, Trial #4 had no major issues, generating a normal score of 72%.

Trial #5—Safety and Engineering Support

For Trial #5, the internal run at rate (IR@R), there was a bit of nervousness. This trial would be scored at a higher standard (Figure 6.9). A minimum of 80% was required to be green. And this trial would introduce additional rigors: an 8-hour run, multiple changeovers, and the rotation of team members.

"Yes, I want to rotate team members—I want to see if our cross-training and job simplification efforts have had an impact," said Ted.

The whole team was present, each with their assigned data collection roles. Also invited were key suppliers, including the supplier who had recently started barcoding their parts, along with their purchasing contact. Steph asked them to be present to offer input—but she also wanted them to have a better understanding of the importance of the barcoding to the overall system.

Date	August 9
Project Name	Franklin
Trial #	5
# Build hours	8
Part #s Run	FA-1, FA-3, FA-4

TRIAL DESCRIPTION	NORMAL	ABNORMAL (SPECIAL ACTION REQUIRED)
Early Trials	50% - 100%	<50%
Practice Run at Rate	70% - 100%	<70%
Internal Run at Rate	80% - 100%	< 80%
Start-of-Production Run at Rate	90% - 100% and a TOTAL score of 30% in Safety & System Readiness	<90% overall or <30% TOTAL in Safety & System Readiness

CATEGORY	% OF OVERALL SCORE	SUB-CATEGORY	% OF CATEGORY SCORE	OBSERVED MEASUREMENT & NOTES
Safety	15%	Safety & Ergonomics Approvals	100%	0%
Quality	35%	Incoming parts PPM	25%	100%
		Mistakeproofing Readiness	25%	100%
		PPM Defective vs. Projected in AR	25%	100%
		End of Line Defects Found	25%	100%
Delivery	20%	Scheduling Information System Operational	40%	100%
		aterials Locations Operational	40%	100%
		unnage & Containers Available	20%	100%
Productivity		cs per Person per Hour vs. Projected in AR	50%	70%
		Operational Effectiveness vs. Projected in AR	50%	70%
System Readiness	15%	All Gauges Available & Approved	20%	85%
		All Tools Available & Approved	20%	88%
		Drawings Available at Correct Release Levels	20%	100%
		Dimensional Compliance of Parts	10%	100%
		Functional Compliance of Parts	10%	100%
		All Documents in Place	20%	0%
		TOTAL SCORE:		76%

Rack incident

"Abnormal" Total Score: Special Action Required

Software not updated; On-call support delays; wrong parts delivered

Figure 6.9 Trial #5 scorecard.

Eight hours was a long time, and it seemed especially long that day. Ted's strategy of rotating team members at each changeover worked fine and had no impact on the output or quality. But during the first changeover, the test machine locked up. The call went in for skilled trades, but it took 30 minutes for them to show up and to discover that the controls software was not properly documented. They could not fix it—they needed an engineer.

This highlighted the fact that although the plant ran on two shifts, the assigned controls engineer did not typically arrive until 8:00 am, and the line was down for an additional 30 minutes waiting for the engineer. The second changeover went smoothly, but the third was another story. The wrong parts were brought to the lineside and placed on the rack. Also, while replenishing the screws on a common part rack, the tugger driver smacked their shoulder on a poorly placed control panel.

"Wait a minute!," said Alexis. "Our scoring system is going to be 'perfect' for delivery, yet the material delivery system is the root of at least half our down time today, not to mention a safety issue. Are we measuring the right things?"

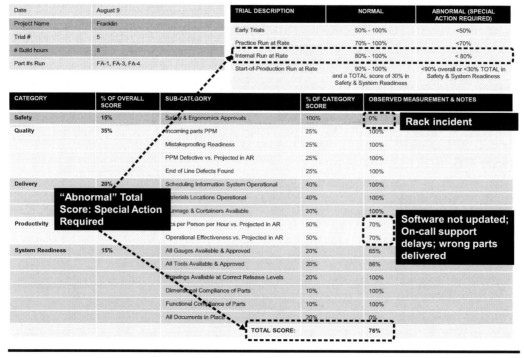

"Let's capture that for the check/adjust phase of our process. I think it is a great question," said Steph. "In some cases, we are measuring that something is present versus the quality of its output.[2] Think about how we might do that differently. Regardless, the process did highlight the problems and overall, we came up red with a score of 70%, but all the issues have simple fixes which we can quickly implement."

Trial #6—The Details

The team ran Trial #6 and to their amazement scored a 96%, which was mathematically green (Figure 6.10). However, the total for both the Safety and the System categories was only 23% versus a target of 30%—therefore the trial was scored red. And it was the Systems category that was causing the problem because the lineside documentation was incomplete. Although easily fixed, that did not satisfy Steph.

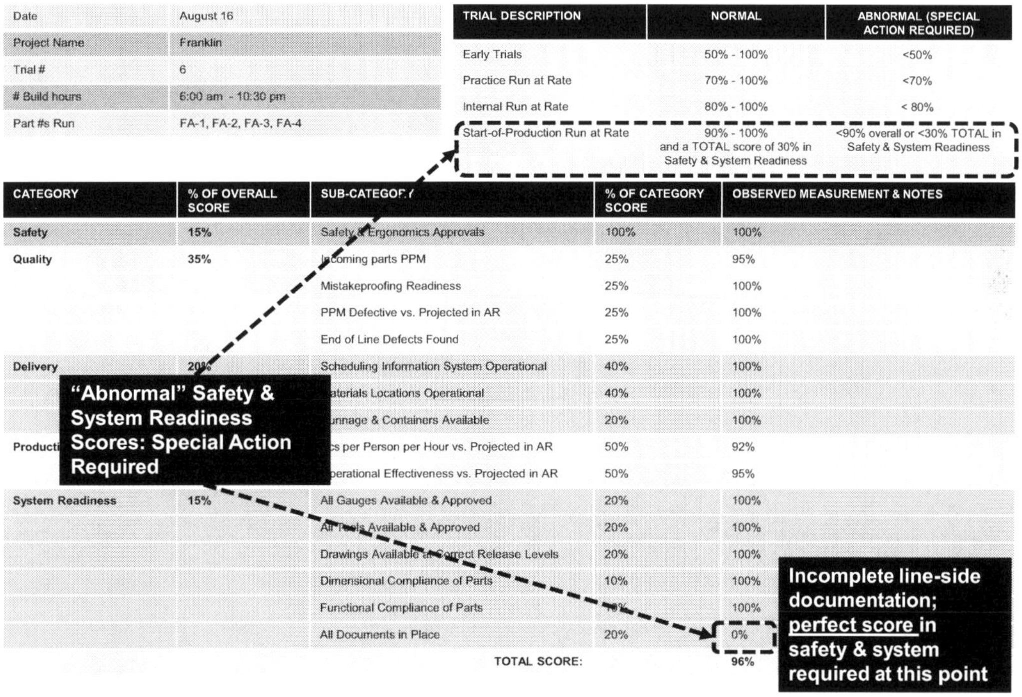

Date	August 16
Project Name	Franklin
Trial #	6
# Build hours	6:00 am - 10:30 pm
Part #s Run	FA-1, FA-2, FA-3, FA-4

TRIAL DESCRIPTION	NORMAL	ABNORMAL (SPECIAL ACTION REQUIRED)
Early Trials	50% - 100%	<50%
Practice Run at Rate	70% - 100%	<70%
Internal Run at Rate	80% - 100%	< 80%
Start-of-Production Run at Rate	90% - 100% and a TOTAL score of 30% in Safety & System Readiness	<90% overall or <30% TOTAL in Safety & System Readiness

CATEGORY	% OF OVERALL SCORE	SUB-CATEGORY	% OF CATEGORY SCORE	OBSERVED MEASUREMENT & NOTES
Safety	15%	Safety & Ergonomics Approvals	100%	100%
Quality	35%	Incoming parts PPM	25%	95%
		Mistakeproofing Readiness	25%	100%
		PPM Defective vs. Projected in AR	25%	100%
		End of Line Defects Found	25%	100%
Delivery	20%	Scheduling Information System Operational	40%	100%
		aterials Locations Operational	40%	100%
		unnage & Containers Available	20%	100%
Producti		s per Person per Hour vs. Projected in AR	50%	92%
		perational Effectiveness vs. Projected in AR	50%	95%
System Readiness	15%	All Gauges Available & Approved	20%	100%
		All Tools Available & Approved	20%	100%
		Drawings Available at Correct Release Levels	20%	100%
		Dimensional Compliance of Parts	10%	100%
		Functional Compliance of Parts	10%	100%
		All Documents in Place	20%	0%
		TOTAL SCORE:		96%

Figure 6.10 Trial #6 scorecard.

[2] For further study see, "Quality of Event Criteria", *Designing the Future*, pp. 86–87, James M. Morgan and Jeffrey K. Liker, McGraw Hill & Lean Enterprise Institute, 2018.

Steph asked, "What's our process fix to ensure this does not happen again on this line? It's easy to say, 'oops' and bring out the missing documentation, but we don't want to be tied to this line and fixing missing documentation forever."

"I'd like to offer a suggestion," said Alexis. "I'll take ownership of an A3 to answer your question, because I think this problem is bigger than Project Franklin. If I stall, I will pull the andon, otherwise, let's move forward toward start of production." Steph nodded her head in agreement.

Trial #6 offered an additional check on readiness beyond the scorecard. The glide path graphs were all indicating on target. With start of production only 2 weeks out, the inventory fill was just a little above target (Figure 6.11).

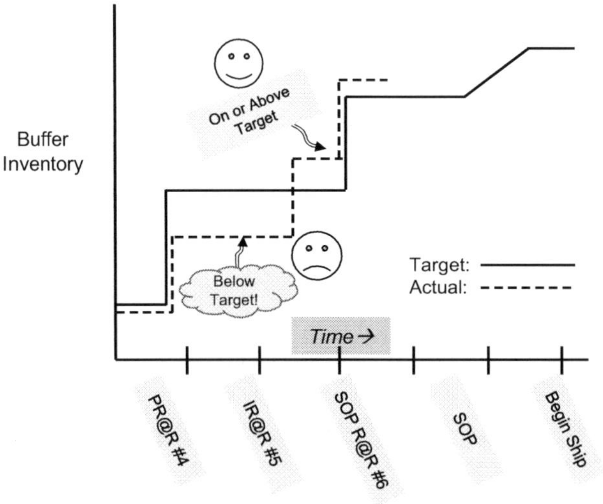

Figure 6.11 Finished goods buffer fill glide path.

The quality, productivity, and operational availability glide paths were also on target as well.

THE STEERING TEAM—CONFIRMED

Jon Jain was ecstatic. It was 90 days after start of production and Dave LaPlace had just done something that had never been done in the history of Acme. Dave checked the original quality, delivery, and cost assumptions in the Project Franklin appropriation request against the actual performance—and they were all on target, and in fact, slightly better.

Jon thought, "Okay, I've been patient for long enough. Time for both the working team and my team to reflect on this experience and determine how to improve the process and how to spread it as well."

Must-Do Actions for Confirm

1. Test and measure the entire value stream to confirm readiness.
2. Use graduated or progressive scoring to prioritize the biggest launch issues.
3. Go and See the process during launch preparation to understand facts, not just data.

Key Questions for Confirm

- What key predictors are you going to utilize in your scorecard (hint: start with our example and modify as you go)
- What is your plan to engage with machine builders and to ensure capability?
- How will you ensure that every trial is executed smoothly and provides the expected learnings?
- Has the entire value stream been exercised to verify sustainability?
- Has the entire spectrum of part tolerances been utilized to test for the impact of stack-ups on the performance of the process?
- What are your indicators for glide paths?
- What is your cadence for learning? (i.e., number of trials, weekly manufacturing readiness reviews, etc.)
- Does the progressive scoring provide the right andon at the right time or does it need adjusting?

Chapter 7

CONtinuously Improve

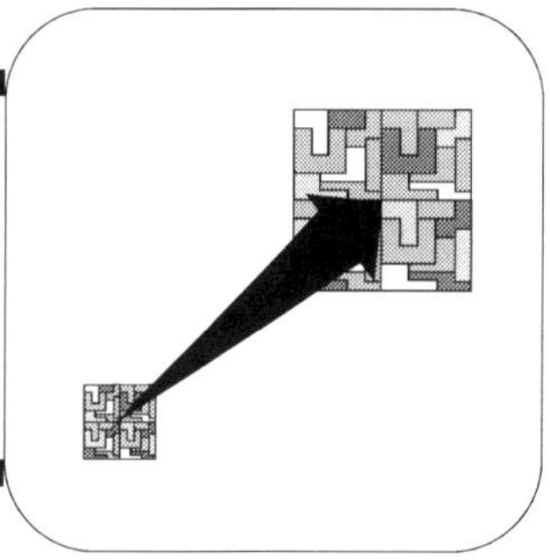

Continuous Improvement is better than delayed perfection.

—Mark Twain

Purpose: making and sustaining consistent improvements over time that will produce even higher levels of performance and delivery of value while providing upstream feedback

Section Prologue: *While the HVS LPC team launched the new process, additional fine-tuning and de-bugging of the process continued in the early months. In addition, the steering committee expanded their scope to craft a plan to enable all future new process development activities to be setup for success with Lean process creation support early-on in the development system.*

The Team Reflects

"Looks like an office supply store exploded in here," said Leslie as she looked around the room. It was a week after the new high-voltage switch had started production and in the spirit of continuous improvement, Alexis and Ted led a reflection event of Project Franklin's development process. The working team had finished the reflection and the steering team was now in the obeya to participate in the report-out. Steph and Jorge were purposely stepping back, so that Alexis and Ted could lead the meeting. If they were to spread this process, they needed to develop more leaders. And this was a first step.

DOI: 10.4324/9781003219712-9

"Before we jump into the results of the reflection, we want to share a bit about the process we used," said Alexis. She continued, "Although we captured ideas and issues throughout the development of Project Franklin, we wanted to take a holistic look at the entire experience."

Ted spoke next, "Most Acme employees, even my production team members, are familiar with value stream mapping. We essentially did the same thing to Project Franklin. We created a product development value stream map, or PDVSM,[1] of the actual flow of the project."

As Jon Jain listened and looked at the map, his mind was spinning. Jon thought, "Lots of ways this approach could be applied, even beyond typical product programs. After all, many of our internal processes are essentially services-as-the-product." He listened intently as Ted explained that after mapping the process, they identified good practices as well as pain points, and highlighted those with green and red Post-It notes, respectively.

"What are the blue stickies?," asked Paul.

"That's kind of embarrassing," said Alexis, "they are the issues we captured and added to our parking lot throughout Project Franklin. The embarrassing part is—let me stop there. What do you notice about them?"

Paul studied the Post-Its, squinting to read some of them, but then he noticed and said, "They are biased towards the front-end of the process?"

"Yes," said Alexis while nodding. "It's the classic case of *I'm not the problem, you are.* During Project Franklin it was easy for us to bash development engineering—if they had only done this, if they had only thought of that. Much of what we documented was through that lens. But when you look at the issues on our final map, you see there is opportunity everywhere."

KEY POINT

As introduced in Figure 3.27 in the Concept chapter, before true improvement will occur in a process or value stream, there must be stability. Standard work as a baseline is a countermeasure to reach stability until the next challenge to improve that baseline. Every new process follows a learning and improvement curve trajectory (Figure 7.1), but the speed that you follow on that trajectory is determined by you. Remember the Improvement Approach hierarchy to help guide you through the trajectory faster and to expand your team's improvement potential.

---

[1] *The Toyota Product Development System*, p. 312, James M. Morgan and Jeffrey K. Liker, Productivity Press, 2006.

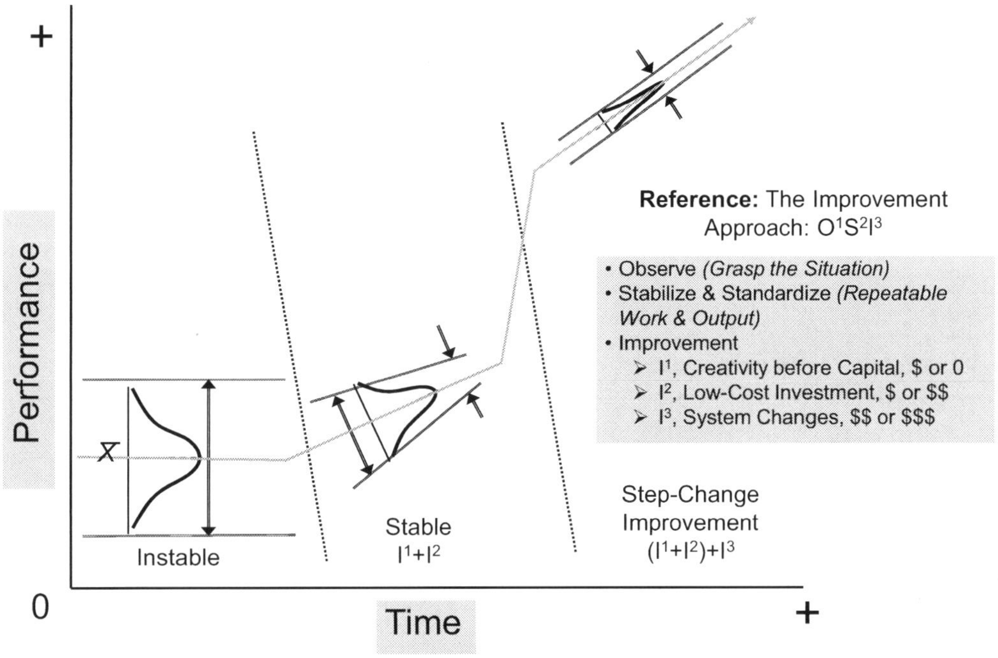

Figure 7.1 The learning and improvement curve trajectory.[2]

As with traditional value stream maps, the PDVSM allowed the team to align around a baseline from which they would improve. The various improvement ideas were prioritized and quantified, and a future state was developed with four timing milestones between now and 2 years out.

THE STEERING TEAM—6 MONTHS POST-LAUNCH

Although the steering team was part of the ongoing Lean Process Development cadence, Jon was anxious for today's steering team meeting. It was their 6-month reflection of how the process was evolving. The PDVSM findings and plans from 6 months earlier served as the baseline for the discussion. As a result, Jorge and Steph would be at this meeting as well, as the rest of the steering team. Jon asked that the meeting be held in the original Project Franklin room, so if any questions came up, they would be able to quickly verify what was actually happening.

[2] Based on thinking presented by Dave Logozzo, "Your Role as the Architect" presentation, slide 17, Lean Enterprise Institute 10th anniversary, 9/18/2007.

Jon walked into the room, sat at the table, and began, "Thanks for coming everyone. This is the first steering team reflection deep-dive, and I think we should do these reflections every 6 months moving forward. From the PDVSM we affinitized our opportunities into five categories—Management System, People, Development as a Process, Tools, and Thinking. Each element was assigned an owner from this team. The role of the owner is to leverage the organization to make progress on the element's maturity, based on the PDVSM recommendations. We are not here to do the work of the project team, but to help them. With that intro, Leslie, I believe you have the management system. What's up?"

MANAGEMENT SYSTEM

All eyes turned to Leslie, who began to speak, "Well, the actual ramp-up of Project Franklin was the best we ever had in Acme history."

"Best is a big and vague word," said Paul. "What's our definition of best?"

Leslie answered, "This will evolve over time, but right now we are looking at how we did with respect to our customer targets of delivery and quality, and our internal targets of profitability. Eventually we want to measure our employee engagement, but it is a bit too soon and our scope on this one program is limited to see a change there. In short, we hit all of our targets when we checked 90 days after start of production."

Leslie added, "And that is something we have never done before. We have always had lingering issues, usually related to profitability. And the profitability is almost always being eroded because of ongoing patches in place to protect the customer from quality or delivery issues we are working. In the meantime, we typically throw loads of people at it. This was not the case on Project Franklin."

Leslie continued, "In short, as we improved the development value stream, we consequently improved the entire business. Last week we just started two new programs that will be based out of this room and use the improved process."

"Just two?," asked Jon.

Leslie responded, "Jon, I know it is tempting to spread this quickly, but we have to be careful to not out-run our learning. We need to create evidence that this was truly better and not the result of some Hawthorne-effect. So yes, two—based out of our tech centers in Austin and Salt Lake City. This will allow us to test the process more broadly and on different products."

Cheryl added, "Jon, I have to agree with Leslie's approach. This isn't just updating software. This is about both improving a process and bringing the people along."

"OK," said Jon, "but what does the next phase of spreading look like and when will it happen?"

"We're currently identifying strategic target programs to be led out of each region," said Paul, "with each pilot being the seed by which we introduce the process, tools, management system, and basic thinking."

"The exact timing of the pilots will vary, but all should be running within the next 6 months," said Leslie. "We have one HR issue to figure out. We are going to need someone to work directly with the teams, rotating from region to region. Someone with deep process knowledge."

"I trust you all will figure that out," said Jon.

PEOPLE

Jon continued, "Circling back to you Cheryl, what is the status of the people element?"

"Internally we are making progress on two fronts," she said. "First, we are *deliberately developing more people to lead this process*. Since Ted and Alexis worked well together on Project Franklin, we have paired them up to lead the Austin effort. In this case, they are going to be engaging earlier as part of the development team for better product and process integration. Likewise, we did the same with Jolene and Carla on the Salt Lake City program."

"What happened to Steph and Jorge?," asked Jon as he glanced at them sitting together at the end of the table.

Cheryl said, "Oh, they are still around. They will be watching over these two programs. Steph will be the lead mentor for Austin and Jorge for Salt Lake. They will continue to collaborate with each other to ensure consistency and to share the lessons learned."

Cheryl continued, "On our second internal front, we are deliberately engaging the value-adding team members upfront in the development process. We've started both of the new programs with a kick-off meeting in the current production facility to review quality and production issues with the legacy product."

"And how did that go?," asked Jon.

"There was the obvious benefit of leveraging lessons learned to improve the next gen product," said Cheryl, "but it also helped to truly build the development team. Holding the initial meeting in the plant removed some of the apprehension of the team members. They felt as though they were actually being listened to. I think this will go a long way to continuing to get their engagement throughout the entire development cycle."

"Finally," added Cheryl, "we've been similarly engaging key suppliers and vendors up-front, and they seem to appreciate the engagement as well."

"Anything have you worried?," asked Jon.

Cheryl thought for a second before she answered, "Yes. Our steering team. We have to reflect more on how we interact with the teams. Both on a regular basis and when we are asked to provide help. If we are to spread all of this, we need to acknowledge exactly what the steering team's role is, figure out what good looks like, and be ready to replicate it to other sites."

"Good point!," said Jon. "We are so close to this and it grew organically. We risk not understanding what we have here."

"Exactly," said Cheryl. "I'll do more research into this and we will spend time practicing better management. And better help."

DEVELOPMENT AS A PROCESS

"Steph, what's the status of the development process itself?," asked Jon.

After finishing a sip of coffee, Steph spoke, "As Cheryl mentioned in the people report, we have added basic reflection to the process. Reflecting on past design results and incorporating countermeasures to past issues into the designs. There has been a people impact, but we can already see benefits to the new design. The introduction of this information into our upfront product study period has really helped us to define and focus on what the customer truly values."

"I would like to add something," began Paul, "we've always had something we referred to as a study period, but it was largely marketing driven. And nothing against marketing, but they should only be one voice among many who contribute ideas to a great product."

Paul's remark gave Steph an opportunity to get another sip of coffee before she continued, "We have also begun creating simple checklists to ensure alignment of all of the functions at each key milestone."

"And how's that working?," asked Jon.

"Better than before, but we already know it is not sufficient. We are looking into how to make it more robust," said Steph, "we are giving ourselves high-fives for doing the items in the checklist, but some items aren't done well. And our current approach does not differentiate that until we get to the launch scorecard during Confirm, and that's too late."

"Glad to see the teams are being honest with themselves. I cannot wait to see what's suggested," said Jon. "Jorge, what's up with the tools?"

TOOLS

"Where should I start?," asked Jorge. Then before anyone could answer, he continued, "We have matured in our use of obeya areas, both maturing the usefulness of the information on a given obeya and keeping the obeya linked as the program matures."

"What do you mean by linked?," asked Jon.

"We stumbled into this on Project Franklin," said Jorge. "At some point the actual work shifts from development to implementation on the factory floor, and when that does, the primary obeya needs to shift there as well. But when we first made the move from this very room to the production line, it wasn't clear how the activities from this room related to the implementation activities on the floor. It was almost like watching a movie and the timing of the sound is off a bit. You can make sense of what is happening, but it is a struggle. Anyway, what we have learned is that the project timing of all the obeya areas needs to share the same major milestones. That will ensure that the timing is aligned. We've also made progress on the use of mock-ups to advance our learning."

"I thought we've been doing that for years?," asked Leslie.

"Sort of," responded Jorge. "We would build a mock-up driven by a checklist, because we had to. But now we are asking ourselves, 'what do we need to learn from this mock-up at this stage?,' and that influences just how sophisticated the mock-up needs to be."

"Can you elaborate?," asked Jon.

"Sure," said Jorge. "If we are trying to get a feel for material layout at each station, we might just need some parts, a team member, a fixture, and some engineers to act as part presentation devices. We can rapidly test the ideal placement of parts relative to the fixture and the team member, and when we get a good solution, take a photo of where the parts are being held by the engineers. The photo is used to remind us of where the actual part presentation devices need to be located. Notice, in this case, we didn't worry about having a perfect representation of the manufacturing process. Later, when we are trying to balance the stations to within a second or two of each other, higher fidelity will be needed. But that level of fidelity would be a waste early on."

"Got it," said Jon. "It seems like there are parallels between this thinking and engineering prototypes built in the tech centers."

"There are," said Paul.

"I'd like to say one more thing," said Jorge. "We're also making progress on improving our Confirmation scorecard, with the help of Dave."

"How so?," asked Leslie.

Dave had been quiet up to this point, but now spoke up, "We've been tweaking what we measure, the weights of the various factors and the timing of the weights. We had a near-miss on delivery during ramp-up. All of our leading indicators were good. We had plenty of finished goods at the plant, but we were not measuring the accumulation of the initial buffer required to fill our distribution system. The pipeline was dry, so to speak."

Dave paused for a moment to judge if everyone was following him, then he continued, "We've added a buffer readiness field that is weighted very low initially, but after PPAP, has a weight that increases quickly. That's just one example. But the moral of the story is that we are looking for holes in the scorecard system and patching them."

"How do you avoid making the scorecard too cumbersome to use?," asked Jon.

Jorge jumped in, "We are aware of the possibility, and we are asking ourselves if we add any criteria, can we remove one. And if not, we are first trying to calculate new metrics off of the data that we are already collecting. If that doesn't work, we then add the new criteria."

Dave added, "I also think that once we better understand this idea of glide paths, we may be able to remove some score criteria and let the glide paths do the talking. But that is for our twelve months reflection."

THINKING

"I guess that leaves you, Paul, to report on basic thinking," said Jon.

Paul explained, "The most fundamental thing to report right now is that we are starting to see the value of making normal versus abnormal knowledge work visible. First, people thought this was going to be an exercise in putting Lean manufacturing tools in the tech center. You know, putting tape around where the laptop goes. Things like that. But then they realized this was fundamentally different, the thinking is the same, but what Lean development looks like in practice is very different. Also, we are starting to plant the seeds of making normal and abnormal look different at our tech centers globally. We need to think of a better, cadenced way to share this thinking. Right now, it's too ad-hoc for my comfort. But we'll figure that out in the next couple of months."

Jon leaned back in his chair and thought for a moment and said, "This is great, transformative activity. And my sense is that we are making progress. And now we have two problems to solve simultaneously. First, sustaining what we learned during Project Franklin and learning how to do that better. Second, spreading this in an effective way globally. How do we move faster without sacrificing the development process quality?"

As though he was waiting for this question, Dave Laplace blurted out, "As a steering team, would we consider creating our own obeya to facilitate this?"

All eyes turned to Dave.

THE STEERING TEAM—12 MONTHS POST-LAUNCH

The steering team gathered in a conference room that had been converted into their management obeya. Gone was the long, rectangular table that occupied the center of the room. It had been replaced by smaller tables that could be quickly reconfigured to meet the need of the day. Currently, that was a square in the center of the room. The walls were now covered with magnetic white boards which displayed the bulk of the transformation status and additional white boards on wheels were available for writing or to subdivide the room when a smaller space was needed.

"This is certainly a more functional space since we've changed it," thought Leslie. "Now, if facilities could just get the temperature stable. This place almost has its own weather patterns."

"We are all here, let's get started," said Leslie. "Let's walk over to the management system board." Central to the management system section of the obeya was a timeline of the standing leadership meetings. The planned scheduled dates were shown as simple open triangles, and the dates the actual meeting took place were indicated by colored-in triangles. If a meeting happened as planned the original triangle was merely colored in. But if the meeting occurred a day or two late, a new triangle was drawn on the actual date and colored in. A simple magnet with a piece of red yarn was at the top of the timeline placed on today's date.

Referring to the schedule, Leslie said, "If we look to the left of the yarn, it looks like all of our key leadership meetings have taken place on time with the exception of the succession planning meeting last week. Why was it skipped?"

"I can explain that," said Cheryl. "Our planned date happened to coincide with the quarterly earnings call, and we have delayed the meeting by a month."

"Okay," said Leslie, "let's add another triangle to the timeline, one month out. I would not be doing my job if I didn't ask, any thoughts on how we avoid similar situations in the future?"

KEY POINT

A Management Obeya is a crucial tool enabling the spread of Lean product and process development concepts. The management obeya needs to be coupled with a defined set of cadenced meetings and escalation paths, providing leadership with structure and focus. The medium is secondary to the method.

"I have asked to get the latest version of the corporate calendar," said Cheryl, "and I thought we could add significant events across the top of our timeline. This way we could plan our management meetings around these anchor points."

"I like it," said Jon, "and I can do my part with my peers to minimize shifting dates on the corporate calendar."

Another section of the management system obeya was tracking the total emails per week that each steering team member received and sent. This was something Paul suggested they do. He had a hypothesis that as the standing leadership meetings matured and became a place for issues to escalate to on a cadenced basis, email traffic for the organization should decrease. Initially the data looked random, but a downward trend was now developing. The team was still uncertain if this information was merely interesting or if it was useful. Paul argued that it might be useful as they expand their new process beyond their division into other Acme businesses.

Another chart was titled, "Andon to resolution lead time." This was the steering team's first attempt at a developing a glide path. The Y-axis of the chart was lead time and the X-axis was actual time. The body of the chart contained two lines. There was one in blue that was the targeted lead time, and a second, hand-plotted line in pencil that was the actual time. The targeted lead time was based on a current state mapping of the issue escalation process, and the resulting improvement plan with action items, estimated impacts, and target dates. A quick glance at the chart revealed that the current lead time was 2 days above the targeted lead time.

"Looks like we are off target," said Leslie, "any thoughts, Paul?"

Paul answered, "Yes, we should be back on target next week. We had to delay the implementation of our next improvement step by a week, but we still think it will generate a 2-day reduction in lead time."

Jon was looking around the room. "What's great," he thought, "is that the lead time reduction chart ties to the steering team's own improvement plan, and that improvement plan ties back to the original PDVSM and the steering team's action items taken from that effort. This was not the shotgun kaizen we have seen before at all levels of the company. This was very purposeful."

Following a quick glance at the rest of the management system boards, Leslie and the rest of the team could see that everything else was on track. "Before we move on to people, any other management system comments?," asked Jon.

"As a segue to People, I want to acknowledge all of the good and deliberate work the steering team has been doing to improve their effectiveness at providing help," said Cheryl.

She continued, "I've been struggling with how we measure this, but I have been receiving great feedback from my staff on the behaviors they see from all of you as they participate in your various meetings. There has been a real change on welcoming problems versus punishing the messenger. And along with that, your efforts towards providing thought-provoking questions, instead of telling everyone how to solve every problem, have been noticed too."

"I sometimes struggle with that," said Dave, "when to shift from ask to tell. What do the rest of you do?"

Leslie spoke up, "There is no single answer to this. On one hand, if we tell people how to solve their problems, they don't improve themselves. When the next problem occurs, they come back to us for another answer. On the other hand, when someone is really struggling and really needs help, another open-ended question can just lead to frustration. Depending on the urgency of the issue, I will typically give the person at least one chance to solve an issue, but after that I may be more direct and tell them what to try next."

"Good advice," said Cheryl. "Any more comments? If not, I want to move to the People board."

The People obeya had two major sections. The first was a trendline of employee engagement scores. This graph showed the employee engagement scores of employees who were using the new product and process creation methods versus the general population. Although the graphs started essentially at the same point, it was clear that those using the new process had much higher engagement scores than the rest of the employees in the division.

Jon commented, "When I see a graph like this, I get even more restless and want to roll this approach out everywhere and fast."

"I think we are ready to go division-wide," said Paul.

"I agree," said Leslie. "Using this approach is now required on all new North American programs with capital requirements over one million dollars, but we have enough experience to do this everywhere now. At our next steering meeting, Paul and I can share a rollout plan that we have been developing with Cheryl. We have even created a glide path for employee engagement scores, taking what we have learned and estimating the impact region by region as we roll this out."

The second section of People obeya was focused on their internal training efforts. A Lean Product and Process Development (LPPD) academy had been formed to spread their newfound thinking and to perform knowledge capture for sharing. The academy had a very small staff of coordinators to handle the logistics of creating and executing learning events, as all the training and knowledge capture was performed by practitioners in the division.

The steering team meeting continued around the room touching on the topics of Development as a Process, Tools, and Basic Thinking. An outside observer would see that Acme Devices was rapidly improving their basic development process, and hence, the rest of the organization was benefiting. There was significant improvement in the purpose and quality of their development milestones. As a new product's design matured at each milestone, the team was understanding just how compatible that design was with the capability of the cross-functional organization's processes. Gone were the late-term surprises of "we can't hold that tolerance" or "our employees don't have that level of skill."

KEY POINT

As noted upfront in the book, poorly thought-out and designed process flows for new products frequently lead to what is really *touzen*, or late-stage improvement that should not have been necessary. In reality, this is not improvement but costly rework. It is critical early-on to recognize this differentiation.

These same discussions provided a natural place to consider common and unique part strategies upfront, as well as the potential benefits that different product architectures could have on the build sequence and quality. They were also understandings on how to scale the new LPPD process to be effective and useful on smaller programs. The same logic was being used.

A casual walk in Acme's buildings showed many examples of the obeya system spreading to the back-office operations. Some examples were better than others, but all were attempting to make normal versus abnormal visible, along with plans for recovery. Acme had established a process development lab that was charged with creating appropriate mock-ups of processes, aiding the quality and speed of the development process.

As the steering team meeting wrapped-up, Jon was rolling all these over in his mind. He said, "I can't express how proud that I am of all this great work, by both this team and the entire organization that we work to support. Although we are only a year into our journey, we have started to impact the whole corporation. The results are getting you all noticed. That said, we cannot become complacent, and we need to continue to push ourselves. It is naïve for us to believe, in this infinite universe we live in, that our current state is the one best way. There is always better."

Jon kept going, "I would like to give ourselves a few challenges for the upcoming year. We have made great progress in our management system, so how do we refine it? How do we continue to reduce the lead time for issue escalation yet encourage issues to be resolved at the lowest levels possible? Corporate has an interest in this steering team approach. How do we help them successfully adopt what we are doing, leveraging our lessons learned from the past year? We can all see that this process is highly dependent on great people and great teams. What can we do to be more deliberate in developing and retaining people? How can we open our learning academy to other divisions and key suppliers while continuing to meet our needs? And Cheryl, the immediate answer isn't a bigger staff." Cheryl smiled and nodded.

Jon continued, "Obeya has made a significant impact on our ability to improve work that is typically invisible. How do we continue to leverage this tool and the process behind it? How do we pass knowledge from the development obeya to the launch obeya to the production obeya? And thinking even further down the road, what is our deliberate process to facilitate continued sharing of lessons learned between product lines, across plants, and across divisions? I know this sounds like a big challenge, and it is, but I think we can do it."

Must-Do Actions for Continuously Improve

1. As a steering team, it is critical to not only support the pilot activity, but also to think ahead of how to create a repeatable routine to share and spread across the organization.
2. The steering team should utilize the same tools and processes (e.g., obeya, glide paths) that the development teams are using, in order to manage and improve their own work.
3. With each new product and process development activity, continue to integrate the functions and sub-teams more closely to reach enterprise connectivity that will understand customer value more completely (further minimizing late-stage, costly *touzen*).
4. The limiting factor in any transformation will be the capability and capacity of the people, so do not outrun your learning curve or the transformation will regress.

Key Questions for Continuously Improve

- How will you build, grow, and sustain the capability of Lean process creation leaders and key contributors?
- What value will your team find when reflecting back at the end of the first pilot?
- What will be your management system for improving the work of process development?
- How will you maintain alignment across the functions and departments when doing the work on future development programs?
- What tools and techniques (e.g., mock-up, launch boards, glide paths) are important to your organization?
- What are your challenges in making technical work visible and manageable?
- Where can you experiment with a leadership obeya to help with integration?

Chapter 8

Conclusion

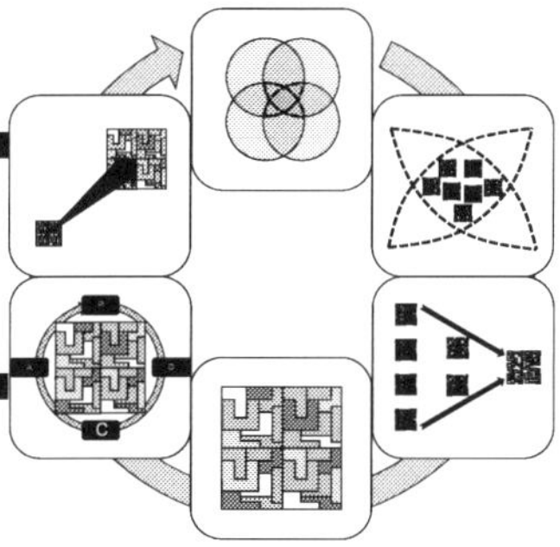

> Reasoning draws a conclusion, but does not make the conclusion certain, unless the mind discovers it by the path of experience.
>
> **—Roger Bacon**

What Now?

Influenced by Womack and Jones from their best-selling book *Lean Thinking*, the steps for getting started with improving how you create Lean processes are shown below.

Change Is Not Easy—Align around a Shared Reason for Needing to Change

As Morgan and Liker wrote about in *Designing the Future*,[1] change is hard, and big change is really hard. Start to build momentum early in your process creation integration efforts within development by setting aggressive goals and targets in order to be the best in your industry from the customer's perspective and to far surpass external threats.

[1] *Designing the Future*, p. 342, James M. Morgan and Jeffrey K. Liker, McGraw Hill & Lean Enterprise Institute, 2018.

DOI: 10.4324/9781003219712-10

Find a System Architect or Chief "Process" Engineer

You will need to find the process creation candidate or pair of candidates that will partner with their product development counterpart. This role will take the responsibility to create the profitable operational value stream and its processes without compromising the innovation and value that will be delivered to the customers and end-users.[2]

Get the Knowledge on the Team—and Develop the People!

The leader will need a team of responsible experts from multiple functions. There needs to be a method to identify the capability that people have and that the team needs, as well as building deeper internal capability. Great products and processes do not develop on their own…talented, technical people with deep expertise and problem-solving capability create the value that customers are looking for in order to exceed their need.

Use the Operational Declaration to Deeply Understand Value and to Share the Vision

The Chief Process Engineer for Lean process creation should use the Operational Declaration (OD) paper to set the vision based on customer value, then work to make it a reality by documenting further details. At the start of a new process creation activity, the OD is a vision paper, which transitions to a contract by the time the team is ready to emerge from the study phase and begin execution.

Forget Grand Strategy for the Moment—Pick Something Critical and Get Started

Do not get paralyzed by indecision or caught up in a cycle of trying to "boil the ocean" of problems or challenges that face your organization. There does not need to be a major engineering functional re-organization or

---

[2] For further study see, *In Search of Value Stream Architects*, Jim Womack, September 2009, Lean Enterprise Institute website: https://www.lean.org/womack/DisplayObject.cfm?o=1123

re-shuffling of the deck chairs at the executive level. Pick a recently developed and launched new program and use that as a leverage point. Then, get people to focus on grasping the current situation related to product and process integration within development.

Map the Product and Process Development Value Stream for the Leverage Point

Use the recently launched new product and process as a learning opportunity by first reflecting back and manually mapping out every single activity, information flows between functions, design changes, program changes, and more. This is an important first step (and usually may be done in 1 day) to get people to truly align around the work that is actually done and the consequences of changes and interruptions to the value creation process.[3]

Select a New Program to Use as Your Learning Laboratory—and Start Quickly

Because change is so hard, pick a critical upcoming new program or one that is in the early stages, and use this as your organizational "learning laboratory" for integrating process creation deeper into new product and process development. Design the future state vision for Lean process creation based on the learning by reflecting on and mapping out the most recent program that completed. This will allow a team to align on how and when the actual work will be organized and be the seeds for visual management later on. Let standards for doing future process creation work emerge but standardize when appropriate.

Practice Set-Based Design for Maximum Learning

During the early stages of development, use set-based thinking to generate multiple process options and then begin to "thin the herd" by de-selecting

---

[3] For further study see, *Why Value Stream Mapping is Essential to Product and Process Development*, Dr. John Drogosz, PhD, November 2020, Lean Enterprise Institute website: https://www.lean.org/-LeanPost/Posting.cfm?LeanPostId=1309

weaker ideas (and generating better ones) based on mock-up, testing, and discussion. In addition, understand where you have "knowledge gaps" related to product and process development. De-risk the back end of the development cycle by identifying and managing the critical knowledge gaps at the front end. When a knowledge gap is closed, it then becomes useful learning for the organization that may be shared through various channels and formats.[4]

Avoid the Development Death Spiral

The nature of the work in Lean product and process development requires the right resources to be in place for earlier activities in the study phase. Your organization may struggle with getting these people to have the capacity to actually do the front-loaded work if they are caught up in a cycle of trying to help do rework on other near-launch or at-launch products from prior generations. You need to overcome this struggle and break the cycle, or you will never get out of it. Be creative in pulling different levers in order to avoid this spiral.

Pace the Invisible Flow of Process Development Work with Milestones and Design Reviews

Utilize milestones during the development cycle for alignment points at critical times for all the functions. In addition, provide clear criteria for the quality of the work that is expected to be completed by each function at the milestone. In order to minimize the risk of missing milestone targets and criteria, allocate time for Design Reviews at the different levels in order to block capacity for technical problem solving and brainstorming on knowledge gaps, issues, and other challenges. As Jim Morgan notes, design reviews are also great opportunities to develop people and the next generation of leadership.[5]

---

[4] For further study see, *Front Loading Product Development*, Durward Sobek, October 2014, Lean Enterprise Institute website: https://www.lean.org/LeanPost/Posting.cfm?LeanPostId=286

[5] For further study see, *The Crucible of Innovation*, Dr. Jim Morgan, PhD, July 2016, Lean Enterprise Institute website: https://www.lean.org/LeanPost/Posting.cfm?LeanPostId=613

Obeya Is Both a Powerful Management Tool and Management System When Done Right

The obeya space has many benefits, including helping teams visualize their mostly intangible work flows and processes. One management challenge is seeing "abnormal from normal" in any work area. When designed properly, the obeya space will provide transparency to enable focus in the right areas where people may then collaborate to exceed challenges. As Alan Mullaly stated at Ford, "You cannot manage a secret," and the obeya should help bring clarity. Start your obeya efforts with a simple, manual system in order to learn and understand the critical social and technical connectivity. Slowly integrate technology and digital tools, but only when they enhance the obeya. Embed the Plan-Do-Check-Adjust (PDCA) scientific method routine into the obeya management system.[6]

Integrate for True Process-Driven Product Development

The purpose is to not do process creation in a vacuum that is separate from new product development and operations or manufacturing. As you evolve and mature, product and process development need to be closely integrated early-on during the development cycle, and ideally, one team. This may be a stretch in your current organization, so strive to start working your way further upstream and downstream with small, yet powerful steps.

An Action Plan for Today

The Prerequisites

Here is a series of key questions that may help your Lean process creation team get started right away in assessing your situation:

- What new product or process design will you use for your ***"Learning Laboratory"*** to test out the new way of working and thinking?

[6] For further study see, *Q&A with Katrina Appell* (on visual management), Katrina Appell, PhD, January 2017, Lean Enterprise Institute website: https://www.lean.org/LeanPost/Posting.cfm?LeanPostId=677

- What is the ***System Architect or Chief Process Engineer*** role for your organization? Who should have this role?
- What is the ***Operational Declaration***? How is this different from the charter? Who owns it?
- How will you gain alignment on how the actual work will be organized to provide the value, from idea to production start? ***(Product and Process Development Value Stream Map)***
- Where will you use ***"Set-based" Design*** concepts to maximize the learning early-on during the *Study Phase*? How will you identify and manage ***Knowledge Gaps*** to de-risk the back end?
- Where will you use the ***Obeya Space*** for effective visual management to see *abnormal from normal*?
- What are the key ***Milestone Integration Points?*** What are the ***Design Review*** types during the development of your new product?
- What is the Management System Routine for ***PDCA*** when developing a new product?

The Work

The 6Con Model and Key Starter Questions from each Chapter

Getting Started: Grasping the current situation and aligning on the performance gaps to close

- What is your current condition for creating new processes? Use a recently launched process and map out the steps taken to deeply understand the situation before jumping to solutions. Include current performance metrics to show the gaps
- Which *post-launch* process improvement work (kaizen) did you experience that could have actually been avoided with proper upfront process design (touzen)?
- What are examples of each of the following process creation failure modes that occurred?
  - Too Much, Too Early
  - Penny-Wise, Pound-Foolish
  - Too Little, Too Late
- What will be your new target condition for Lean process creation? Learn from the *6Con* model to link to your current Development System milestones
- Who will lead the process creation for your next program?

- Which responsible experts will you dedicate to the team?
- How will leadership support, engage, and learn with this process creation team and their experiment? Use the Acme-style steering team in the early stages

Context: understanding each customer's value proposition, the high-level value stream design, and the value stream's key attributes

- What are the *Financial Health and Factory Health* Measures?
- What are the objectives and targets for this process flow? What is value from the customer perspective, and how will this process exceed it?
- What may be learned from observing similar processes that exist today?
- What is the Operational Declaration?
- What is the Future State Value Stream Design and Operating Plan?
- What are the takt time (demand) levels and planned process cycle times?

Additional key questions that could be included:

- How will you understand and identify the operational vision and value from the customer's perspective, and how will you maintain it?
- How will you create flow, eliminate waste, and minimize variability with the actual technical work of developing the Lean process?
- How will you create and capture new knowledge early-on and during the Lean process creation cycle?
- Key tools:
  - Obeya space, Program Schedule wall
  - Operational Declaration

Concepts: discovering the key knowledge gaps and exploring multiple process design options to facilitate learning in the converge phase

- What are the key points of your Operational Declaration? Are they being met? What needs to be adjusted?
- How many different process concepts will you develop before convergence?
- What will be the Lean-style cost model that you plan to use for comparing the value of the different process concepts? How will you measure progress with regard to Safety/Ergonomics, Quality, and Delivery as well?

- What are the fundamental operations that make up the process, including their precedence?
- How will you get a 3-D image of each operation to support fast learning and testing at different fidelity levels?
- How will you quickly capture the motions required for every step in the process concept, as well as data, facts, and opportunities?
- What is your Natural Cycle Time target?

Converge: testing/modeling the initial design concepts and narrowing them down to select an optimal design through rapid learning cycles

- What were the key points of your Operational Declaration? Are they being met? What needs to be adjusted?
- What is the proper degree of automation for your process?
- Where are the opportunities to use low-cost automation to support the people doing the work?
- What process design challenges would help to improve the value?
- What product design challenges would help to improve the value?
- How will you quantify the new concepts that emerge during this phase?
- How balanced is the flow of the product through the operations in your process?

Configure: engineering and arranging the selected process concept to create value and minimize waste with a reasonable management system, while linking the material and information flow system to upstream suppliers and downstream customers

- What were the key points of your Operational Declaration? Are they being met? What needs to be adjusted?
- What degree of mock-up is required for which stations?
  - Table-top
  - Rough
  - Detailed
- What is your quantity control plan at each station? (WCT, SOS, JIS, Set-up Reduction, PM)
- What is your quality control plan at each station? (Quality Diagnostic Matrix, Error proofing)
- How will you signal for and replenish materials with minimal delay? (PFEP, Common and Unique Parts, Connection Map)

- What is the design for Lean zone control?
- What layout shapes will best support the customer demand? How will you enable stations to be rearranged easily?
- What is the decouple strategy?
- What is the updated Material and Information flow for the Value Stream Map?
- What is the management system to detect abnormal from normal as well as the response mechanism?

Confirm: leveraging a robust launch readiness approach to finalize the process while ensuring it meets the targets set in the business plan

- What key predictors are you going to utilize in your scorecard (hint: start with our example and modify as you go)
- What is your plan to engage with machine builders and to ensure capability?
- How will you ensure that every trial is executed smoothly and provides the expected learnings?
- Has the entire value stream been exercised to verify sustainability?
- Has the entire spectrum of part tolerances been utilized to test for the impact of stack-ups on the performance of the process?
- What are your indicators for glide paths?
- What is your cadence for learning? (i.e., number of trials, weekly manufacturing readiness reviews, etc.)
- Does the progressive scoring provide the right andon at the right time or does it need adjusting?

Continuously Improve: making and sustaining consistent improvements over time that will produce even higher levels of performance while providing upstream feedback

- How will you build, grow, and sustain the capability of Lean process creation leaders and key contributors?
- What value will your team find when reflecting back at the end of the first pilot?
- What will be your management system for improving the work of process development?
- How will you maintain alignment across the functions and departments when doing the work on future development programs?

- What tools and techniques (e.g., mock-up, launch boards, glide paths) are important to your organization?
- What are your challenges in making technical work visible and manageable?
- Where can you experiment with a leadership obeya to help with integration?

Index

Note: *Italic* page numbers refer to figures.